Your Premature Baby

*The Complete Guide to
Premie Care During That
Crucial First Year*

Your Premature Baby

*The Complete Guide to
Premie Care During That
Crucial First Year*

Robin Marantz Henig
with Anne B. Fletcher, M.D.

Foreword by Dr. Benjamin Spock

Illustrations by Deborah Addison

Photographs by Jerry A. McCoy

BALLANTINE BOOKS   NEW YORK

Library of Congress Catalog Card Number: 83-91166

ISBN 9780345313652

This edition published by arrangement with Rawson Associates

Manufactured in the United States of America

146604632

Dedicated to my family, with love;
and to yours,
with admiration and with hope.

Contents

viii   *Contents*

II. FINALLY, HOME

x   *Contents*

III.   THE OUTLOOK

APPENDICES

Acknowledgments

Many people have contributed their time, confidence, and ideas to the shaping of this book. First mention should go to Dr. Anne Fletcher, my co-author and medical adviser. I met Anne in the course of my research for the *New York Times Magazine*, for which I was writing an article on the stunning advances being made in neonatal intensive care. It was then that I became acquainted with the range of Anne's knowledge, and especially with her sharp, perceptive thinking about the ethical aspects of her work. Only later did I discover her other skills as an editor and communicator. Her commitment to this book has exceeded my fondest expectations. Anne has put in countless hours of work on the manuscript, has guided me through a maze of scholarly research on premies, and has been a trusted first reader—and conscientious rewriter—of every word in the book. How she managed to devote so much time to our project, and still to keep pace with her demanding job as director of the intensive care nursery at Children's Hospital, remains a mystery to me.

Michaela Williams and Deborah Pines, my editors at the *New York Times Magazine*, first let me explore the fascinating world of neonatology in an article for the magazine. Eleanor Rawson, my publisher at Rawson Associates, provided much-needed support and encouragement as that article turned into a book. And Lynn Seligman, my agent, worked with me on this book during what for her was a terrible time to be thinking about premies: while she was at home on bed rest awaiting the birth of twins. (Lynn's twins, a boy and a girl, were born three weeks early.)

I have talked to dozens of premie families, all of whom were generous with their time and lavish with their suggestions about what information other premie parents would need. The quotes from parents that appear in this book are all from my interviews with these parents, but their identities have been changed to protect their privacy and the privacy of their families. My thanks go to all of them for their help and advice. The image of their kids' faces stayed with me long after our visits and reminded me of how miraculous premie lives really are.

My own kid's face also lit my motivation to write this book. Jessica was a healthy, full-term baby when she was born in 1980, and she has been a constant reminder to me of how thoroughly a mother can love a child. It's as a mother that I came to the writing of this book; it's as a medical journalist that I found the information I wanted to present. The facts herein will, I hope, ease the leaden grief of loving a child who is sick—a grief I've been fortunate enough not to know, yet, firsthand.

Since my old school friend, Deborah Addison, is addicted to children's books—she always sends us the books that end up being Jessie's favorites—she was delighted to try her hand at illustrating the special pull-out section of this book.

All the drawings in this story for siblings, "My Baby Sister's Too Small to Come Home," were done by Debbie, who in her other life is an art director at a major advertising agency. I'm grateful to her for the time and talent she devoted to making the story and its characters come alive.

The photographs in the center section of this book are the handiwork of Jerry McCoy, a talented young photographer I was fortunate to meet in the media resources department of Children's Hospital. Jerry's pictures, I believe, capture the drama and poignancy of the intensive care nursery—and tell you more than my words alone can just how your premie will look during the long weeks in the hospital.

Finally, my love and thanks go to my husband, Jeff. As always, he helped me with his incisive comments on each chapter as it was written and formulated with me the ideas that I hope make this book especially worthwhile. But, more important, he provided me with the time, and the confidence, to take this project on in the first place. Jeff ferried Jessie to the park or the babysitter's when my deadlines loomed large, did without a clean house or home-cooked meals for yet another year, and put up with the emotional highs and lows that come with writing a book. Especially now that Jessie is part of our lives, my work would be impossible if Jeff weren't Jeff.

Foreword

Nothing could be more accurate than the word "complete" in the subtitle of this book. It explains everything that any parent would want to know about prematurity: The anatomy and physiology of the baby; the incredibly complex and miraculous apparatus of the nursery; the stages of the parents' feelings—grief, guilt, anxiety, acknowledgment, bonding, learning; a full discussion of all the scary diseases and complications to which premies may be susceptible; the questions about breast or bottle, circumcision, and how far to go in sustaining life by heroic measures when serious and permanent impairment seems likely; the transition to home and the care at home, including monitors and the prevention of infection; the special problems of caring for twins, who are often premature; a developmental chart for frequent reassurance; some more scary diseases and disturbances of development that show up later in the year; the quandary about what is wise protection and what is overprotection; questions about subsequent pregnancies; and finally, the special attachment and joys that come with bringing a baby through such crises, even in cases where there are residual effects.

Robin Henig, with the able assistance of Dr. Anne Fletcher, has done a skillful job in researching, digesting, and presenting clearly all the modern data on prematurity without lapsing into jargon. She shows a consistent awareness of the feelings of the parents which, in a way, are as crucial as the baby's survival. Particularly admirable, to me, is the good sense and sensitivity with which she has balanced her explanation of the various dangers of prematurity, which are enough to keep most parents painfully anxious in the early stages, with the reassurance that can be drawn from the statistics on survival—especially healthy survival—which have improved dramatically over the years.

I myself would have been constantly tortured by trying to strike this balance, for my inclination is to reassure at all costs short of lying. That's not hard to do with full-term babies, who are incredibly tough despite their appearance of helplessness. But parents of prematures know from the start that dangers are lurking and they are constantly reminded of this by the awe-inspiring apparatus and the hustling staff in the nursery. So the parents are anxious already; what they want to get is a fuller understanding of the disturbances their baby is showing, and the survival chances. They will certainly get these to their satisfaction in Robin Henig's book. But there's still the likelihood that in reading they'll stumble on other complications or disturbances that their baby doesn't have and that they hadn't heard of before, which will give them more to worry about. My advice would be to confine your reading about diseases and problems to those your baby has already shown. That advice is logical but it doesn't take account of human nature and human curiosity.

I'll add one more hopeful note. Just as the outlook for premies has improved remarkably in the past decade, it is likely to keep on improving, year by year. So each time you read a statistic here on survival and recovery, you can reasonably assume that it has already changed for the better in the months or years since the book was written.

Dr. Benjamin Spock

Preface

You've had your baby. It's weeks, or maybe even months, sooner than you expected it, but suddenly you've had your baby and here you are—somebody's parent. Why do you feel so let down?

You're letdown because your baby was premature. And when your baby is premature, nothing happens the way you planned.

Most significant, of course, is the fact that your child is sick. You had envisioned an idealized "bonding" hour with your child after an easy, "natural" birth, but as soon as your baby was born she was scooted out of the delivery room into the intensive care nursery—or, worse, to a nursery at a hospital clear across town. How can you start to fall in love with your baby when she isn't even there?

In a way, you might be secretly disappointed in the baby you just delivered. She's not the cuddly "Gerber baby" of your private fantasies, but a scrawny, elongated infant who might be very sick. It's hard to feel attached to her when you wonder whether you'll soon lose her.

In a way that most newborns don't require, a premie demands that you act grown-up and responsible. You must talk to doctors and nurses about your baby's well-being, make decisions about certain courses of therapy, transmit information to your other children or your parents in a level-headed, reasonable way. At the same time that you're trying to act adult, though, you may be cowering with fear. You're worried about the baby's health, her comfort today and her prospects for a normal life tomorrow. It's incredible to you that you must juggle so many churning emotions— and all before you've even had a chance to attend your first childbirth preparation class!

But perhaps the hardest part of being a premie parent is going home to an empty house. While your baby is in the intensive care nursery, your own house echoes, and you long to fill it with your baby's sounds. Whether the baby stays in the hospital for an extra two days, an extra two weeks, or an extra two months, the wait before her homecoming can be interminable. And that is why I wrote this book.

When my friend had a premie, years before I was even considering motherhood, she used to talk about sitting in her baby's room at night—a room she had finished decorating just days before his early birth. She would sit, she said, in that green-and-white nursery, in her rocking chair, waiting for her baby. Sometimes she pumped her breasts so she could bring breast milk to the hospital the next day. But sometimes she just sat, and rocked, and waited.

With this book, I hope you can do more than wait. You can prepare. In the long, lonely hours before your baby comes home, you can read this book for an idea of what to expect. The book is written chronologically, and it takes you through the whole first year of your baby's life. It may be hard to believe, but twelve months from now your baby, too, will probably weigh more than three times her birthweight, will probably be able to sit unsupported, will probably be moving and laughing and exploring. What wonderful compensation for these trying early days.

This book begins at the beginning—in the hospital. There's a great deal of emphasis here on the medical problems your baby might encounter. We also describe theories about what caused your baby's premature birth and ways in which the environment of the intensive care nursery is unique—not quite the womb and not quite like home. There are chapters, too, about how you feel during your baby's hospitalization—and how you can make yourself and your loved ones feel better—and about the decisions you'll be asked to make regarding the way your child is treated and fed. These weeks in the hospital, you'll find, are weeks when anything can happen.

The book then follows you home, to clue you in on ways in which a premie, even after she's out of medical danger, is different from her full-term peer. It will alert you to warning signs of impending problems and, even more important, help you pinpoint highlights of your baby's growth and development. As long as you measure her progress in small steps—remembering, always, to "correct" her age for the weeks of development she missed in utero—your loving encouragement will serve to hasten her growth and to cement the bond that's been growing between you.

A word about the use of "he's" and "she's." Boys make up just over one-half of the premature babies born—just as they make up just over one-half of all babies born—but that is not sufficient reason to justify calling your premie "he" throughout the book. All the special problems, and special wonders, of premies are as valid when applied to girls as to boys. To avoid the stilted phrase "he or she" each time I use a pronoun, I have settled on a compromise: when referring to a premie, I will alternate the use of "he" or "she" from one chapter to the next.

For the sake of flow, I've also settled on a conventional use of pronouns when referring to the adult actors in your premie's drama. Doctors generally will be referred to as "he," nurses as "she," and parents, when a gender must be applied, as "she." This is done only to make the book easier to read. It is not intended as a political statement. If you had to stumble upon female doctors and male nurses throughout the book, you'd be giving more attention to these matters than I think they deserve.

Introduction

Neonatology is a rapidly changing and promising medical specialty, and it has advanced a great deal in the past decade. The main beneficiary of these advances is, of course, your premie. Ten years ago, most premature infants who were born weighing less than two pounds rarely survived beyond the first days of life. Today, many of these tiny infants—perhaps your baby among them—will not only survive, but will go on to lead healthy and normal lives, provided they receive appropriate care.

While newborn technology and care have advanced rapidly, attention to the needs of the parents of premature newborns has often not kept pace. The birth of a premature infant, no matter how large or small the baby, comes as a shock. Inconsequential worries might bother you at first: the baby's room at home, for example, might not be ready. In the meantime, other, more serious problems might arise.

Your premie is, in many ways, still too young to manage alone in the world outside the uterus, and in the days or weeks to come might need much medical help in order to grow and thrive.

Immediately after birth, your newborn might be whisked away to the hospital's intensive care nursery. If the hospital has no such facility, the baby might be transported in a specially equipped ambulance to a different hospital to receive better care. If your baby is transported to a different hospital, it's not necessarily because of serious illness. It might just be that the hospital where you gave birth cannot care for infants who are premature.

Having the baby in a different hospital is an added worry, and it complicates an already complicated situation during the first few days after birth. The baby's father might have to oversee details of admission to the referring hospital, make hurried plans for the care of other children in the family, and be torn between calling at two hospitals at once during visiting hours. The baby's mother, if she's lucky, will have a picture of her infant, but this is a poor substitute for the opportunity to see, touch, and hold the child.

Amid all this unexpected activity, the mother might be left alone during her period of greatest pain and sorrow. She has, perhaps, too much time to ponder the possibilities of what will happen to her infant and to the family.

The more you understand, the better able you will be to cope with being the parent of a premature infant. In that spirit, we present this book. We will try to take you through the griefs and joys of having a premie. We will introduce you to the health care professionals who will care for your child, and the procedures and equipment they will use. And we will tell you about the special wonders, and special problems, that might await you even after you bring the baby home.

As you read this book, keep in mind that there are many excellent hospitals throughout the country, each of which might have a slightly different way of managing a particular problem. There is no way to explain exactly how your hospital will treat your child; in fact, there often is no one absolutely correct way. Do not be upset if our description of a disease or a treatment differs from one you receive from your own doctor or nurse. Just remember that it is important to discuss the details of your infant's care with the nursery team at your hospital.

You might have heard about the importance of parent-infant bonding during the first days of life. Researchers now know that the opportunity for bonding is not lost if your baby is hospitalized during these early days. Bonding can take place later and become just as strong. And bonding can take place in the hospital, too. The hospital staff will give you every opportunity to feed and bathe and hold your baby during the nursery stay. Your doctors and nurses will work with you to arrange the best possible follow-up plan. By the time your newborn is discharged, and probably even before, you will begin to feel the joys of your premature infant, even if everything is not completely normal or perfect. Remember, too, that you can always call the hospital even after the baby is home if new questions arise.

As a neonatologist at a major teaching hospital, I know that physicians, nurses, and other members of the hospital staff might at times seem very formal or unapproachable. We look busy, and we are. But this should never make you reluctant to ask questions. On occasion, the intensity of your infant's illness might make us forget to call you or talk to you as often as we should. If this is the case, do not be silent. Share your concerns and questions with us, and never hesitate to call. We need to work together for the best outcome of your infant.

Those of us who have worked with many families of premature infants know that all parents need time to mourn the loss of the expected full-term infant, and to make adjustments to the reality of parenting a premie. We have found many ways of helping you adjust during this difficult time. Many of these ideas will be discussed in the following chapters, especially Chapter 3 on "Premature Parents." One of the first things you can do to work through your shock and grief is simply to give your child a name. Do not be afraid to do this. Hospital staff members want to call all babies by name, even the smallest ones. Furthermore, during this difficult time, you'd be wise to keep open lines of communication not only with the hospital staff, but also with members of your family and concerned friends.

You do not need to read this book from cover to cover. Read only those sections that apply to your baby. In Chapter 5, "The Hospital Roller Coaster," we have described in detail certain difficulties that occur frequently in very small premies. If your infant is not critically ill, do not read this chapter. You will be encouraged to know that many premies do beautifully from the very beginning. They thrive during the first weeks of life, grow steadily, and go home in perfect health.

We physicians cannot always answer all of your questions. You will sometimes have to be content with an "I don't know." We realize that this is seldom a satisfactory response; however, in many cases it is the only honest one. Some things that you want us to predict simply cannot be predicted. The brain of the premature infant is immature, and patterns of development, normal or abnormal, might not appear for months. Bear with us, for as hard as it is for you to hear "I don't know," it is just as hard for us to have to say it.

Finally, as you read this book, know that all of us caring for your premature infant firmly believe in the saying "Primum non nocere"—"First, do no harm."

Anne B. Fletcher, M.D.
Director, Intensive Care Nursery
Children's Hospital National
    Medical Center
Washington, D.C.

I

In the Hospital

1: The Premie: More Fetus Than Baby

THE INTENSIVE CARE NURSERY is an awesome place for a first meeting between parent and child. Your baby seems so far away, so alien, so tiny. Surrounded by tubes, plugs, and machines, he looks as though you can never reach him. Surrounded by competent doctors and nurses, he looks as though you can never do enough to make him well.

"I just wanted to put him back inside me," Katie Lee says about the first time she saw her baby, John. Her feelings are echoed by premie mothers everywhere. With their babies separated from them long before they were ready to let them go, these women experience a sense of loss that is almost as profound as if the baby had died.

In fact, something *has* died, something that can never be recovered: the special bond between a pregnant woman and her unborn child. Lost, too, are the parents' fantasies about their baby, their dreams about how the baby will look and behave. In the place of beautiful dreams are now harsh images of reality, images sometimes too painful to bear. It is for the loss of fantasies, and for the symbolic death of the healthy, round-cheeked baby they did not have, that many parents grieve.

A premature birth is, first and foremost, a surprise. "But you don't understand; I can't be having a baby. It's too early," Ann Foster said to the medical resident who examined her when she went to the hospital complaining of cramps. "And anyway, my husband and I are going away for the weekend!" When Ann finally resigned herself to the idea that her baby would indeed be born that night, events proceeded so quickly that she was left breathless. "I didn't realize that premies can just pop out," she recalls. "Once I was admitted to the hospital, at about 5:30 P.M., we expected to have a long night and have the baby no earlier than midnight. But suddenly I had a son, and I had even eaten dinner—and it was still only eight o'clock."

In this maelstrom of emotions, parents must come to grips with some of the toughest feelings they've ever encountered: feelings of grief, of guilt, of profound anxiety. These feelings are perhaps most difficult for first-time parents, who might not have been ready yet to think of themselves as parents at all, much less as parents who might have to fight for the very life of their tiny child.

The majority of "premie parents" are frightened, grieved, and sometimes even a little repulsed by the first sight of their stunningly tiny babies. It's important to recognize and accept these feelings—and to remember that a very small premie is still, by rights, a fetus. He is at a stage in his development in which he is perfectly designed for survival inside the womb but ill equipped—especially his respiratory, circulatory, gastrointestinal, and nervous systems—for life outside. That's why he needs special care in the neonatal intensive care nursery, and that's why he runs special risks.

A premature baby is born approximately once in every ten births. In the United States today, nearly one-quarter of a million infants a year are born prematurely—that is, before the 37th week of gestation (out of a full-term pregnancy of 40 weeks). The name "premie" can be applied to a wide variety of newborns, from the baby born six weeks early who weighs nearly five pounds, to the baby who is three months early and weighs two pounds or less. Generally, the smaller the baby, the more immature he is; and the more immature, the more problems he is likely to encounter during his first weeks of life.

No one knows for certain what causes prematurity. Doctors do know, though, that some women are more likely than others to give birth early. This "high-risk" group of pregnant women includes those who have had a previous premie or were themselves premature; who receive inadequate medical care or nutrition during pregnancy; who are younger than sixteen or older than forty; who weighed less than 100 pounds before they got pregnant; or who waited less than one year from their last child's birth to get pregnant again. Some physicians who have studied the association between lifestyle and premature labor have found that women in high-stress careers seem statistically more likely to give birth early. They say that women who work during pregnancy as doctors, nurses, salespeople, hairdressers, domestics, or in other occupations that involve strenuous physical effort, standing, and continuous nervous tension, are at some added risk of going into premature labor. This would also include women who are home full time with two or more preschoolers and no domestic help. Cigarette smokers have been found, too, to be more likely to give birth too soon.

Dr. Robert K. Creasy, an obstetrician at the University of California, San Francisco, and Marie A. Herron, a nurse who works with him, have made a study of which women go into premature labor, and why. According to Dr. Creasy, most premature births cannot be explained. Only in about 3 or 4 percent of the preterm births he's seen is the mother's anatomy to blame. In the vast majority of cases, he says, there's nothing physically wrong with the mother's uterus. (An exception to this rule is found in women whose mothers took the synthetic hormone DES while they were pregnant with them; these women are more likely to have a "T-shaped" uterus that makes them prone to miscarriages and premature births.) Dr. Creasy says the single most significant factor in explaining premature birth is a woman's own obstetrical history; if she's had one premie, her risk of having another premie is about 40 percent. We will describe Dr. Creasy's work in greater detail in Chapter 12, in our discussion of special considerations that will face you during your future pregnancies.

A Close Look at the Premie

When you first see your premie, his size is the greatest shock. How can someone so tiny survive? He looks fragile, vulnerable, and far too small to be real. Many of the premies we will be describing in this book—and perhaps your premie, too—are so very tiny that it's hard to imagine their size until you've held one in your hand.

Try to picture four good-sized grapefruit, or a big city's Sunday newspaper, or a small roasting chicken. That's the weight of some of the babies we're talking about here. They can be, head to rump, no bigger than an adult's hand, and their limbs can be no wider around than a quarter. When Aaron Wynn, a premie who weighed 940 grams (2 pounds 1 ounce) at birth, was a week old, his father slipped his wedding ring around Aaron's wrist, like a tiny bracelet—and Aaron had room to spare.

But your premie is not simply a smaller version of a full term baby. He will look different from a term baby, not only in his size but also in his texture, his proportions—everything. He will behave differently, using a set of motions that seem disjointed and unrelated to his environment. He will function differently, equipped as he is with organs that are still in many ways incomplete.

The way your premie looks depends on where he was in gestation when his intrauterine growth was interrupted. Very early in pregnancy, the basics of a human form are laid out: fingers, toes, facial features, all encased in a very thin layer of skin. But the last weeks of gestation are devoted to finishing work, including completion of such fine points as the cartilage in the ear, the nipples, and the genitals. Because this finishing work is still undone, the newborn premie is in many ways more like a fetus than like a fully formed baby.

The first way in which your premie differs from a term baby is seen on the surface—his skin. Even if both parents are Caucasian, a premie's skin can be ruddy in color, and, after the first day, it can become wrinkled like the skin of a wizened old man. Premies born to black parents often appear white, but their skin color darkens over the course of a week or so as their pigment reaches its mature level.

Unlike term babies, who have spent the final weeks in utero fattening up, the premie has no fat deposits beneath his outer skin layer. Without this added layer of fat, the skin is almost transparent. You may be able to see straight through to the veins and arteries—a disconcerting sight. Even more disconcerting is the fact that the premie seems to "change color," his skin coloration reflecting whether he has recently been moved or fed or even whether he has had a bowel movement.

Many premies are covered with a fine layer of downy hair called "lanugo." This hair serves in utero to help protect the fetus's skin from the amniotic fluid in which he is suspended. It usually disappears during the last month of gestation, but when pregnancy is ended early, lanugo can still be found on the newborn's forehead, back, shoulders, and arms. The lanugo is harmless and will soon thin out and disappear, but it does tend to make the scrawny, wrinkled premie look all the more like a little monkey.

Other differences between a premie and a term baby are less noticeable to the unpracticed eye. Premies' ears, for instance, are often unformed. They can be bent back upon themselves into a flat fold, failing to resume their normal shape without help. This is because the fetus does not begin to make firm cartilage—which, among its other functions, serves as a semirigid spine for the ears—until the last weeks of gestation.

Similarly, the genitals in both boys and girls are still incomplete. In boys, the testicles usually have not yet descended into the scrotum, and the foreskin does not yet completely cover the head of the penis. In girls, the outer folds of the labia are not yet fully formed, so the inner folds can be seen more clearly than they will in a few weeks. These signs of genital immaturity are insignificant, since the premie will grow out of them, but they can be quite worrisome to parents. Many parents focus on them as the most obvious indication that their baby is "abnormal." Be assured that, even if it does not seem that way to you yet, your little boy or little girl is *all* boy or *all* girl.

The premie's breasts are unformed, too, with no fat beneath them and only a small nipple and no areola (the pigmented area around the nipple). This, too, will change in a few more weeks, as the premie does some additional growing outside the womb—growing that nature had intended him to do in utero.

Reflexes: Relating to the World

A newborn is far less helpless than he seems to be. Infants are equipped from birth with a group of reflexes—the so-called "primitive reflexes"—that enable them to participate in their own survival. They can suck, swallow, find a nipple, grasp onto a supporting hand, even make stepping movements when stood on their feet. Many of these reflexes are vestiges of reflexes that assured the survival of our primate ancestors. Except for sucking and swallowing, most of them are today unnecessary for the survival of a modern newborn, who will have his needs taken care of whether he can grasp his mother's finger or not. But still, these reflexes contribute to our generalized image, conscious or unconscious, of what a baby acts like. Parents learn that if they stroke a baby's cheek, he will turn his head to that side; they learn that if they slam a door loudly, the baby will swing his limbs in distress.

Premie parents need to learn something else: that premies often don't behave in these predictable ways. Many primitive reflexes, such as sucking and swallowing, simply are not imprinted in the fetus's brain before about the 34th week of gestation. That means that a baby born before then will be unable to carry out some very basic functions that we usually take for granted in newborn babies. Among the reflexes with which term babies are born, and which are slow to develop in the premie, are:

1. Sucking. Term newborns are able, after an early adjustment period, to suck on a breast or a rubber nipple in order to receive nourishment. But premies often are too weak to suck. The premie's suck is not strong enough for drinking until he reaches 32 to 34 weeks gestational age; until then, he will probably need to be fed in some other way. Your baby's doctor will either use an intravenous line (which goes from a bottle—filled with sugar water, protein, and fat—directly into his vein via a needle in the baby's arm, leg, or head) or a feeding tube (running from the milk or formula bottle, through the baby's throat, and right into his stomach) to supply nutrition to your baby. When he gets bigger, he will be fed from a bottle. At first he will probably need to use a small "premie nipple," made of very thin rub-

ber to help babies with a weak suck. Later still, he will be able to use a regular nipple on a regular bottle, and finally to nurse directly from the breast.

2. Swallowing. Like sucking, this is a process that most term newborns do instinctively, but one that is extraordinarily tiring for a premie and that requires a coordination premies do not have. Although fetuses are able to swallow from about 20 weeks gestation, they cannot coordinate this with sucking until about 34 weeks. The methods used to feed a premie who cannot suck well—intravenous lines and feeding tubes—also are useful in feeding a premie who cannot swallow.

3. Rooting. This reflex allows the full-term newborn to find a nipple and grasp on to it. When the newborn's cheek is stroked gently, he will instinctively turn toward whatever stroked him. A premie, though, is too disorganized neurologically to accomplish this reflexive movement. For a premie to be fed, his parent or nurse must rely not on the rooting reflex but on a rather more direct approach—actually pushing the nipple into the baby's mouth, and at times even moving his lips for him until the baby gets the feel of sucking.

4. Startling. If a full-term newborn hears a sharp, sudden sound, the startle reflex occurs. When a newborn startles, he opens his hands, throws out his arms, and brings his arms together again. Often, the baby will then cry. But a premie is too small and too immature to mount this primitive response to surprise. If he hears a sharp, sudden sound, he lies quietly. Early signs of the startle reflex, which is also called the Moro response, can be seen at about 28 weeks. It usually is not complete until the baby reaches a gestational age of 37 weeks. Once the baby begins startling, he generally will maintain this reflex for about three months.

5. Crying. Crying requires a surprising amount of strength and maturity to accomplish. A term baby quickly learns to use his cry to signal hunger, discomfort, loneliness, or pain,

and a parent learns to respond to crying in ways that supply the newborn with some of his basic needs. But a premie may offer no such cues. Some premies, especially sick premies, can be so silent that their parents might wonder whether the baby is deaf or mute. As the premie gains strength, he also gains the ability to cry—but his cry still might be different from the cry of a term baby. Variations in pitch, intensity, duration, and reasons for crying have been studied recently as clues regarding a premie's general state of health.

6. Grasping. The grasp reflex is one of the strongest in the term newborn's repertoire. It probably originated in mammals whose young needed to grasp onto the mother as she carried them around foraging for food or eluding predators. But for the premie, the mere act of moving his fingers into a clamped fist is difficult. Unlike term babies, who spend most of their time curled into themselves, premies tend to lie flat, like little frogs. They have almost no muscle tone (doctors call this hypotonic limbs, or hypotonia) and remain limply in whatever position they are placed. As they grow and mature, they begin to assume the curled-up position of term babies, but this often does not occur until they reach about 34 to 36 weeks gestational age.

A Look Inside the Premie

In ways you cannot see, your baby is also different internally from a baby born at term. Like the surface differences, his differences beneath the skin are due to the fact that certain stages of intrauterine development have been interrupted. The last organs to develop in utero are the ones that will be most incomplete when a premie is born, and are the ones that will present the gravest problems in neonatal intensive care. These organs are the lungs and the brain.

As a fetus, your baby did not need lungs to get oxygen. Throughout pregnancy, oxygen was delivered directly to the fetus's bloodstream through the placenta, an organ connecting the fetus to the uterus. The fetus's oxygen came from the mother's bloodstream through the placenta, via the umbilical cord. The fetal lungs played no part in this scheme.

The fetus does not develop the capability of true, effective breathing until quite late in pregnancy. In about the 24th week of gestation (and later in many cases), fetal lungs begin manufacturing small amounts of a substance called surfactant. Surfactant, secreted by cells in the small air sacs within the lungs, is needed to keep the air sacs (called alveoli) pliable. If we had no surfactant, every time we took a breath our lungs would collapse. With it, the air sacs can contract and expand with ease.

Many premies are born before their lungs learn how to make sufficient quantities of surfactant, and before they even have sufficient numbers of alveoli. Their lungs are so immature that each breath is labored and potentially hazardous.

Surfactant production increases sharply at about the 35th week of gestation. But lung maturation can occur at different rates in different babies. Fetuses under stress throughout pregnancy—those born to drug-addicted mothers, for instance—often are born with mature lungs even if they are born prematurely. The stress of intrauterine life for such fetuses probably led them to secrete certain hormones, called corticosteroids, that are known to hasten lung maturation in utero. Similarly, premies born at least twenty-four hours after their mothers' amniotic sacs have ruptured seem to have more mature lungs than other premies of similar gestational ages. Once again, the stress of intrauterine life probably causes the fetus to secrete additional corticosteroids, which in turn promotes the secretion of surfactant from the fetal lungs.

The brain is the other organ that develops late in pregnancy. Although the basic structure of the brain is established early, usually before the 20th week of gestation, the bulk of brain growth occurs in the last trimester (that is, between weeks 26 and 40). In addition, the brain cell fibers are raw, lacking the protective coating (called myelin sheaths) that begin to form during the last trimester. When they are fully formed, myelin sheaths facilitate the transmission of impulses from one brain cell to the next. This process, called myelinization, is thought to continue until the child reaches the age of about two.

With myelinization still incomplete, the premie is neurologically behind a baby born at term. In many ways, this deficit is a blessing. Since the neurologically immature premie is less responsive to his environment than is a full-term newborn, many of the procedures he will undergo during his first rough weeks of life will cause him less pain than they would cause a term infant or an older child. In addition, the premie is not yet primed to attend to the sights and sounds of the world, and might find it easier than a full-term baby would to shut out the nonstop growl and glare of the intensive care nursery. Be assured, though, that as your baby matures and his nervous system becomes better integrated, he will begin acting—and responding—more and more like a full-term baby.

The blood-flow pattern in the brain of a premie also is significantly different from that of a full-term newborn. Between the 24th and 32nd weeks of gestation, the brain contains a gelatinous structure, called the germinal matrix, that is filled with prominent veins, arteries, and capillaries. The germinal matrix shrinks and disappears by 38 weeks, but when a baby is born prematurely, this region is still an important feature of the brain. Because blood flow to the germinal matrix is so great, and because the blood vessels— especially the capillaries—are so tiny and fragile, ruptures of these vessels can be a frequent occurrence among very small premies.

Figuring Gestational Age

Laurie Falk was so concerned about her daughter's health that she barely glanced around the intensive care nursery during her visits there. All she did was sit beside the isolette and stroke tiny Jennifer's leg. But one day, Laurie happened to overhear the nurses discussing Eric, the premie in the next isolette. She perked up her ears when she heard Eric's birth date: May 10, the same as Jennifer's! Laurie later peeked into Eric's isolette and was startled to find a baby more than twice her daughter's size. If they were both the same age, Laurie thought, then surely something must be terribly wrong with Jennifer. Otherwise, why would Eric, who was born prematurely on the same day, be so much bigger?

There was a perfectly good explanation for Eric's bigger size: he was older than Jennifer. The fact that both babies were born on the same day does not mean that both babies are the same age. *Not all premies are the same age at birth.* This is a fundamental point to keep in mind as you compare your baby to the baby in the next isolette. But it can be a difficult concept to grasp. Think of it this way: From the moment of conception, your unborn child develops along a predetermined schedule, forming a heart by the 6th week after conception, a brain by the 18th week, fingernails by the 20th. When we describe the milestones that occur in utero, we talk about the fetus's "gestational age"—that is, the amount of time that has passed from the moment of conception until that point. (The word derives from the Latin "gestare," to carry.)

Jennifer, who on her May 10 birth date weighed just 1050 grams (2 pounds 5 ounces), was due to be born on August 10. That means she was conceived on approximately November 17, giving her a "gestational age" at the time of her birth of 27 weeks. (Actually, 25 weeks had elapsed between conception and birth, but doctors always add 2 weeks to this figure so they can calculate gestational age from the date of the mother's last menstrual period, which usually occurs 2 weeks before conception.) Eric, on the other hand—who at birth on May 10 weighed 2100 grams (4 pounds 10 ounces)—had been due on June 20. That means he was conceived on approximately September 27, seven weeks earlier than Jennifer, and at birth had a "gestational age" of 34 weeks.

Jennifer's stay in the hospital will probably be much longer than Eric's, and because of her tiny size and her profound immaturity she is likely to encounter more and different problems along the way. That's why doctors, when describing the outlook for premies in the 1980s, talk about two very different groups of babies. Eric belongs to the "low birthweight" group—any baby born weighing less than 2500 grams (about 5½ pounds) but more than 1500 grams (about 3 pounds 5 ounces). (Physicians will be talking about your baby's weight in grams; a chart for quick conversion from grams to pounds appears in Appendix A. Within a short while, you will be thinking metric, too—especially if your baby has trouble gaining weight, and every added gram becomes a cause for celebration.)

For babies in the low birthweight group, the prospects are bright indeed: More than 95 percent of these premies survive the newborn period, and the vast majority of them— about 90 percent, by most estimates—will bear no scar of their early introduction into the world.

Jennifer belongs to the "very low birthweight" group—all those babies who weigh less than 1500 grams at birth. The prospects for these babies are bright, too—far brighter than anyone dared hope a decade ago. The babies who do best are the biggest babies in this group, those who, like Jennifer, weigh between 1000 grams (2 pounds 3 ounces) and 1500 grams. Most hospitals are saving about 85 percent of the babies they treat in this weight category, and again the majority—about 75 percent nationwide—are absolutely normal. (For the remaining 25 percent, the problems are usually quite mild—nearsightedness, learning disability, a tendency toward upper respiratory infection—and often reversible. We will describe all these problems, and the ways doctors and parents can treat them, in Chapters 5 and 10.)

A premie's size usually relates directly to his gestational age. But this is not always the case. About one-third of "low birthweight" babies are in fact full-term babies who suffered growth retardation in utero. Because their organs are fully mature but chronically malnourished, these babies—whom doctors call "small for gestational age," or "small-for-dates"—encounter problems that are quite different from those that face babies whose growth in utero was normal but abbreviated.

Figure 1–1 is a "growth curve" for the size of a typical fetus between the 25th and 38th weeks of gestation. Your neonatologist might use such a chart to see where your baby fits in. The top line represents the 90th percentile—that is, 90 percent of premies with a corresponding gestational age should be expected to weigh less than the weight indicated by that line. The bottom line represents the 10th percentile—only 10 percent of premies of that gestational age will weigh less. Most probably, your baby's weight and age will place him somewhere in between those two lines. If he is below the 10th percentile line, he is considered small-for-dates.

Small-for-dates babies look and behave differently from premies whose size is "appropriate-for-dates." The main problem of extremely small full-term babies is that their growth was stunted in utero. This creates a unique set of potential difficulties during the newborn period: hypoglycemia (dangerously low blood sugar levels), birth defects, chromosomal abnormalities, and other disorders. Extremely small premature babies, on the other hand, face a different set of potential problems. Their main liability is that their growth period in utero was stopped abruptly, and the difficulties

A GROWTH CURVE FOR PREMIES AT BIRTH

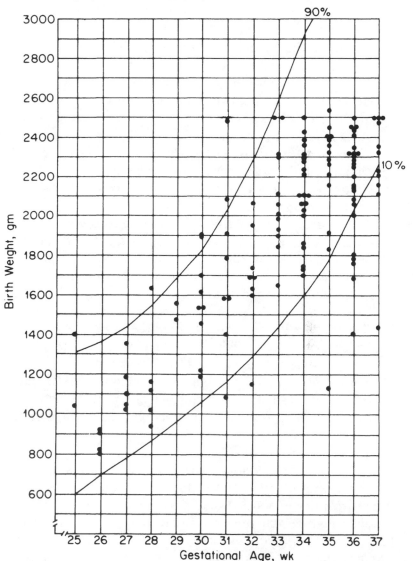

they face arise more from their immaturity than from their size.

Because the two groups of babies differ in such important ways, doctors must assign small babies to the correct group even before treatment begins. When a neonatologist first sees a tiny baby, his job—after stabilizing the baby—is to try to determine the baby's gestational age. This is essential in setting the subsequent course of therapy.

To make this determination, your baby's doctor will have to depend on more than simply your report of when your baby was due. It's not at all unusual for a mother (based on the due dates her obstetrician had been giving her) to be convinced her premie is a 28 weeker, only to be told by the neonatologist that the baby, on examination, is shown to have a gestational age of 30 weeks. How can this discrepancy come about?

The main source of the confusion is the relatively imprecise nature of most methods used to figure a baby's due date. When an obstetrician tells you when your baby is due, he bases his calculation on the date of your last menstrual period (in doctors' lingo, LMP). From the first day of the mother's last period, the physician counts ahead 40 weeks— and then he tells you your baby will be born on that day, "give or take a week." The 40 weeks assigned to the length of an "ideal" term pregnancy is a somewhat arbitrary number based on doctors' knowledge of certain averages: the average of 2 weeks between a woman's menstrual period and the date of conception of an embryo, plus the average of 38 weeks that it takes for an embryo to grow into a fully-formed fetus ready to be born.

But the LMP technique of assigning gestational age can be wrong, for several reasons. For one thing, many women have irregular periods. If they miss a period for one or two months and become pregnant in the third month, dating on the basis of menstrual history is thrown off kilter; the developing fetus might in fact be one or two months younger than the doctor thinks it is. For another thing, some women experience episodes of spotting in the early months of pregnancy. Often, the spotting occurs around the time of an expected period, and it can produce stains that look very much like menstruation—even though the woman is already pregnant. When this happens, a woman might tell her obstetrician that her last period occurred on a date when she was really one or two months pregnant, and the fetus might in fact be one or two months older than the doctor thinks.

Because of the limitations of the LMP method of dating a pregnancy, obstetricians and neonatologists have tried to be more precise in establishing exactly when a conception took place. These more elaborate methods are reserved for cases in which there is a special need to know precisely how old a fetus or a newborn is. If the mother is diabetic, for instance, and is likely to encounter serious problems in the last weeks of pregnancy, an obstetrician might want to know the fetus's exact age so he can safely schedule an early delivery. This is usually done through an ultrasound examination, or through amniocentesis, or both.

Another special case is, of course, the very tiny infant. Several tests of a newborn's maturation have been developed recently. Among the quickest and least intrusive—essential considerations in the evaluation of sick babies—is the so-called Dubowitz assessment. In making these assessments, the doctor will very gently move your baby's arms, legs, and torso to see how well they assume certain positions. This positioning is your doctor's clue to the baby's neurological and muscular maturity. A 28-week-old premie, for instance, lying on his back offers no resistance when an examiner touches the baby's heel to his ear. By 32 weeks, this extreme flexibility has diminished, and at about 36 to 38 weeks it is impossible for an examiner to bring the baby's heel to his ear.

Baby's First Test: The Apgar Rating

A quick way to determine how a newborn is doing in his first few minutes of life is by the Apgar rating. This test, developed by Dr. Virginia Apgar in 1958, is administered to a newborn at one minute of age and again at five minutes of age. The baby's score at five minutes, on a scale of 1 to 10, has been shown to correlate significantly with such later measures as performance on tests of mental and motor development.

In doing an Apgar rating, this is what the doctor looks for:

What is the baby's heart rate?
If there is none, score 0.
If it is below 100 beats/minute, score 1.
If it is above 100 beats/minute, score 2.
What is the baby's respiratory effort?
If there is none, score 0.
If it is weak and irregular, score 1.
If it is good, and the baby is crying, score 2.
What is the baby's muscle tone?
If it is flaccid, score 0.
If there is some flexion of extremities, score 1.
If the baby is well flexed, score 2.
What is the baby's response to having a catheter placed in his nose or to having the sole of his foot tweaked (this is called reflex irritability)?
If there is no response, score 0.
If the baby grimaces, score 1.
If the baby coughs or sneezes, score 2.
What is the baby's color?
If it is blue and pale, score 0.
If the body is pink but extremities are blue, score 1.
If the baby is completely pink, score 2.
Doctors use the Apgar rating primarily to determine whether the baby needs to be resuscitated—that is, whether

he needs oxygen pumped into him for help in taking his first breaths. They will refer to it again during the premie's hospital stay to determine whether any subsequent problems (the ones we will discuss in Chapter 5) might have been related to difficulty immediately after birth.

A Few Premie Families

In the following chapters we will describe the special problems—and the special joys—that await you as the parent of a premie. At the same time, we will include the stories of a few families whose babies, like yours, were born too soon. These families' experiences were, of course, unique, and they may differ in significant ways from the events you will encounter in the months ahead. As we have seen, the category "premie" is a broad one, spanning three months of gestational age, and there is therefore no typical premie story. But these stories may well be closer to yours than the ones you'll hear from friends and relatives about their term infants—even term infants born on the same day as your premie. Premature infants are not just smaller versions of infants born at term. They are different in significant ways. And you are likely to recognize your own child's differences in the stories of other premie families, which will be scattered throughout the book.

Some of the families we will meet are actual families, whose words and experiences are recorded here exactly as they occurred. Some of the families are composites, with the details of their stories changed for the sake of clarity. In all cases, the names of family members have been changed to protect their privacy.

The Lees, whom we have already met, are an Oriental couple with two children. Ken, in his early forties, is a surgeon; his wife, Katie, in her late twenties, has a master's degree in social work. Even though their first child was born five weeks early, the Lees never worried about the next baby being born too soon when Katie got pregnant again one year later. In the seventh month of her second pregnancy, Katie went into labor. John was born the following evening, weighing 1190 grams (2 pounds 10 ounces). His breathing was good in the first two days, but he suffered a large brain bleed in his third day of life. Today, John is retarded and totally blind.

The Fosters, whom we met as well, are a white couple whose first child, Charles, arrived six weeks early. Stuart is an attorney; his wife, Ann, is an office manager. Charles weighed 1980 grams (4 pounds 6 ounces) at birth and, except for some early breathing difficulties, his hospitalization was without incident. But when he came home two weeks later, a surprising range of problems arose—extreme irritability, feeding difficulties, an immature esophagus that led to unusual amounts of spitting up. Within six months, though, Charles settled down to a normal pace of development.

The Wynns' first child, Aaron, was born at 27 weeks gestation weighing 940 grams. The Wynns are a black couple; Donald is a carpenter and Stacy is a hairdresser with her own small shop. In her seventh month of pregnancy, Stacy, who was herself born two months early, went into active labor that could not be stopped with antilabor drugs. Fifteen hours later Aaron was born. During Aaron's two-and-a-half-month hospital stay, he required the use of a ventilator, treatment for jaundice, and treatment for an infection. But today he shows no scars of his extreme prematurity.

We will meet these men and women again, as well as other premie families, as we describe the various paths a premie's first year might take. They will have much to tell us about what can happen to a tiny baby in his early months of life, what special feelings about parenthood are involved in being the parents of premies, and the ways in which caring for premies—both in the hospital and at home—demands a very special combination of knowledge and love.

2: A Tour of the Intensive Care Nursery

WHEN YOU FIRST WALK into the intensive care nursery, you will be struck by the constant cheeping of monitor alarms and the constant buzz of activity. As you zero in on your tiny baby in the midst of all this hubbub, she will seem lost indeed; a fragile-looking creature surrounded by an awesome life support system many times her size.

Don't be frightened by the knobs and buttons, the tubes and plugs, the busy nurses and doctors. At first glance, the cast of characters and the high-tech equipment might be dizzying, and the professionals you encounter might seem frazzled, or preoccupied, or lost in conversation about someone else's child. But you mustn't be cowed by this brave new nursery. *You* are still your baby's parent, and you have every right to expect the best care modern neonatology can deliver.

When you've just had a premature baby, you're probably

feeling more scared and more vulnerable than you've ever felt in your life. At a time like this, it's easy to be intimidated by the intensive care nursery and all the busy professionals in it. Your baby's hospitalization might even be your first introduction to doctors, nurses, and the strange rituals and routines of the modern hospital. No wonder you feel overwhelmed.

The most reasonable way to deal with your dizzying feelings is to try to learn all you can about neonatology—the medical care of newborns. The more you know about premature infants, about what care they should receive and what problems they could encounter, the better able you'll be to talk to your baby's caretakers as their intellectual equal. And, the more you know, the more you'll become part of the nursery team, working with the professionals there toward the same goal: the health of your child.

The pace of the intensive care nursery can seem frenetic, especially to a parent still reeling from the unexpected birth of a premature, often sick child. Typically, the first parent to see the baby in the nursery is the father. The mother is usually too weak from her delivery to visit her infant right away. And if the hospital where the baby was born has no intensive care nursery, the premie might even have been taken to a distant hospital with more sophisticated facilities—to be cared for there while Mother recovers at a different hospital clear across town.

Many fathers bear their sudden solo responsibility beautifully—but many others don't. Men are not used to the medical setting. Unlike women—who regularly see gynecologists and pediatricians, and who, during pregnancy, undergo routine prenatal checkups for months—men haven't had a chance to learn how to talk to doctors.

Will Davidson, one premie father, experienced an extreme case of the bewilderment many fathers face during their first visits to the intensive care nursery. Within hours of the precipitous birth of his son, Matthew, in a rural community hospital, Will rushed to the distant special care nursery to which the baby had been transferred. When Will arrived, alone, at a strange big-city hospital, he was directed to the nursery, shown how to scrub up, and told to put on a gown. But no one told him which baby was his. Overcome with shyness, confusion, frustration, and loneliness, Will couldn't even bring himself to ask. He just took off his gown and made the 50-mile drive back home.

A tour of the intensive care nursery might relieve some of the overpowering confusion that helped account for Will's behavior. First, let's take a quick look at the cast of characters who will play a major role in caring for your baby, the folks who will explain her medical and psychological growth to you, and who will make decisions about how to treat her, what to feed her, and when to send your baby home.

The Nursery Team

At most intensive care nurseries, the medical team is headed by the neonatologist. A neonatologist is licensed in both pediatrics and neonatal/perinatal medicine. To qualify as a neonatologist (which gets its name from the Latin word "neonate," meaning "newborn"), a physician must complete four years of medical school, three years of residency in pediatrics, and two years of a fellowship in neonatology at one of North America's 160 hospitals with special programs in neonatal care.

If your baby is in the hospital for more than one month, chances are you will encounter more than one neonatologist who will be your child's primary doctor. The doctors at most large newborn nurseries serve on one-month-long rotations, so that in any given month one or two doctors are responsible for all the babies in the unit. The next month, one or two different doctors take over.

The neonatologist on duty in March will tell you, before the end of the month, who will be the doctor in charge in April. He'll also give you an opportunity to talk to the new neonatologist a few days before he comes on duty. (To reflect the sex distribution of these professions accurately, we are using the generic "he" to describe doctors and the generic "she" to describe nurses—even though there are plenty of female doctors, especially among neonatologists, and many male nurses.) If he forgets to do this, ask him to. It will be much easier on you to be introduced to your baby's new doctor *before* you must discuss with him your baby's medical progress.

It might seem as though there are a great many people making decisions about your infant's care, but that's not really so. Ultimately, only one person is responsible for what happens to your baby—the neonatologist. The other members of the nursery team are added resources from whom you can seek basic information about your baby's progress, but the neonatologist is the person who makes the final decision. Bear this in mind when you talk to the doctors-in-training, nurses, or surgeons called in on your baby's case. Different individuals might interpret a particular condition in different ways, and might differ in how they tell you their opinions about your baby's health and prognosis. But the individual whose opinion matters most is the neonatologist.

"Our neonatologist warned us about the brain surgeon who was going to put a shunt into Meredith," recalls Eddie Pines, whose daughter required brain surgery for treatment of a severe bleed in the head. "The surgeon's an older man, in his late fifties, and still remembers the bad results of the surgery he did for this condition twenty years ago. The neonatologist was right, too. The first thing the surgeon said to me was, 'She has a 50–50 chance of being retarded, even if the operation is a success.' I'm glad the neonatologist had warned me about him."

If your baby is in a teaching hospital—that is, a hospital affiliated with a local medical school—the neonatologists will be assisted by neonatology fellows. Fellows are trained pediatricians who are studying for licensing as neonatologists. Ranking slightly behind them are the pediatric residents, young doctors who have been out of medical school for two to three years and are completing their hospital-based training before they can be licensed to practice pediatric medicine. Generally, fellows intend to remain involved in neonatology, and residents do not. (Pediatric residents are more likely to devote their careers to general pediatrics or to a different subspecialty, such as pediatric cardiology.) These doctors-in-training are all qualified to render medical opinions, but if you are at all disturbed or confused by what they tell you, don't feel shy about seeking out the neonatologist for an explanation.

At a teaching hospital, you are likely to see medical students and nursing students rotate through the unit. Depending on the students' personalities and abilities, you either will have very little to do with them, or you will find yourself seeking them out for information and advice. Again, remember that they are just part of a team, and if at any time you are confused by what they tell you, the neonatologist should have the final word.

Perhaps the most important caregivers in the neonatal intensive care unit are the nurses. Neonatal nurses are Registered Nurses (R.N.s) with special training or experience in dealing with newborns. Theirs is considered by many to be the most difficult job in nursing; working year in and year out with a constant succession of premies can be emotionally exhausting. In addition to its psychic stresses, the logistical stresses of the job are quite real: long hours, low pay, little status, and inconvenient work schedules. Even the best hospitals experience a high rate of turnover among nurses, as their good nurses "burn out," seek administrative jobs, or leave to have babies of their own.

Most neonatal nurses consider their charges to be uniquely beautiful and brave, and the attachment they form with these babies can sometimes mimic the mother-child bond. This can be especially hard on a mother, who might already envy the nurses for being able to spend all day or all night with her baby while she can only visit. Only rarely is a mother able to appreciate this affection for what it is: a sign of truly loving care, a sign that her infant is being emotionally enriched during her hospital stay. If you find yourself uncomfortable with your baby's nurses, ask yourself if you are, in part, jealous of all the time they can spend with your child. Try to understand that a nurse who loves your baby will be a better nurse—and that, no matter how good a nurse she is, she will never be your baby's mother.

A new kind of nurse is now making an appearance in many intensive care nurseries: the nurse practitioner. This is a nurse with a bachelor of science degree, plus one year of training beyond the R.N. Her extra training enables her to take on some additional medical responsibilities of her own. In the units that employ them, neonatal nurse practitioners behave much like resident physicians, inserting intravenous lines, intubating babies, and ordering medications (with a doctor's countersignature). They are always under the supervision of a fellow or a neonatologist, and they make daily rounds with the team. They're especially nice to have around because they don't rotate; unlike almost everyone else involved in your baby's care, the nurses and nurse practitioners will be there from one month to the next.

Because caring for a premie is a team effort, you will notice the medical professionals in frequent consultation. Every morning, they go on rounds—a regular review of each baby's progress, in which all professionals involved in the baby's care gather around her isolette and review the events of the previous day. Rounds are usually made early in the morning, and if you are visiting your baby you might be asked to step outside for the five or ten minutes that the doctors and nurses will be discussing her.

Many intensive care nurseries also have their own social workers. Some parents think a social worker can help them only if they are on welfare, or if they anticipate trouble paying the hospital bill, or if they want to arrange for foster care for their baby. That's not the case. Neonatal social workers can provide crucial emotional support while your baby is in the hospital and in those long first months at home. And you don't have to be "crazy"—or impoverished—to need their help.

At some hospitals, social workers have taken the lead in initiating parent support groups. The theory behind such groups is that a social outlet can help ease the pain of suffering alone. The self-help groups can take several forms. Some are a weekly evening meeting attended mostly by parents with babies still in the hospital and led by the social worker or another professional. Some are entirely parent-sponsored, with "graduate" parents whose babies are now home serving as counselors for new parents with babies recently born. A listing of self-help groups from around the country appears in Appendix C.

Other specialists include physical therapists, occupational therapists (an odd designation for a nursery full of new-borns, but for this age range stimulation and play are a baby's "occupation"), and psychologists. We will have more to say about the services they provide—which you will probably find of most use after you get your baby home—in Part II of the book.

An Artificial Womb

Once you learn who everyone is in the intensive care nursery, you'll want to know how they can help your baby. Remember that your child has missed some of the most important weeks of anyone's life—her last weeks in utero, when her body was meant to undergo dramatic growth and development. It is the goal of all those working in the intensive care nursery to simulate the conditions of the womb, to provide for your child a nurturing, warm, supportive environment that allows her to get on with the business of growing into a fully formed baby. Mimicking the womb is a theme you will hear over and over again, as you're introduced to the array of gadgets and enclosures designed to keep your baby healthy.

But if this is a womb, it's a bizarre womb indeed. How can anything so bright, so metallic, so mechanized be likened to the dark, soothing ocean of the fetus's first home? Rather than bouncing gently in a sea of amniotic fluid, your baby in the intensive care nursery will lie supine on a bed, her position changed frequently to ease the stress on any one part of her body. And rather than being housed in your uterus, your baby will find herself either in an isolette (what your mother called an "incubator") or on a warming bed.

A warming bed is a small mattress that can be adjusted to any position (head elevated, feet elevated, or flat). Above it hang two radiant heaters. A sensor, called a "servo-control," might be attached to the baby's skin to regulate her body temperature. It serves as a thermostat that directs the warming lamps to switch on or off. In nurseries that don't use this device, the nurses keep the baby's temperature constant by taking frequent readings and adjusting the isolette accordingly. Using servo-control, if the baby's skin temperature drops below body temperature (36° Celsius), the lamps turn on. And they stay on until the skin temperature again reaches 36°.

A warming bed does not regulate body temperature quite as well as an isolette does. But it does carry one important advantage: it allows quick, easy access to the baby. In her early days of life, the premie must be attended to constantly, especially if she is on a ventilator. Although a doctor or nurse can insert an intravenous line or prick a heel or take a temperature on a premie in an isolette, it is far easier to do these manipulations—and the even bigger manipulations required for sicker babies—when the baby is lying on a mattress that is open on all sides.

Within a short while, the premie will graduate to an isolette. An isolette is much like a warming bed, but it is more self-contained and therefore better at maintaining the baby's body temperature at an even level. Regulation of body temperature is crucial during a premie's early days, especially if she is so premature—younger than 32 weeks gestational age—that she cannot shiver, and has not yet laid down the layer of "brown fat" cells that full-term babies use to keep body temperature constant. Some premies need so much help staying warm that they require special isolettes within their isolettes—that is, double-walled units that hug closer to the babies' bodies—or need added layers of plastic, or even aluminum foil, on the isolette walls to keep precious heat from escaping.

The isolette is a see-through plastic bassinette, closed on top, that usually sits on a cart (with casters) housing a storage cabinet below. It has four portholelike openings on its sides, through which nurses, doctors, or parents can insert their scrubbed hands to manipulate the premie, to give her a bottle, or just to stroke a tiny arm or leg. At some hospitals, premies in isolettes are kept on waterbeds rather than regular mattresses; the theory is that for some babies, especially those with breathing problems, the simulation of the movements of the fluid-filled womb can have a beneficial effect.

Monitors

The premie lying in the isolette is usually naked. She might be wearing a diaper, and in some nurseries she might also be wearing a tiny ski cap, since doctors have found that as much as one-half of the heat lost from a premie's heat-starved body escapes from the head. Typically, the premie will have several wires attached to her body to keep tabs on her breathing, heart rate, and perhaps blood pressure or other functions. The wires, called "monitor leads," rest on top of her skin, and are fastened with small disks glued to the baby's chest or back with electrode jelly. It does not hurt the baby to have the disks on, and it does not hurt her to have them removed. The leads are connected to a large machine that you'll see at the top or side of the baby's isolette. These machines, called monitors, vary from hospital to hospital, but their purpose is always the same: to record, either through a visual screen display, a numerical reading, or both, the baby's vital signs.

On most monitors, you will see a small screen with squiggly moving lines. This is an oscilloscope, and the lines reveal the pattern of the baby's breathing and heartbeat. Nurses and doctors can look at the screen and tell from the frequency of highs and lows, as well as the height of the extremes, how well a baby is doing. When the baby's rate of respiration or heartbeat gets too high or too low, the monitor will sound a high-pitched alarm, and a tiny red light will begin flashing.

The first few times the alarm goes off, you may panic. But you'll relax after you see how calmly the nurses take these apparent crises. When a monitor alarm sounds, a nurse will first check all the leads to make sure they are still attached—often, even a slight movement from the baby will set off an alarm—and then will take further steps to get the baby behaving normally again. This may be as simple as tapping the isolette to remind the baby to start breathing, or as elaborate as grabbing the oxygen mask that always lies nearby and pumping oxygen directly into the baby's nose and mouth (a procedure called "bag and mask").

Tubes and Lines

If your baby is very small, she probably will have had several tiny hose-like attachments inserted into her. Some of these, called "catheters," are made out of special plastic compounds (most typically polyvinyl or Silastic) and are placed into a vein or artery. They are the route by which doctors and nurses can provide nutrients or medications to the baby and from which they draw out blood. Another attachment, called a "tube," is usually inserted into the stomach to remove air that could otherwise cause the stomach to enlarge and interfere with breathing.

When a catheter is in place and working, you will hear the doctors and nurses refer to it as a "line." There are two kinds of lines—peripheral lines and central lines. Peripheral lines are the more frequent. They can be inserted into the blood vessels at the periphery of the baby's body: her hands, her feet, even the top of her head. Through a peripheral line, doctors can administer nutrients or drugs, but it is generally difficult to draw samples of the premie's blood from this route.

If your baby has a peripheral line in place, you might also notice a splint and some bandages on her arm or leg. This does not mean the baby has broken a bone. All it means is that the doctors want some extra reinforcement for the tubing to make sure that the baby does not pull it or dislodge it as she moves.

Central lines tend to be used on sicker babies, and they have many uses. They stay in place for longer periods of time (that's why they're known as "indwelling catheters") and facilitate continuous monitoring of the baby's body functions. When a central line is inserted into a baby whose blood needs to be sampled and tested every half hour, the doctor won't need to reinsert a new catheter time and again. This helps protect the premie's fine, thin veins and delicate skin, which can be damaged when new tubes are frequently inserted.

In addition, the doctor can use the central line to deliver drugs or nutrients to the baby more easily, without damaging the fine veins in the baby's skin. A central line can be sent through one of several routes: through the saphenous vein (in the baby's leg), through the subclavian vein (in the arm), or through the umbilicus (the stump left behind after the obstetrician cuts the umbilical cord that had connected the fetus to the placenta).

An umbilical artery catheter is usually the first line placed, and it's the one you are most likely to see. It is used for keeping tabs on the levels of oxygen and acidity in the bloodstream when the infant is breathing additional oxygen, and it is used as well for continuous monitoring of blood pressure. Once the central line is in place, doctors need only open the spigot to draw off a little blood for analysis. Thus, frequent blood samplings can occur with a minimum of disruption to the baby. An umbilical artery catheter is used only as long as it is needed to measure blood gases. (In an adult, an artery is a blood vessel that carries oxygen-rich blood away from the heart and to the other organs in the body; a vein carries oxygen-depleted blood back to the heart.)

A central line inserted into the umbilical vein can be used for measuring venous pressure, drawing blood, or giving medications. In veins elsewhere in the body (such as the saphenous or subclavian vein), a central line can be used to give intravenous nutrition. When a line is used for nutrition, it is never used for anything else.

Central lines make the tasks of caring for your premie much more efficient and much less traumatic. But they also carry some risks. Infections or blood clots can develop, for example, where the indwelling catheter was inserted. For this reason, central lines are used for no longer than they need to be. In general, they will be removed as soon as your baby's condition has stabilized, especially once the baby is breathing a lower concentration of enriched oxygen.

Bili Lights

Premature babies are especially susceptible to a condition called neonatal jaundice, and your baby might need treatment for it while she's in intensive care. Jaundice is caused by a sluggishness in the functioning of the liver. The immature liver is unable efficiently to remove waste (called bilirubin) from the bloodstream. Bilirubin comes from the breakdown of the extra red blood cells the baby required in utero. When the liver functions poorly, bilirubin accumulates in the blood, giving a yellow tinge to the skin.

Treatment for neonatal jaundice consists of "phototherapy"—in other words, treatment with light. If your baby has jaundice, she will be placed under a special fluorescent lamp called a bilirubin light (affectionately known as a "bili light") around the clock. The bili light emits light waves at a wavelength that has been shown to hasten the breakdown of bilirubin in the bloodstream. She will stay under the lights until her liver is mature enough to take over.

The bili light is not harmful to the baby. To protect the baby's eyes from discomfort and possible damage, nurses will put on eye patches or a ski cap pulled down to the baby's nose. Parents often are distressed to notice that their infants cannot see when they're placed under the light. Just remember that phototherapy usually lasts for only a few days.

At many hospitals, nurses are instructed to turn off the bili lights whenever parents visit the baby, so the eye patches can be removed and the parents can engage in normal social interactions. If this is not done routinely at your hospital, ask your baby's doctor or nurse whether her condition is stable enough that she can do without phototherapy for half an hour or so.

Help for Breathing

If your baby has trouble breathing on her own, as 20 percent of premature infants do, she is likely to need some equipment to help her. Several possibilities are available, ranging from a simple oxygen hood to a sophisticated mechanical ventilator. The oxygen hood is about the size and shape of the plastic bowl of a food processor; it is a clear plastic cylinder that rests above the baby's head, with a hose coming out one end attached to a tank of oxygen outside the isolette. The air may seem foggy inside your baby's oxygen hood; if it does, it's because the doctors have warmed and humidified the oxygen to moisten the baby's air passages. The oxygen controller outside the isolette determines the percentage of oxygen delivered to the infant. From there, the oxygen is passed through a humidifier, which also has a temperature control. Ordinary room air has 21 percent oxygen; your baby's doctor might order a mixture of anywhere from 30 to 100 percent oxygen, depending on the child's needs.

If the baby needs even more help breathing, she may be given a trial of CPAP—continuous positive airway pressure. CPAP is a particular way of delivering oxygen, through a tiny tube inserted into the baby's nose or mouth. For CPAP the oxygen is also mixed, warmed, and humidified in an oxygen controller outside the isolette.

The last step in an effort to help the premie breathe is to place her on a ventilator. (This machine is often called a respirator; although you, your relatives, and even your doctors and nurses will probably use the two terms interchangeably, we will stick here to the term ventilator because it is the more accurate. The machine is breathing for your baby by helping to open the lung's air sacs more efficiently. She might also be doing some breathing on her own; you can check this by reading the number of breaths per minute coming out of the ventilator, and then counting your baby's actual breathing rate.) At most hospitals, about one-third of the babies admitted to the intensive care nursery eventually require assisted ventilation.

If your baby needs a ventilator, the doctors first will put a breathing tube down her throat. Through this tube, oxygenated air will be delivered directly into the baby's lungs.

The procedure of putting in the breathing tube is called intubation. You probably will not be allowed to watch your baby being intubated, but this is what happens: the doctor takes a long plastic tube, inserts it into the baby's nostril, and guides it through the nose, down the throat, and into the windpipe (the trachea). A tube inserted in this way is called a nasotracheal (that is, nose to trachea) tube.

Another way of intubating a baby is through the mouth instead of the nose. This is called an endotracheal tube. After it is inserted, the tube is held in place on the baby's face with tape or a special device for stabilization.

At one end of the tube, then, is the baby's trachea; at the other end, the part you can see, is the ventilator. Several kinds are in use today in the intensive care nursery: they generally can be categorized as time-cycled, volume-cycled, or pressure-cycled. We will discuss the different ventilators in more detail in Chapter 5, in a description of the treatment of respiratory problems in the premie.

3: Premature Parents

CONTRARY TO CONVENTIONAL WISDOM, most newborn babies are not instantly lovable. Our culture has tried to convince us that all newborns are pink, chubby, cherubic little bundles—the bundles we see in baby food ads. But the "Gerber baby" is really three months old. Newborns often are mottled, flat-faced, disconnected-looking creatures with dozens of tiny imperfections. Many parents love their babies instantly, but many others do not—and there's nothing wrong with the parents who don't.

For premies, love at first sight is even more unlikely. As we've already seen, a newborn premie is a wrinkled, scrawny, floppy thing who looks more like a newborn puppy than a baby. And mothers trying to "bond" with their premature babies already have one important strike against them: they have missed out on the final weeks of pregnancy that are designed to make bonding easier.

The Routes to Attachment

In 1974, Dr. A. C. Turnbull and his colleagues found that the blood level of the hormone called estradiol increases dramatically during the last seven weeks of pregnancy. Estradiol is a potent maternal hormone: it has been shown to induce mothering behavior in virgin female rats, and even in male rats. If a woman misses out on those last seven weeks of pregnancy, she misses out on those high levels of estradiol. She doesn't receive the benefit of hormones that probably make it easier for her to connect with her newborn baby—and to know what to do to care for him.

The leaders in the study of parent-infant attachment are Drs. Marshall Klaus and John Kennell. When they were both pediatricians at the Rainbow Babies' and Children's Hospital in Cleveland, they coined the term "bonding." Largely because of their research, many hospitals in the United States now allow parents of healthy newborns to keep the baby in the recovery room for an hour or so after birth. During this time, the mother might try to nurse the baby, and both parents spend a great deal of time stroking him, looking into his eyes, cooing to him, and holding him close.

The acceptance of bonding, which spread through the nation in the 1970s and 1980s, went a long way toward improving the relationship between new parents and their children. Because the hours after birth are a time when both mother and infant are physiologically primed to respond to each other, the bonding hour enabled more parents to go home from the hospital feeling as though their new baby was really theirs. But as with so many other trends in child development, the bonding trend carried with it its own guilt trip. Parents who, for one reason or another, missed out on the early moments of interaction with their newborns began to question whether their relationships with their children would forever be inadequate.

This has been especially true of parents of premies. The scene in the delivery room of a premie birth is quite different from the scene described in books about gentle birth, bonding, and instantaneous attachment. Parents struggling through premature labor and delivery are already under stress because of the uncertainty of the outcome; when their efforts are met only with a baby's weak cry—and no child to hold—the disappointment is enormous. Instead of receiving the baby to admire, to nurse, and to touch, bewildered parents receive only silence—or, worse, snatches of anxious conversation from the neonatal team working on their baby in a corner of the delivery room. Once the premie is stabilized, he might be held up briefly for his parents to see. But more often, he is whisked away altogether, sometimes even to a different hospital, and the parents are left wondering whether they really even had a baby at all.

Drs. Klaus and Kennell have made a study of what premie parents go through when left in this lonely situation. They describe one patient of theirs, whom they call Ann Dixon, and her terrible first days after the premature birth of her daughter, Kimberly. Kimberly was six weeks premature and had to be transferred to a hospital across town while Ann recovered on the maternity floor of the hospital where her baby was born.

"It was terrible in the hospital," she told the doctors. "At six o'clock in the morning they would come in and say, 'Would you please wake up, Mrs. Dixon, your baby's coming in,' and I was there for six days. Every day they'd come in and say, 'Please wake up, Mrs. Dixon, your baby's here— it's time to feed her.' I'd say, 'My baby isn't here.' The nurse [would say], 'Honey, you're just asleep—your baby's here.' I [would say], 'I know my baby is not here—please don't wake me up.' That was very hard. The girl next to me got her baby and fed her baby and she sort of felt bad. She said, 'Do you want me to pull the curtain because I have my baby and you don't?' "

Drs. Klaus and Kennell found that, though it might require more ingenuity and more perseverance, bonding can occur in the intensive care nursery quite as effectively as in the recovery room. There are more barriers—physical, psychic, geographic, logistical—but, given enough motivation, any parent can walk right up to his child's isolette and announce, in a style that is the parent's alone, that Mother or Father is there.

How do you begin the difficult work of bonding with your premie? Much the same way any other parent gradually learns a baby is really his—by sight, by feel, by sound, and by action.

1. Take a picture. If your baby will be transported to another hospital, an instant picture of the child is usually taken by the transport team. However, if you can, invest in a Polaroid camera and take some pictures of your own. That way, while the mother recovers in one hospital, she at least has a piece of her baby in another hospital. Each time Father visits the intensive care nursery, he can take more pictures. A photograph is almost always more reassuring than the pictures in one's imagination. They are almost as good as real life in easing Mother's fears as she tries to envision how her tiny baby looks, and where the tubes and wires she hears about fit on the baby's little body. Many hospitals routinely provide such photos for premie parents; ask whether yours does.

2. Visit as soon as you can. If the baby is in the same hospital in which he was born, both Mother and Father can soon go to see him in the intensive care nursery. Mother might need a wheelchair for the trip—don't be afraid to ask for one. When you first visit the intensive care nursery, a nurse will be on hand to show you where the gowns are and to instruct you how to scrub up. Usually, hospital policy requires that all parents, especially if they intend to touch

their baby, scrub their hands and arms to the elbow with antiseptic soap for two to three minutes, and put on a gown over their street clothes before entering the room. The nurse will show you where the sink, soap, paper towels, and gowns are kept.

Both parents might need to have a chair or stool near the isolette for the first meeting with their premie. No matter how well doctors and books prepare you for what he will look like, the actual sight of your baby—plus the sight of rows of other premies and sick infants, and the strange sounds and smells of the high-tech nursery—might make you feel faint. There's no shame in that. If you start to feel dizzy, sit down.

If your baby has been transferred to another hospital while Mother is still recovering from the delivery, Father will have to take on the parenting responsibilities alone at first. Many fathers say they feel closer to their premies than to their other children for just this reason—because with their premies they were actively, and uniquely, involved in those important early days.

A premie with jaundice will be treated with bilirubin lights, which require that he wear a blindfold to protect his eyes. Ask the nurse whether your baby's lights can be turned off at least for a while during your visit so you can take off his blindfold and look into his eyes. According to Drs. Klaus and Kennell, the authorities on bonding, an inability to make eye contact is one of the greatest obstacles to bonding with a premie, and one of the greatest sources of frustration for premie parents. You can expect to feel greatly relieved, and feel much more as though your baby is a "real" baby, once you can look him in the eyes.

3. Touch! As soon as the doctors say you can, put your hands in the isolette and touch your baby. You might wonder at first where on his tiny body you can find enough skin to touch, but it's there. Try his arms, his legs, the soles of his

feet. The extremities are less sensitive than the torso, so they are the best place to start.

You are relating to your baby each time you touch him. A stroke through a porthole might not seem like much, especially when you had envisioned episodes of nursing, cuddling, and caressing. But that will come later. Right now, your baby needs the quiet, reassuring presence of your fingertips, your palms. He will soon learn to recognize those hands as the ones that are there to comfort him, the ones that do not prick him or poke him or put in new tubes.

Touching your baby is important not just for your relationship, but for your baby's health. Premies have been denied weeks of the most sensuous period of human experience—the time in the womb, when the sway of the mother's body, the warmth of the uterus, the buoyancy of the amniotic fluid envelop a fetus in a world of peace and nurturance. This is the ideal environment in which to grow. You can help recreate it by your touch. Studies of premies have shown that those who were touched an additional twenty minutes a day beyond the amount involved in routine care gained weight more rapidly, had fewer episodes of apnea (breathing stoppages), and scored higher on tests of mental and motor development in the first year.

4. Talk! The next important stimulus you can provide for your premie is your voice—especially when it is combined with your touch. The bulk of the stimulation that premies receive in the intensive care nursery is disjointed—the sounds they hear are unrelated to the sights they see, which are unrelated to the medical procedures they feel. Only your input is coherent. By talking gently to your baby as you stroke him, you can let him learn to incorporate input from two different senses—an important step on the road to intelligence.

While your baby was in utero, he was able to hear his mother's and father's voices, filtered through the pulsing sound of the placenta and the mother's digestive and circulatory systems. Now, as he lies in his isolette—which carries in its motor a steady hum equal in noise level to that of moderate automobile traffic—he will be soothed once again by those familiar voices. Keep talking to your baby, even if you feel a little foolish to be cooing in the middle of such sterile-looking equipment. In a little while you will notice that your baby really does perk up when he hears your voice. As one premie mother recently told a reporter, "Somewhere in her brain, I think she knew, 'There's that voice that doesn't hurt me.' "

5. Don't let the nurses do your job. As soon as your baby is out of danger, you'll be able to do the things for him that all parents do—change his diapers, feed him, give him baths. These caretaking chores might seem boring—and, in fact, they are!—but they are what cement the bond between parent and child. The more you do to comfort and nurture your baby, the more he learns to love you and the more devoted you feel toward him. Don't make the nurses do these tasks for you; they are more than willing to teach you how to do them for yourself. Nurses might be warm and loving, but they are not your baby's parents. Only you can give him the feeling that he is the most special creature in the world.

At first, it will be terrifying to take on any of the care of your child. Even lifting him out of his isolette is frightening when the baby is attached to apnea monitors or oxygen machines. But it can be done. Nurseries that have experimented with allowing parents to take over routine child care as early as possible have been pleased with the results. In some cases, parents have become wholly responsible for their premies when the babies weighed as little as 1700 grams—about the size of two dense loaves of bread.

At the Rainbow Babies' and Children's Hospital, Drs. Klaus and Kennell were involved in a program in which mothers could "room in" with their premies when the babies weighed between 1720 and 2110 grams (3 pounds 12 ounces to 4 pounds 11 ounces). During this period, which the doctors referred to as "nesting," Mother and baby stay together in a private hospital room, and Mother is wholly responsible for the infant's care. It's considered a prelude to discharge— but it occurs when the baby is still too small for most hospitals to allow him to go home.

"It was interesting to observe that the mothers rearranged the furniture, crib, and infant supplies [in the hospital room], resembling in some ways the nesting behavior observed in animals," the pediatricians have reported. "Eight of the first nine mothers were unable to sleep during the first 24 hours, . . . [but] in the second 24-hour period the mothers' confidence and caretaking skills improved greatly. . . . The babies seemed to be quieter during this living-in period. In some mothers there were physical changes, such as increased breast swelling accompanied by some milk secretion." Once they were given total responsibility for child care, these premie mothers finally were able to look and act maternal.

Many nurses and parents become quite creative in the ways parents are allowed to take over care of their premies. The fact that a baby is being fed by a nasogastric tube, for instance, does not necessarily mean he can't be lifted out of his isolette and held during feedings. If Mother or Father pins the tube to a collar or lapel, the baby can be cradled in two arms throughout the feeding. It might not look like a Mary Cassatt painting, but it's an important step in cementing the bond between parent and child.

Don't be shy about coming up with similar techniques of your own. If what you long to do is bathe your child, but you can't figure out when or how, talk to your nurse. Together you can decide when is the best time for your baby's bath, and what special efforts might be needed to keep certain tubes or other equipment out of the bath water. If you want to try changing his diaper, or feeding him, or even cleaning his tubes or replacing his monitor leads, ask if you may. Remember, he is your baby, and you're the one who will go home with him and take care of him for many years to come.

Grief, Guilt, Anxiety

"She still doesn't really feel like my daughter," Lorna Jackson confessed three weeks after Jade's premature birth. "She feels like she belongs to the hospital. My husband's office has given him a baby shower, but I don't really want presents yet. I don't want to get her anything, or even fix up her room, until we know for sure that she's coming home."

Like Lorna, many premie parents feel and act reserved about their babies. This doesn't mean they don't care; usually, they're the very parents who care tremendously. Mother, especially, might feel an overwhelming desire to caress and protect her tiny baby. But she holds back—out of fear, or sadness, or guilt. She might already blame herself, rationally or irrationally, for the baby's premature birth, and she might feel she would endanger her baby by holding him, feeding him, or loving him.

"I didn't want to touch John the first time I saw him," Katie Lee recalls. "I felt so responsible for putting him through this, and I didn't want to hurt him anymore."

The guilt felt by premie parents is very normal—and it can be enormous. "What did we do wrong," they ask each other time and again, "to bring on labor too soon?" Almost every couple can find something to fret about. We shouldn't have had sex, they might think; we shouldn't have gone sailing; we shouldn't have moved to a new apartment.

Mother can come up with dozens of things she should or should not have done: I should have stopped working, I shouldn't have lifted my older child, I should have been more sure about wanting this baby, I shouldn't have had those two glasses of wine. And underlying the self-recriminations is her unspoken thought that she can't be much of a woman if she can't even carry a baby to term.

The only way to deal with these feelings is to talk about them—to your husband, your friends, your doctors and nurses and social workers. A premature birth creates a crisis of confidence, especially for the mother. "For mothers of premature infants," notes Dr. Marjorie J. Seashore, a sociologist at San Francisco State University, "the typical hospital care procedures may themselves induce feelings of inadequacy. . . . By placing the infant in an intensive care unit in which he is cared for by trained medical personnel rather than by his mother, the hospital is not only increasing the physical distance between mother and infant but is communicating to the mother that her infant requires care that she is not able to provide." A typical feeling for a premie mother, notes Dr. Seashore, is a profound lack of self-confidence. She tends to think that other people—the child's father, grandmother, nurses, or doctors—are always going to be better able to comfort, clothe, and feed the baby than she is.

The birth of a premie has been described by psychologists as an "acute emotional crisis." Far more than the crisis of new parenthood, which in itself is incredibly stressful, the crisis of premature parenthood demands all the inner resources of an individual and a couple. At no other time is a relationship under such strain. The patterns of communication you establish early during this crisis will help determine whether your baby's special needs draw you apart—or closer together.

The important thing for a couple to remember at this difficult time is that one must not judge the reactions of the other. There is no "right" way to react to a premie; all feelings, ranging from profound, instantaneous attachment to revulsion and rejection, are normal. And one thing is certain: However you feel about your premie today, you won't feel that way forever.

Both Mother and Father will experience wide swings of emotion, one day euphoric about the baby's chances and the next day in a deep depression about whether he'll be normal. Chances are the emotions will be mirror images of each other: when Mother is gleeful, Father will be sad; when Mother is at her lowest, Father will be at his best. Don't blame the other parent for being insensitive; just be glad he's there to complement your own emotions.

This balance is lost, of course, for premie mothers who are single. For them, the grief and isolation of premature parenthood can be profound. No one understands quite how worried you are; no one knows quite how to say the right thing. The other women on the maternity floor, reveling in their healthy babies, seem an affront, and there's no one on your side to soften the hurt. If you feel especially lonely during this time, ask the social worker on the unit to put you in touch with other single mothers, either with premies currently in the hospital or with babies who have "graduated" from the intensive care nursery.

The Four Stages of Premie Parenthood

The experts say there are four stages to be accomplished on the road to healthy premie parenthood. All these stages, ideally, are encountered while the baby is still in the hospital. You and your mate must work through the stages both together and separately. This will probably occur even without your conscious effort, as you find yourself experiencing the following emotions on your way toward building a feeling of closeness and commitment to your tiny new baby:

1. Anticipatory grief: the preparation for the possible loss of the child. In this stage, which usually occurs immediately after delivery, the parents withdraw emotionally from the

child so that, while they hope he will live, they brace themselves for his death.

2. Facing up: the acknowledgment and acceptance of the mother's failure to deliver a normal full-term baby. This can occur simultaneously with the first task, so that by the time the baby is out of danger, the mother has recognized her own feelings of guilt and failure, and is ready to move on. Sometimes, though, the feelings of guilt persist for a long time and are eased only through counseling and demonstration that the parent really is able to provide good care for the child.

3. Bonding: the resumption of a relationship with the new baby. In a healthy term delivery, bonding ideally begins in the moments after birth. For a premature birth, especially one in which the baby is very sick, it does not truly begin until two or three days later, when the baby begins to recover. Usually, it is only now that parents feel ready to allow themselves to believe that the baby is really theirs, will really be all right, and will really come home.

4. Learning: the development of an understanding of the ways in which premies differ from full-term babies. By the time they're ready to take the baby home, parents must view him as a premature infant with special needs. But, at the same time, they must understand that these special needs are temporary and that, eventually, the premie will look and behave like any other child.

Grandparents and Other Loved Ones

Often, in the tense atmosphere of the intensive care nursery, parents can become a tight little twosome who see themselves as all alone in the world. But there are many other people who love your baby, too—and who worry about him almost as much as you do. Your own parents, your sisters and brothers, your friends—all the people who love you already love your child. And their concern about your baby is enlarged, and complicated, by their concern about you.

Since a tendency for premature births can run in families, many grandparents of premies were premie parents themselves. They have some pretty gruesome memories of the high-risk nurseries of thirty years ago, when the majority of babies with hyaline membrane disease died and when a significant number of survivors of intensive care were sent home blind, or with cerebral palsy, or with some other major problem. Those memories now color the feelings they have toward you and their tiny grandchild; they don't want their nightmares to be relived in yours.

The baby's grandparents are, first and foremost, your parents. Their concern for your child is overriden, in most instances, by their concern for you. Don't get angry at them if you think they're being unfair to your baby when they suggest that you stay away from the hospital, or decline naming him, or hold off on buying a crib just yet. They are only trying, in the best way they know how, to protect you.

Sometimes their efforts to protect you might seem misguided—and might, in turn, prompt efforts on *your* part to protect your child, even from your own parents. "I don't think I can ever forgive my mother for the things she has said about Aaron," says Stacy Wynn. When her mother suggested that Stacy and her husband, Donald, try to relax a little rather than spend every afternoon and every evening sitting beside Aaron's isolette, Stacy flew into a rage. "She keeps saying we should go out to dinner or to a movie," Stacy says. "She says she doesn't understand why we're knocking ourselves out coming here twice a day. But I'm here all the time because I want to be. The only time I'm not worried about Aaron is when I'm with him."

Another premie mother, Vera Stone, had a similar experience. "My mother had six children of her own, plus three adopted children, and has two other grandchildren," Vera says. "She's the most loving mother I can imagine. But after Ben was born, she said to me, 'If I were you, I wouldn't go to visit him every day. You don't want to get too attached to him in case something happens.' If anyone should know, she should know that there's no way you could get less attached to your child, whether you go every day or once a week."

The comments made by grandparents can be especially hurtful if they underscore some underlying conflicts already running through their relationships with their adult children. Some grandparents, for instance, can't stop themselves from assigning blame for the baby's prematurity to a son-in-law or daughter-in-law with whom relations are already strained: "If he had stayed home with you rather than taking all those business trips. . . ." "If only she hadn't insisted on working throughout her pregnancy. . . ."

In families that have experienced a premature birth before, a grandparent's reaction to a new generation of premies can be especially chilling. "While my daughter was in the intensive care nursery, my mother told my brother that the baby might be better off dead," one premie mother recounts. "The baby weighed only two pounds at birth, and my mother was worried that she would be retarded. But I was a 4-pound baby myself, and now I keep wondering: is that what she thought about me when I was born?"

In these premie-prone families, the reaction of grandparents is usually complicated by another emotion—the grandparents' own feelings of guilt. This is most likely to be the case for premies born to so-called "DES daughters," young women whose mothers took the synthetic hormone DES during their pregnancies. The drug was used widely in the 1940s and 1950s to prevent miscarriage, and only recently has it come to be associated with a wide range of problems in the offspring exposed to DES in utero. Among these problems: a tendency, among DES daughters, toward premature labor.

Ironically, the women who took DES when they were pregnant twenty-five to forty years ago are the very women for whom childbirth often meant tragedy. They took the powerful drug in the first place only because they had a history of difficulty becoming and staying pregnant; many of them had tried for years to have families before DES finally made it possible. "I only took it because I wanted you so much," one mother apologized when she told her daughter she was a DES daughter. When "DES mothers" become "DES grandmothers," their tiny, sick grandsons or granddaughters become a personal affront. Many of them see these premies as yet another generation that must suffer because of their own incomplete femininity—a view that is certain to complicate their ability to approach the new baby with happiness or hope.

Your parents, your brothers, and your sisters don't know your baby yet the way you do. To them, your baby is primarily someone who is causing you pain. Try to remember this when they say things that to you seem incredibly callous and hurtful. And if you react to some of their comments with fury on behalf of your child, remember that the protective, all-consuming love you are feeling for your baby at that moment is the very same love that they're feeling for you. When they see the pain your baby causes you, their first instinct is to protect *you*. Your relatives wouldn't say the things they do about your child if they didn't love you so much.

Your Older Children

Difficulties with your premie's older siblings might create an especially wrenching problem. How do you explain to a preschooler that Mommy and Daddy are sad, and that they must divert all their psychic and physical energy for the sake of a faraway baby? How do you explain to an eager kindergartner that she won't be able to play with her new baby for a while?

If your premie is the second child in the family, you probably could have anticipated some sibling rivalry anyway. It's not easy for a youngster to learn to share her parents' love, attention, and time. But the extent of the jealousy and resentment that can bubble up against a premie can run far deeper than ordinary sibling rivalry. The new baby is, and remains, a stranger to your older child. He is someone your child has no chance to get to know—yet he does more to preempt the firstborn's central place in the family than any newborn at home possibly could. Sometimes, the disarray of family harmony following a premie's birth occurs with absolutely no warning, if the second baby is so premature that Mother and Father have not even told their older child yet that Mother is pregnant.

If the firstborn is old enough, she will be grieving, too—grieving not only for the loss of her parents and their exclusive attention, but for the loss of the baby whose arrival had been so eagerly anticipated. If an older child is properly prepared for an addition to the family, she looks forward to the new baby as a potential playmate, friend, and ally. She has waited patiently—and, more often, not so patiently—during the long months of pregnancy, looking at her friends' baby brothers and sisters with envy and planning the activities she will embark on some day with her own live-in companion. In many ways, she is almost as disappointed as you are that the ideal birth and joyful homecoming you envisioned together did not occur.

Chapter 4 is a special illustrated chapter specifically designed for your older children. It is meant to help you in guiding the adjustment of your premie's older brother or sister. "My Baby Sister's Too Small to Come Home" is a short story that might help your youngster verbalize her own fears and resentments.

If your firstborn is two or three, cuddle up with her and

read as much of the story as she is interested in. If she's older, she might want to use the pages as a coloring book, or even read the story herself. But the important thing is for you to try to use the story to get your firstborn talking about how she feels.

The protagonist is named Chris, so she can be either a boy or a girl. You might want to turn Chris into the same sex as your child to make it easier for your child to identify with Chris's thoughts and emotions. Ask questions about the story: "Isn't Chris lucky to have Grandma staying over?" or "Would you like to go to the hospital to visit your new baby, like Chris did?"

Some hospitals now allow short sibling visits in the intensive care nursery, but the rules vary. Ask your doctors whether your older child can scrub up, put on a gown, and come in to touch the baby some day when the nursery is relatively quiet. If not, perhaps she can at least see the baby through the nursery window.

If your older child is going to visit, think about ways to prepare her. Remember what a shock your baby was to you—how much greater a shock he will be to your firstborn, whose imagination already turns some not-so-scary sights into the stuff of nightmares! Elizabeth Hawkins-Walsh, a nurse at Georgetown University Hospital in Washington, D.C., who specializes in counseling families of intensive care nursery patients, suggests what she calls "hands-on" experience. Buy your child a tiny, tiny doll and borrow some cast-off catheters and monitor leads from the nursery. Let her play with the doll and the equipment, explaining to her why the tubes must be positioned in the baby's mouth, nose, arms, or legs.

Talk to the staff about using an idle isolette for your child to place the doll in; if that's unworkable, consider buying some sort of plastic box, like a sewing box from the dime store. According to Ms. Hawkins-Walsh, the most troublesome aspect of a child's first sight of a premie is that the

baby is lying in "that box." Children are especially concerned because the box has a lid on it, and they can't figure
out how the baby breathes.

Stimulating the Premie

You might think, when you're inside the non-stop hubbub of the intensive care nursery, that the last thing a premie
needs is stimulation. Look at all the "inputs" he's receiving—the sound of the nurses' conversation and perhaps the
music from their radios; the touch of the doctor's stetho-
scope and the nurse's thermometer; the sight of the lights,
the equipment, the faces passing by.

But think again. The intensive care nursery might seem
stimulating to you, but to a premie it's not stimulating at
all—it's downright deafening. In self-defense, most premies
learn to tune out all the inputs. Rather than try to make
sense of a world that to them is chaotic and disorganized,
premies try desperately to find some quiet, some solace,
comparable to the sensations of the womb.

Only you, the baby's parents, can provide that solace.
While your baby was in utero, he eavesdropped on your
surroundings, your conversations, even the sounds of your
body functioning. He learned whose voice was his
mother's—and, often, whose voice was his father's, too.
When those voices call out to him from the harsh new world
he entered too soon, the baby takes comfort and, finally, can
rest.

This sounds like an idealized, romantic notion of the parent-infant bond, but it's not. It's based on the findings of sci-
entific studies. One researcher, for example, played a tape
recording of their mothers' voices to a group of premies six
times a day at two-hour intervals until the babies reached a
gestational age of 37 weeks. The premies who received this
input exhibited greater response to a bell or rattle, and

scored higher on motor maturation when tested at 36 weeks. The premies in the control group (that is, those who did not receive this stimulation) exhibited lower visual response to a red rattle, and lower scores of touch adaptability.

One recent study found that just by stroking and flexing a premie's legs for seven minutes an hour over ten days, a researcher could improve the baby's development along several dimensions. When compared to nonhandled infants, the babies who were handled exhibited better body tone, more alertness, better head control when they were pulled up to sit, more rapid avoidance of noxious stimuli, better ability to recognize familiar light and sound patterns, and greater hand-to-mouth facility. And—perhaps most important to the parents—the handled babies were more easily consoled.

Other studies of extra stimulation in the intensive care nursery—usually in the form of prearranged periods of stroking or rocking by the nurses, or something as simple as hanging some colorful objects outside the isolette—almost always find that the stimulated babies do better. Visual and tactile stimulation tend to make premies sleep better, gain weight better, learn better, and respond better.

Although most such studies involve only very small numbers of babies, when taken as a whole their message is clear: premies benefit from being touched. What scientists are trying to determine now is just what kind of touch is best, and in what amount, and for what duration. That is where the parents come in.

The problem in most intensive care nurseries is not that there's not enough stimulation, but that it's of the wrong kind. Psychologists call it "disjunctive stimulation," or "non-contingent stimulation"—events that occur seemingly at random, with little relationship to any action the baby might initiate. "Although infants in special care units do not suffer from a lack of visual, auditory, and tactile stimulation, they have relatively little coordinated or integrated sensory experience," notes Dr. Allen W. Gottfried, a psychologist who tested the kinds of stimulation received by premies at the University of Southern California Medical Center Women's Hospital in Los Angeles.

In a typical home, with a typical term baby, there's a clear cut meaning to certain rituals. The baby cries and someone soon will come to him. The sound of footsteps means Mother is coming; the sight of the breast or bottle means food is coming; the sound of Mother's voice, combined with the feel of her arms and smell of her body, means he is taken care of and loved. By putting all these inputs together—over and over again, day after day—the newborn learns to make sense of his surroundings.

But the only sense in the intensive care nursery is the parents. If the parents are there frequently, talking to the baby in tones that became familiar while he was in the womb, they can provide an oasis of coherence in an incoherent world. Doctors and nurses are too busy attending to the baby's medical needs to worry, at least at first, about his emotional ones. That is the job of the parents, a job that is as important in the hospital as it will be for the rest of the child's life.

One nice way parents have found to stimulate their babies is to make a tape recording of their voices to leave in the isolette. You can't be with your premie round-the-clock—but a tape can be. It's noisy inside the isolette—the motor sound can reach 75 or 80 decibels (a radio at full blast, by comparison, is 60 decibels, a factory about 75)—and any sound that's not loud and harsh is especially welcome. Talk into a cassette recorder for half an hour or so, using your baby's name frequently. Sing lullabies, describe his room at home, tell him about his grandparents, recite Mother Goose rhymes. Then bring the recorder and the cassette into the nursery, have them sterilized if the hospital requires it, and ask the nurses to turn the tape on every now and then. Your baby will eventually learn that those are your voices, and they will keep him company.

From one day to the next, your feelings about your premie are bound to change. But you are that baby's parent,
now and forever, and no amount of separation or illness is
going to change that. If you allow yourself the freedom to
feel, and if you make sure you have the opportunity to
express your feelings to your child, you and your baby will
help each other through the coming difficult weeks until it's
time, triumphantly, to take him home.

4: A Special Illustrated Section

"My Baby Sister's Too Small to Come Home":
A Story for Siblings
Illustrations by Deborah Addison

LAST WEDNESDAY MORNING when I woke up, Mom and Dad were gone. Next to my pillow I found a green envelope with a piece of paper inside. And then Grandma came into my room! She said she would be staying at our house for a few days. I gave Grandma my green envelope, and she read from the piece of paper inside. It said, "Dear Chris, We went to the hospital to have our baby. We love you—see you soon! Love, Mom and Dad."

I was so excited. Grandma told me she made my favorite breakfast—cream of wheat. We had a good time eating breakfast, and then we played together with my new blocks. Later, Grandma read some books to me. But Grandma didn't seem to be having too much fun. She kept stopping in the middle of a page and looking away. Then she'd hug me and sigh and start to read again.

That afternoon, Daddy called on the telephone. "You have a new baby sister!" he said. But Grandma was looking worried.

When Dad came home that night, he looked worried, too. "Your sister's name is Megan," he told me. "She's beautiful, with lots of pretty brown hair and big blue eyes. But she's very, very small—much smaller than new babies usually are."

"Why is she so small?" I said.

"Because she was in such a rush to be born. She wasn't supposed to be born for another two months, and her body really still belongs in Mom's belly where it can grow best. But Megan was in a hurry. She wanted to see you and me and Mom as soon as she could. The doctors at the hospital have put her in a special kind of crib to keep her warm and protected. She has to stay there for a while until she is big enough and strong enough to come home."

I wanted to ask Dad why she couldn't grow bigger in her own house, in her own room, in her own crib that used to be mine. But I didn't because Daddy looked so sad.

Every day since then, Daddy has gone to the hospital on his way home from work to visit Mom and Megan. When he comes home, it's late at night and he's very tired. He hardly has any time to play with me before I have to go to bed.

That baby! She made everything different by coming so early. She made Daddy tired, she made Grandma sad, and, worst of all, she made Mom go to the hospital and stay there for a long time. If it weren't for that baby, Mom would be home with me and Dad would be able to fly me in the air like an acrobat after dinner.

When I came home from school on Friday, I started to cry because Mommy still wasn't home from the hospital. "Don't worry, Chris," Grandma said. "Mommy will be home soon. And when Megan comes home things will be even better. Mom and Dad will be happy, because it will mean Megan's not sick anymore. And you will be happy, too. You'll like having a little sister around to look at and play with and tickle and hug."

Yesterday was Saturday, so Dad was home all day. He took me with him to the hospital, and the nurses let me go upstairs to see Mom in her room. She looked so pretty sitting in her hospital bed wearing her robe with the yellow flowers all over it. I was happy to see her. When I hugged her, she cried and cried.

Mom took me down the hall to see Megan in the special hospital room for tiny babies. "She'll look a little funny to you," Mom said, "because she's so tiny. And she has a lot of wires attached to her so the doctors can help her get well." Mom said there would also be a hose in Megan's mouth to blow air into her. She said Megan needed that extra air to help her breathe better.

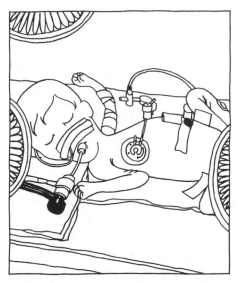

Megan was lying without any clothes on inside a little plastic box. No wonder she had trouble breathing—the box had a cover on it!

Megan was smaller than any of my dolls. Her arms and legs were real skinny, and I couldn't see her face at all because of that hose. She looked very sick to me. I also thought she looked sad, lying there all by herself without anyone to play with.

Last night I had a dream about Megan. I dreamed she was trying to swim in a big lake, but she couldn't hold her breath under water. So I had to lift her up and carry her on my back to a boat, Mom and Dad were in the boat, and they laughed and said, "Chris! Chris! You saved our baby! Now we can all be together!"

Today Dad told me Megan doesn't need that hose to breathe with anymore. I'm glad. I think it would hurt to have a hose stuck in your mouth all the time.

When Mom comes home on Tuesday, I'm staying home from nursery school. I'll help Grandma make lunch for Mom and put it on a tray so she can eat it in bed, if she wants to. But I hope she'll want to eat her lunch with me, in the kitchen.

Grandma says Mom might be sad when she comes home, because she really wanted to be able to come home with a baby instead of all alone. But Dad says Megan will be coming home, too, just a few weeks after Mom. And besides, Mom won't be all alone at home. She'll still have me.

5: The Hospital Roller Coaster

WITH PREMIES, anything can happen. One day, the baby might seem fine, and the next morning he could wake up with a severe infection that takes weeks to clear. Premie parents soon learn not to take anything for granted.

The metaphor most often used to describe a premie's hospital stay is that of a roller coaster. Optimism about a rapid and intact recovery skyrockets one day and plummets the next. And, of course, the parents are along for the ride.

Parents of premies, especially very tiny premies, telephone the hospital first thing each morning or visit the intensive care nursery first thing each afternoon with one thought uppermost in their minds: Is my baby the same as he was yesterday, or did something new come up while I was away?

This chapter is not meant to scare or worry you—although it probably will. It's agonizing to think that, just when you imagine your baby is out of the woods, something wholly unexpected could arise and set his progress back for weeks. But bear in mind that the odds against even any *one* of these problems affecting your baby are great—and the odds against any two or more of them affecting him are greater still. Most of the complications outlined here happen, if they happen at all, to premies of very low birthweight—less than 1500 grams. In general, the bigger your baby, and the greater his gestational age, the less likely he is to encounter setbacks on his road back home.

The conditions described here are listed in alphabetical order. All problems that premies typically encounter are included, no matter how minor and reversible they might be. The more information you have, the better able you'll be to talk to your doctor about your baby's prospects. And, perhaps even more important, information will help you to ration your worry. If you fret about every medical downturn, and wonder with each new diagnosis about what it portends for the future, you'll have no energy left to think about your infant as a real baby rather than a collection of medical charts. Although hospitals differ greatly in the ways they treat the same problem, we present detailed information here in the hope that it will help you intelligently decide which conditions you should worry about, and which you shouldn't.

Anemia

Anemia is a blood disorder characterized by an insufficient number of red blood cells, which contain the iron-rich compound called hemoglobin. It occurs in almost all premies because they have missed out on the last weeks of gestation, during which red blood cells ordinarily are produced in great numbers. A full-term baby is born with enough iron stores to last him for approximately six months, but a premie typically has enough iron to last him only a month or two.

There are two kinds of anemia: the kind caused by a relative deficiency of red blood cells, and the kind caused by an absolute deficiency of blood. The latter form, more properly called volume loss, is caused in large measure by the ministrations of doctors—the very efforts, ironically, that are needed to save the premie's life. Problems caused in this way are known as "iatrogenic illnesses," from the Greek "iatrikos," for physician, and "genic," caused by.

At the time of birth, most newborns get a large amount of blood from the umbilical cord. Obstetricians usually wait to clamp the cord until after it stops pulsing—that is, until after it has emptied all of its blood supply into the newborn's body. But a premie birth is often an emergency, and the obstetrician must clamp the cord immediately so life-saving efforts can get under way. This rapid severing of the blood supply can cause the premie to suffer a loss of blood volume that must somehow be replaced.

Another type of iatrogenic anemia occurs when blood samples are taken frequently from very sick, very small infants. The amount of blood a baby can spare depends on his weight. Most premies can tolerate no more than 5 to 10 percent of their blood volume being taken within forty-eight hours. Thus, a 1500 gram premie might become anemic after just 10 cc's of blood are removed for study. To avoid this complication, doctors routinely administer replacement transfusions to premies from whom a great deal of blood must be taken.

Research has been conducted recently into the role of vitamin E in the development of anemia. Premies are born with extremely low stores of vitamin E. A premie weighing 1000 grams might have a vitamin E level as low as 3 micrograms, compared to 20 micrograms in a full-term newborn. Vitamin E serves as an antioxidant, inhibiting the blood cells from interacting chemically with the oxygen they carry through the bloodstream. In the absence of vitamin E, the cell membrane—composed of the fatty acids that tend to react with oxygen—is quickly broken down. The result: destruction of the red blood cells and, eventually, anemia.

Treating anemia with large iron supplements may only worsen the disease in vitamin E-deficient premies, because iron acts as a catalyst in this chemical oxidation process. Some hospitals have been successful in administering oral vitamin E supplements to their premies, sometimes in combination with iron. Other hospitals have found that premies fed breast milk, which contains both vitamin E and a therapeutic proportion of saturated (as opposed to polyunsaturated) fat, do well without any supplements.

Transfusion is usually required when the anemia is severe. A transfusion, which takes about two to three hours to accomplish, sends a fresh supply of healthy red blood cells into the baby's bloodstream via an intravenous line. After a transfusion, you'll notice that your baby's color is pinker, healthier, and he might seem more alert than he did just before the transfusion.

For sick premies, transfusions might be needed as often as once every two or three days. They carry some risk, but the risk is usually minimal. Most commonly, infection can occur at the site of the intravenous line (this is a hazard caused by the line, not the transfusion). Rarely, an infection can be introduced through the blood itself. Some hospitals are beginning to use washed red blood cells, which lessens the likelihood of infection. In any event, within ten days to two weeks, the transfusions probably will no longer be needed. Anemia is one of the most common problems seen in the intensive care nursery, and it is also one of the easiest to treat.

Apnea and Bradycardia

Apnea and bradycardia are really two separate problems—the first is a difficulty with breathing, the second, a slowing of the heartbeat—but they occur together so frequently that they often are uttered as one word. About one-third of premies under 1750 grams suffer from apnea and bradycardia. Indeed, these problems are so common that doctors and nurses now consider them relatively minor hazards that the baby almost certainly will outgrow.

Apnea (literally, "no breath") occurs when the baby forgets to breathe. Apnea that is part of the pattern known as "periodic breathing"—when the baby breathes strenuously for a few moments and then stops altogether for five or ten seconds before he resumes—is seen in almost all premies in their first days of life. But when the apnea persists for longer than 20 seconds, it's not considered normal.

The most common time for apnea to occur is as the baby drops off to sleep immediately after eating. Premies who are prone to apnea are wired to a respiratory monitor that is set to beep whenever the apneic period extends past a pre-determined level. The length of an acceptable "pause" in breathing varies from one hospital to another; usually, the alarm is set to go off after about 15 to 30 seconds.

Within five seconds of the start of an apneic episode, the premie frequently will experience a coincident episode of bradycardia—that is, a significant slowing (from "bradys," Greek for slow) of the heartbeat ("kardia" is Greek for heart). Bradycardia also will set off a monitor alarm, usually when the heart rate drops below about 100 beats per minute.

Frequently, doctors treat apnea with drugs. The most useful such drug is theophylline, which has a direct stimulant effect on the respiratory center of the brain. The active component of theophylline and its related drug, aminophylline, seems to be caffeine. Caffeine itself is also occasionally used to treat apnea. Side effects from these medications are rare but can include a fast heart rate and, occasionally, abdominal distention.

Apneic episodes are worrisome to parents—especially when the alarms start beeping. "Aaron's biggest problem was apnea and bradycardia. It really bothered me," says his mother, Stacy Wynn. "The worst part was when he'd stop breathing when I held him. He'd relax so much in my arms that he'd forget to breathe. It was awful to watch him turn blue just when I was most enjoying him."

But apneic "spells" generally do the baby little harm. Almost 90 percent of the time, a nurse can get the baby breathing again with a gentle reminder: she flexes the baby's leg, strokes his skin, or taps on the isolette wall. Some doctors now are asking nurses not to tap on the isolette, because the noise it makes, to the premie's ear, can be quite loud. They suggest instead that nurses tie a length of fabric to the baby's ankle so they can pull on it without having to open up the isolette for every apneic spell.

If gentle stimulation is not enough to prod the baby back to breathing, the nurse will try administering a puff of oxygen to the baby through a "bag and mask" that is usually available right alongside the isolette. If that fails to revive the premie, or if the apneic episodes become too frequent, the neonatologist might order that the baby be placed on CPAP. (For a description of oxygen hoods, CPAP, and artificial ventilation, see the section in this chapter on hyaline membrane disease.)

Babies who are especially prone to apnea are sometimes placed on waterbeds, tiny water-filled mattresses that can be laid inside the isolette. Some of these waterbeds can also be rocked. Studies have shown that the gentle movement of the waterbed seems to stimulate rhythmicity in the infant's breathing, minimizing the likelihood that his breathing will skip a beat. Waterbeds have the added advantage of mimicking the movements of the womb, thus recreating many of the sensations nature intended to accompany the growth and development that take place during the last weeks in utero.

Brain Bleeds

Despite the best efforts of modern obstetric care, many premies experience episodes of birth asphyxia. Asphyxia (from the Greek words "a," meaning not, and "sphyzein," to throb) indicates a loss of consciousness (or, as the Greeks would have it, a stopping of the pulse) that results from too little oxygen and too much carbon dioxide in the bloodstream.

Although newborns tolerate transient deficits of oxygen far better than do children or adults, birth asphyxia can have a devastating effect on certain of the premie's organs. The primary effect of asphyxia is constriction (that is, narrowing) of the blood vessels. This in turn reduces the supply of oxygen to certain essential organs, especially the kidneys and intestines. And in one organ, where an adequate supply of oxygen is most critical and the blood vessels are the most delicate and lacking in support, the tiny blood vessels, when denied oxygen, can actually burst. That organ is the brain.

Bleeds inside the head (most commonly called intraventricular hemorrhages, or IVHs) are frequent in very small premies. In hospitals that routinely screen for brain bleeds, as many as one-half of all premies weighing less than 1250 grams are found to have bleeds.

It's important to remember, though, that not all bleeds are severe. Most of them simply are reabsorbed and disappear. Even those bleeds that seem massive in the first days of life can, occasionally, turn out to have little impact on the child's eventual mental functioning.

Doctors generally categorize brain bleeds into four groups, Grades I through IV. (At some hospitals, the bleeds are categorized in only three groups, based on approximately the same criteria.) The grade is determined after either an ultrasound scan of the brain or a special brain x-ray called the CT scan (pronounced either "C-T scan" or "cat scan"). The mildest bleeds—Grades I and II—tend to disappear with little apparent ill effect. But the more severe bleeds—Grades III and IV—tend to create relatively more severe problems later.

Brain bleeds are thought to be caused by a number of factors. Birth trauma seems to be one of the major causes of brain bleeds, which is why more and more obstetricians are willing to deliver very premature infants by cesarean section. But other important causes of brain bleeds probably occur during the first days of life. When all grades of bleeds are studied, the majority have been found to occur between twelve and seventy-two hours after birth. What could be happening to these babies during those crucial sixty hours?

Large-scale hospital studies have shown that babies with bleeds tend to be those who experienced asphyxia, respiratory distress, extremes in blood levels of oxygen and carbon dioxide, pneumothorax, and the need for CPAP during their early days in the nursery. They are susceptible to the effects of these events, it seems, because of the differences between their brains and the brains of full-term newborns.

Between the 24th and 34th weeks of gestation, fetuses have an unusually high proportion of tiny unprotected blood vessels, called capillaries, surrounding a certain area of the brain's ventricular system. The ventricular system comprises the brain's fluid-filled spaces, which occupy several distinct regions arranged like a series of canals: the lateral, third, and fourth ventricles. The ventricles are usually small and filled with small amounts of cerebrospinal fluid. Ordinarily, the fluid drains out of the brain into the spinal cord and also surrounds the surface of the brain, bathing the entire nervous system.

The brain is particularly vulnerable to damage in a premie's first days of life for several reasons: because it has these unprotected capillaries around the ventricular system; because it is still undergoing development of certain brain cells (called neurons and glial cells); and because it has not yet evolved mechanisms to protect it from changes in blood pressure.

Although premies generally can keep their blood pressure within a constant, normal range, they may have periods alternating between hypertension (high blood pressure) and hypotension (low blood pressure). Each extreme of blood pressure can do damage to the brain. High blood pressure, scientists think, can overload the capillaries of the premature brain, causing them to burst. Low blood pressure can result in a diminished flow of oxygen to the brain, causing damage similar to the damage caused by birth asphyxia.

Occasionally, bleeds are discovered only as part of a routine screening test. The mildest bleeds are usually found in this way. Years ago, before routine CT scans were performed, the fact that these babies experienced Grade I or Grade II bleeds might never have been discovered. And these unsuspected bleeds, minor as they were, would probably have made no difference in the child's eventual well-being.

But in many other premies, the bleed is detected days before the routine CT scan—and it's discovered because it makes the baby behave differently. Some babies, for example, have seizures at the time of their bleed. Their limbs stiffen, their eyes roll, and they may even, briefly, lose consciousness. Once the baby is revived, the neonatologist will probably order a CT or ultrasound scan, and the likely finding is that the baby had a bleed of some significance.

The four grades of bleed indicate how far from the ventricles the blood clot has spread. The grades are assigned on the basis of the baby's CT scan. In a Grade I bleed, the bleeding is extremely localized, remaining only within the small region of the brain in which it originated. In a Grade

II bleed, the blood has extended into the ventricles, but it goes no farther.

Grade III bleeds include some dilation of the ventricular system. This dilation, or expansion, indicates one of two things: either the excess blood is directly causing the ventricles to balloon, or it is interfering with the drainage of cerebrospinal fluid. Any amount of dilation—no matter how small or how large—qualifies as a Grade III bleed.

In a Grade IV bleed, the blood has extended beyond the ventricular system into the brain itself. The prognosis for premies with Grade IV bleeds, while far more grim than for those with milder bleeds, is difficult to pinpoint. As your doctor will tell you, the likelihood of a healthy, intact outcome depends on many elements: the condition that caused the bleed in the first place, the regions of the brain that were affected by the seepage of blood, the degree of scarring or damage left after the blood clot dries up. Generally, premies who stayed relatively healthy at the time of the bleed—that is, who did not suddenly need mechanical ventilation or other forms of more aggressive therapy—tend to recover better from their brain bleeds.

The initial treatment for a bleed that has caused ventricular dilation is to ease the pressure inside the brain. This is called decompression. It can be done through implantation of a tiny "reservoir" that collects the fluid for daily emptying, or through a series of spinal taps to accomplish the same end. The method of treatment varies from one hospital to another; ask your physician what method he thinks is best.

If your baby has had a severe brain bleed, he might develop hydrocephalus, a condition commonly (and incorrectly) called "water on the brain." In hydrocephalus, something obstructs the normal flow of cerebral spinal fluid from the brain to the spinal cord, and the fluid accumulates dangerously inside the ventricles. The added pressure of the enlarged ventricles could interfere with normal development of the rest of the brain, which could result in mental retardation.

To avoid this possibility, doctors will follow your baby with frequent ultrasound scans. If hydrocephalus develops, they might implant a device under the skin and into the brain. This device, called a brain shunt, allows the fluid in the ventricles to drain off as it should. It is a long plastic tube that is surgically inserted into the baby's ventricles. The tube is attached to a valve under the skin in the baby's head, which in turn is attached to another tube that runs along the inside of his neck and into his peritoneal (abdominal) cavity. There, the cerebral spinal fluid can safely empty.

The procedure of inserting the brain shunt is relatively simple, but it must be repeated several times as your baby grows, so that doctors can replace the plastic tube with a longer one to adjust for the child's increasing length.

If your doctor considers your infant too small for the shunt operation, he might try a temporary measure to stem the development of hydrocephalus. Once hydrocephalus has been confirmed through CT scan or ultrasound, the doctor might first try a temporary method of decompression, such as repeated spinal taps. (These can be done only if there is a connection between the ventricular system and the spinal cord, so that taking fluid out of the spinal cord will have a beneficial effect.) Another possibility is an external brain shunt. This is a small plastic tube that goes directly into the ventricles from the top of the skull and drains the cerebral spinal fluid into a closed bottle near the baby's head.

Parents whose babies receive this shunt often express dismay or horror at seeing a tube emerging from the baby's head. "I looked at John with that thing coming out of his head, and all I could think was, 'What have I done to you?' " says his mother, Katie Lee. "When we knew John had a Grade III bleed, we asked the doctors not to do anything heroic to save his life. Our greatest fear was retardation. But now, John is ours, and if anything threatens his safety, I will do anything in my power to protect him."

Chronic Lung Disease

One of the most common complications of long-term intensive care for premies is a chronic lung condition called bronchopulmonary dysplasia (BPD). In this case, "chronic" does not necessarily mean "permanent": most children with BPD recover completely normal lung function by the age of two or three. But BPD is chronic in that it will affect a child long after his initial illness (the so-called "acute" phase) is over, and will serve as a distressing reminder of his time in intensive care.

Bronchopulmonary dysplasia has been called "concrete lung" because that's how it makes a baby's lungs look: stiff, hard, solid. And it's been called "respirator lung" because that's how it usually comes about: after too long a period of artificial ventilation in the intensive care nursery.

When a baby is on a ventilator, his lungs are traumatized by the forced flow of air. This can be especially damaging to a premie's lungs. As we have seen, a deficiency of surfactant often makes the lungs of premature babies extremely stiff.

At most intensive care nurseries, approximately 1 to 8 percent of babies with hyaline membrane disease will develop BPD. The likelihood of long-term lung problems for these babies increases as the severity of their disease increases. For babies who need artificial ventilation and supplemental oxygen for more than twenty-four hours, especially if the ventilators use a form of air flow delivery called intermittent positive pressure, the chances of developing BPD might be as high as one in five.

A premie who develops BPD might be hospitalized for

months. Before he can go home, he must be "weaned" from the ventilator. In weaning, the doctors turn down the setting on the baby's ventilator, using progressively smaller doses of oxygen and progressively decreased respiratory rates, until the baby finally is able to breathe on his own. Once he's weaned, the baby must recover sufficient lung function to be able to return home to his parents' care. For the most severe forms of BPD, a baby might be sent home on oxygen and his parents taught how to use the oxygen tank and how to insert the breathing tube (called a cannula) into their child's nose.

Babies with BPD can be unhappy babies. One nurse, Jerri Oehler of Duke University, has written that BPD babies are "small tyrants who squirm, kick, twist, turn blue, and refuse to be comforted. Chronic air hunger," she says, "seems to create an unpleasant personality."

The child can be a frustration to his parents, his caretakers, and even himself; no baby likes to be sad and cranky. His progress is slow, and often he regresses with bouts of upper respiratory tract infections, pneumonia, or other complications. There's not much that nurses or parents can do to speed the child's recovery except to make him comfortable. This often includes chest physiotherapy, in which the baby is placed in various positions and tapped on in a prescribed pattern so that the mucus that collects in his lungs is allowed to drain.

But the good news is this: within two or three years, most babies with BPD have outgrown their earlier lung problems. Fresh lung tissue has grown in sufficient quantity to take over for the older, scarred tissue. "When Stephen finally was off oxygen at one year, I felt incredible relief," says Eve Markham, his mother. "And, maybe because he was so sick during that first year, his accomplishments were even more precious to me. He's two and a half now, and I still have with Stephen a very special tie. That specialness, I think, I'll feel for the rest of his life."

HYALINE MEMBRANE DISEASE

Many premies who weigh less than 1500 grams at birth have some trouble breathing. A large group of them also suffer from a lung abnormality called hyaline membrane disease, or respiratory distress syndrome. (The two terms are often used interchangeably.) The incidence of hyaline membrane disease increases as the baby's birthweight and gestational age decrease. About two-thirds of premies under 30 weeks develop hyaline membrane disease; the incidence decreases to less than half of those born between 30 and 32 weeks, less than one-fourth of those born between 33 and 34 weeks, and about 0.05 percent of babies born at term.

Every year, an estimated 40,000 premies in the United States are afflicted with hyaline membrane disease. This is the disease that President Kennedy's premature son, Patrick, died of in 1963, and it is the disease to which most premie deaths can still be attributed today. But the mortality rate of hyaline membrane disease has changed dramatically since Patrick Kennedy died. Even as recently as ten years ago, nearly three-fourths of infants who had hyaline membrane disease died before they reached one month of age. Today, the vast majority of babies with hyaline membrane disease (nearly 80 percent) are fully recovered within ten days to two weeks.

In your mother's day, the diagnosis of hyaline membrane disease was almost a death sentence. Today, while still a serious complication of prematurity, it is a disease that most babies survive.

Hyaline membrane disease gets its name from the word "hyalos," which is Greek for "glass." The name describes the pink membrane seen in some of the lung's air sacs after the infant tries breathing on his own. It is caused by a deficiency of surfactant, the substance that healthy lungs secrete to keep the air sacs (the alveoli) soft and supple. Alveoli work something like air-filled balloons. They let air out slowly at first and, when they are almost empty, they quickly expire the last bits of air and totally collapse. Surfactant prevents that last burst of air from escaping; instead, the alveoli are able to fill with air once again and avoid collapse.

When surfactant is secreted in sufficient amounts, the alveoli never collapse completely. But when surfactant production is insufficient—as happens in premies whose immature lungs don't yet have the equipment they need to make enough surfactant—the alveoli frequently collapse.

The result, ultimately, is that breathing becomes inefficient, and great amounts of pressure are required to reopen the air sacs. In addition, the chest wall is likely to collapse, because in premies it tends to be poorly formed.

Because of the hazards of hyaline membrane disease, and because of its high incidence in premies, neonatologists are constantly on the lookout for breathing difficulties in all babies born at less than 37 weeks gestational age. If they catch it early enough, they can treat hyaline membrane disease—and cure it.

Your doctor will suspect hyaline membrane disease in your baby if he sees the child breathing with difficulty. The most easily detected sign is called "tachypnea"—that is, rapid breathing rate—although the baby also grunts, flares his nostrils, and heaves his chest mightily as he breathes.

CURRENT TREATMENT: WARMING AND WATCHING

The treatment of respiratory distress is designed to assist the premie in his efforts to breathe. The first step is simply to place him in a controlled temperature environment, either a warming bed or an isolette. When the baby is kept warm, his need for oxygen declines, and often the simple regulation of his body temperature helps ease the baby's breathing considerably. If this is not enough, the next step is to place your baby inside an oxygen hood.

In the initial stages, nurses and doctors monitor the baby round-the-clock, taking hourly readings of his color, activity, heart rate, respiratory rate, and skin temperature. They also obtain measures of certain "blood gases" as often as they are needed. The blood gas measurements—which denote the levels of carbon dioxide, oxygen, and pH (acidity) in the bloodstream—might seem to you to be disrupting your baby needlessly. But they are essential to prevent the development of severe acid-base imbalances. Metabolic acidosis or respiratory acidosis, two conditions common in hyaline membrane disease characterized by an excess buildup of acid and carbon dioxide in the bloodstream, can have serious consequences to the baby's ability to get oxygen properly to all his organs, and they are easily prevented when doctors and nurses are monitoring blood gases frequently.

A premie with respiratory difficulties requiring additional oxygen receives an umbilical catheter (or some other arterial catheter). This allows the nurses to take frequent blood samples quickly and with a minimum of disruption. The blood is then studied for levels of oxygen (O_2), carbon dioxide (CO_2), and pH. The neonatologist also will see that your baby is given some calories intravenously, along with sufficient fluids to keep his body chemistry in balance. If time passes and your infant still cannot eat anything by mouth, the doctor can administer more calories through the intravenous line.

OXYGEN HOODS

If your baby's blood gases are abnormal while he's breathing room air, he is almost immediately placed under an oxygen hood. This is far less drastic than it sounds. An oxygen hood is simply a plastic cylinder, about the size and shape of a food processor bowl, that fits over the infant's head. Into the hood, a long hose delivers oxygen from an oxygen source outside the isolette.

The neonatologist determines how much oxygen to deliver—30 percent, 50 percent, 100 percent, or anywhere in between. (Room air, by comparison, is 21 percent oxygen.) Oxygen in the correct amount is mixed with compressed clean air in a special blender outside the baby's isolette, where it is also warmed and humidified. Doctors have found that extra heat and humidity make it easier for premies with lung problems to breathe. You might be frustrated to find that all the moisture in the air your baby is breathing creates a slight mist inside the hood that makes you unable to see his face clearly. Just remember that he probably won't be under the hood for very long.

While your baby is under an oxygen hood, the nurses obtain blood gas readings intermittently to make sure the O_2, CO_2, and pH readings are in the normal range. This is to minimize the chance of damage to the baby's eyes, which can occur if oxygen levels get either too high or too low. (More on this topic appears later in this chapter, in the section on RLF.) Measurements of CO_2 also will help determine whether the baby needs the next step in hyaline membrane disease treatment—artificial ventilation.

In the majority of cases, close monitoring, combined with additional oxygen delivered through a hood, will give the infant's lungs time to mature, and the hyaline membrane disease will resolve itself within about two weeks. But for approximately 10 to 30 percent of babies diagnosed at birth as having hyaline membrane disease, treatment will involve something more elaborate—breathing assistance, in the form of either CPAP or artificial ventilation.

CPAP (CONTINUOUS POSITIVE AIRWAY PRESSURE)

Sometimes, an oxygen hood is not enough. If your baby's blood level of oxygen gets too low even while he's under a hood, the doctor usually increases the percentage of oxygen going in, particularly in the early stages of the illness. But he can't turn up the oxygen knob forever. At a certain point, the doctor is likely to try maintaining the baby's oxygen level through another means: CPAP. This usually happens when the baby is getting approximately 70 percent oxygen in the first twenty-four hours of life, yet still is having trouble keeping his blood level of oxygen within the range considered safe.

CPAP (pronounced "see-pap") works by forcing a constant flow of gases (air and oxygen) into the alveoli to keep them from collapsing each time the infant draws a breath. It is especially well suited to babies with hyaline membrane disease because of the stiffness of their lungs; CPAP counteracts the lung's tendency toward collapse.

The gas, at an oxygen concentration and humidity level determined by the physician, is forced into the alveoli through a tube in the baby's nostrils or throat. Although CPAP is far less intrusive than the next step in respiratory assistance—mechanical ventilation—it does carry some problems of its own. A few babies on CPAP might rupture a lung, leading to excess air lying outside the lung but within the chest cavity (a condition called pneumothorax). But CPAP today is considered one of the most significant factors in the improved outlook for hyaline membrane disease. The majority of premies who require CPAP need nothing more in making the transition to breathing on their own.

MECHANICAL VENTILATION

Your doctor will move on to mechanical ventilation if the baby doesn't do well on CPAP. Usually, this means that even with 80 percent oxygen, the baby's oxygen levels are low, carbon dioxide levels are high, and pH is dangerously acidic. Other indications that your baby needs ventilation: if he won't breathe or if he's in shock.

There are three kinds of ventilators: time-cycled, pressure-cycled, and volume-cycled. Respiration can be measured according to three parameters: the frequency of and length of inspirations and expirations per minute (time), the strength (pressure) of each respiration, or the amount (volume) of air forced in with each breath. Any one measure depends on the other two. What the various kinds of ventilators do is keep one of the three measures constant, so that the other two measures can be adjusted.

In general, the more work the ventilator must do for your baby, the sicker he is. You can watch him get better as the ventilator settings change. When the doctors can begin to lower the number of breaths per minute, or when they reduce the pressure or volume of air being delivered, you'll know your baby is improving.

Most mechanical ventilators today use what is called intermittent positive pressure. They force air into the chest, creating pressure inside the chest wall. The baby must breathe out in order to relieve the pressure. Another type of ventilator, one that is used at only a few intensive care nurseries, uses intermittent negative pressure. If you are interested in the mechanics of ventilation, ask your doctor how your baby's machine works. There are many good ventilators in use in intensive care nurseries, all of them scaled down for premie-sized lungs. Your nursery probably uses only one or two kinds of ventilator, and with good reason: the variation from one machine to another is small, and it's far more important to enable all health care professionals to become well-acquainted with a particular brand so they feel comfortable using it.

FUTURE TREATMENTS

Some researchers have reasoned recently that if hyaline membrane disease is caused by a deficiency of surfactant, then surfactant should be useful in treating it. In 1980, Dr.

Tetsuro Fujiwara of the Akita University School of Medicine in Japan tried using natural surfactant—culled from the lungs of cows and lambs—to treat hyaline membrane disease in ten very small premies (their average gestational age was 30 weeks, their average birthweight about 1500 grams). Dr. Fujiwara dripped surfactant directly into the windpipes of these babies—all of whom were doing poorly twelve hours after birth—and then blew 100 percent oxygen into their lungs for two to four minutes. Within three hours, most babies were able to have the settings on their ventilators lowered from about 80 percent oxygen to about 40 percent.

The study has yet to be replicated, and surfactant still is not available for experimental use in intensive care nurseries in this country. But it holds promise as being more effective than current treatment for hyaline membrane disease.

Other scientists are experimenting with new, less traumatic ways of ventilating premies with hyaline membrane disease. For example, at some hospitals, particularly in Canada and Sweden, doctors have tried delivering oxygen to the babies at extraordinarily high rates of respiration—as high as 150 to 200 breaths per minute. In addition, a special experimental ventilator, which delivers air in an oscillating rather than a regular breathing pattern, has also been used with some early signs of success. In the next few years, neonatologists should have an idea of whether these new treatments prove more effective, and less traumatic, than current methods of treating the major disease of prematurity.

Infections

Neonatal infections are frequent among premies. Not only do premies have fewer defenses against infection than do full-term infants, but they also exist in an environment in which infection is more likely to develop: the intensive care nursery.

Infection can be passed on to a newborn in one of two ways—from the mother, either while the baby is in utero or as he emerges through the birth canal; or from the environment, that is, the other babies, adults, and equipment to which he is exposed.

Birth is a dirty business. As the baby passes through the birth canal, which is inhabited by several kinds of bacteria, his skin is covered with foreign, potentially dangerous, organisms. Contamination with bacteria always occurs during labor and delivery, except during a Cesarean section. Usually, these bacteria are easily washed away, and pose little threat to the baby's health. But for premies, especially those who also have other difficulties in addition to prematurity, these bacteria can create serious problems.

Ordinarily, the infant's skin and mucous membranes serve to shield his body from outright invasion by the bacteria that contaminate his surfaces. But when the skin breaks, the bacteria invade the system and begin to colonize. Any manipulation can lead to a break in the skin, including those that are common in a premature labor and delivery: fetal monitoring, obstetrical handling, vigorous resuscitation after birth, and the use of indwelling catheters in the intensive care nursery.

Infections are also more common among premies because mothers who carry particular organisms in their vaginal tracts tend to give birth earlier. These bacteria usually cause no symptoms in the mother, but they are passed on to the baby during birth. The most common of these infections is from the bacteria streptococcus Type B. Maternal cytomegalovirus (CMV) infection, syphilis, and toxoplasmosis are other organisms causing the problem known as chronic intrauterine infection.

Infections in newborns can be difficult to diagnose. The

symptoms they create can be subtle and often look like the symptoms of a normal premie: abdominal distention, apnea, jaundice, lethargy, poor muscle tone, or poor feeding. If one or more of these symptoms lead doctors and nurses to suspect an infection, they will do what is called a "sepsis workup." (Sepsis means infection.) Samples of the baby's blood, spinal fluid, and urine are sent to the lab for culture to see whether any dangerous organisms are growing there. Immediately after birth, the doctor might also do a culture of the infant's body surfaces.

If your baby does develop an infection, he may or may not be isolated. The decision about quarantine depends on many factors, especially the type of infection your baby has and the availability of space. Usually, hospitals try to place infected babies in rooms where they and all other babies are in isolettes. The isolettes, with their individualized air supplies, serve as a kind of miniquarantine.

Some infections lead to respiratory problems. Your infected baby might therefore need to receive supplementary oxygen or artificial ventilation. He might also need to be taken off oral feedings and given only intravenous feedings until the infection clears.

And, of course, there are antibiotics. A wide range of drugs now exists to treat a wide range of bacterial infections. The most popular antibiotics have names that end in the suffixes "mycin"—gentamicin, kanamycin—or "illin"—ampicillin, oxacillin, penicillin. The drugs are effective against particular organisms, but they can be risky, especially when they are used for extended periods. Among the most common side effects of antibiotics, especially those of the "mycin" family, are kidney damage and hearing loss. These side effects are rare in the newborn, though, and are usually reversible.

The most effective, and least risky, therapy for infection is prevention. That is why you must always wash your hands thoroughly (to the elbow, for two to three minutes) before you enter the intensive care nursery. The doctors and nurses are scrubbing up, too, and are keeping the equipment and the babies as sterile as possible. With tiny babies who are already susceptible to so many other problems, hospital staff members want to take every precaution they can in trying to ensure that the incidence of at least one problem—infection—is minimized.

Jaundice

Jaundice is the excessive buildup in the bloodstream of bilirubin, a biological waste product ordinarily excreted through the liver. When bilirubin accumulates, it causes the skin and eyes to take on a yellowish color.

Bilirubin is produced by the breakdown of red blood cells after they have reached the end of their useful life (about four months in an adult, two and a half months in a newborn). At birth, infants produce bilirubin at a rate more than twice that of an adult. Their livers, therefore, must excrete bilirubin at twice the adult rate. Compounding the added workload is the fact that the newborn liver functions less effectively than an adult's.

The job of the liver is to convert bilirubin in the bloodstream into a water-soluble form (called "conjugated bilirubin") that can be excreted through the feces. But with so much bilirubin to account for, the newborn liver quickly becomes overburdened.

Thus, a newborn—even a healthy, full-term newborn—is likely to experience a rise in bilirubin as his liver tries to cope with the backlog. As many as one-half of all newborns born at term develop a condition called "normal" or "physiologic" jaundice between the second and fourth days of life. It's a condition that almost all healthy babies outgrow.

For premies, jaundice can be a more serious problem. Estimates are that as many as 70 percent of premature infants experience physiologic jaundice. In order for bilirubin to be converted successfully, adequate amounts of both glucose (sugar) and oxygen are needed. Many premies, especially those with hyaline membrane disease, low body temperature, or acid-base imbalance, are likely to experience deficiencies in either glucose or oxygen or both.

Usually, the yellow tinge to the skin characteristic of jaundice appears on about the fifth or sixth day of life in premies and disappears by the ninth or tenth day. When the doctors and nurses notice that a premie looks yellow, they will take blood samples from the baby's heel every six to twelve hours to test for the amount of bilirubin and conjugated bilirubin in the bloodstream. They also will measure the rate at which these levels are increasing; if they increase too rapidly, the doctor is likely to consider the jaundice to be more than merely "physiologic."

If jaundice requires treatment, the first step is to place the baby under fluorescent lights—the so-called "bili lights." These deliver light at a specified wavelength to accelerate the breakdown of bilirubin, thus helping the liver in its task of converting bilirubin to a form that can be passed through the urine. The light works primarily through the skin, so a baby under the bili light is nude, except for a protective bandage over his eyes.

While the baby is under the lights, he may eat poorly, experience an increase in water loss, and have very loose stools. The nurses will take his temperature frequently, because the lamps can make his isolette quite warm.

If your baby's blood level of bilirubin continues to climb, his doctors will consider an exchange transfusion. This is a two-step procedure in which the baby's blood is removed and then replaced with healthy blood. It's a dramatic measure, but it's sometimes necessary to avoid the buildup of bilirubin in the bloodstream, which can accumulate in the brain and central nervous system if left untreated.

An exchange transfusion is a minimally risky undertaking. Usually, at least two physicians plus one nurse are in attendance throughout the procedure, which lasts about an hour and a half. Complications, while rare, can be significant, including NEC (described in the following section), infection, transfusion reaction, some changes in blood chemistry, and, quite rarely, cardiac arrest, vein perforation, or blood clots. Nurses will monitor the baby closely for several hours after the exchange transfusion to catch any complications early.

NEC

NEC is shorthand for necrotizing enterocolitis, an intestinal disorder that affects about 2 to 15 percent of very small premies. It occurs most often in premies who have suffered from episodes of asphyxia or shocklike conditions, either at birth or afterward. Infection may play a part in NEC, which develops most frequently in premies after they have been fed milk or formula by mouth.

In most intensive care nurseries, all very small premies are considered "at risk" for developing NEC. Doctors routinely test the babies' bowel movements for the presence of blood and delay oral feedings of these babies for at least seventy-two hours after birth. When feedings are begun, they are begun carefully, either with a dilute formula or, whenever possible, with breast milk—either pumped from the mother or, for those premies whose mothers have decided not to nurse, taken from a hospital "milk bank" of donated milk.

After the babies' first feedings, they remain under close scrutiny for early signs of NEC. Their abdomens are measured frequently and their stomach residuals checked before each feeding to determine whether any milk remains undigested in the stomach.

The development of NEC is thought to begin at birth, when a premie has difficulty taking his first breath. An episode of birth asphyxia can lead to scarring of the intestinal tract, a sort of burn-like sloughing of the intestinal lining caused by a transient loss of blood flow to the region. This scarring is harmless until the baby's first feed. Then, the milk or formula begins to pool in the intestinal tract, settling around these areas of damage, and acts as a substrate on which bacteria can grow. The bacteria multiply, and NEC results.

Most cases of NEC develop just when a baby seems to be out of the woods—when he is about ten to fifteen days old and has been growing and tolerating oral feedings for a few days. NEC is suspected when the abdomen gets excessively large, when the baby begins to do poorly, and when blood appears in the stool. It is confirmed by an abdominal x-ray. Many "cases" of suspected NEC turn out to be false alarms, and the diagnosis is discounted when the baby's abdominal x-ray shows no abnormality.

If it's caught early enough, NEC can be treated easily. The baby is taken off oral feedings (this is called "NPO," or "nil per os"—Latin for "nothing by mouth"). He is given nutrients through an intravenous line and is also given an antibiotic to attack the bacteria thought to be associated with NEC. After two weeks of intravenous feedings, if the NEC has cleared up, oral feedings are gradually reintroduced.

Sometimes, however, NEC begins insidiously and may result in actual rupture of the bowel. Then, by the time it's detected, it can be treated only through surgery.

Surgery does not cure NEC, but it does repair the damage the disease can do. An operation for NEC usually consists of cutting out the intestinal tissue that has been damaged by the infection and bringing a healthy piece of intestine to the surface of the abdomen to form an "ostomy"—an external sac for collecting the baby's stool. The ostomy stays in place until the infant recovers, at which time the intestine can be hooked together again.

The first thing to remember about an ostomy is that it will not be there forever. When the baby is out of danger and some additional intestines have regenerated, surgeons can operate once again to close up the ostomy hole and reroute the gastrointestinal tract. The age at which this is done varies, according to the child's condition.

The next thing to remember about an ostomy is that it's not as bad as it sounds. Even though your baby's ostomy will probably bother you, it will not bother your baby. He is too young to be embarrassed about the way he passes his stool, and he has no conception of there being another way to do it. And, if it is kept clean, an ostomy is not at all painful or inconvenient to your child.

Your nurses, you'll see, handle ostomy care with ease. They will teach you how to keep the area around your baby's ostomy clean and dry. Many hospitals have an "ostomy nurse" who specializes in instructing patients and their families in ostomy care. You might also want to look for *Your Infant with an Ostomy*, a pamphlet for parents published in 1978 by the Duke University Medical Center. The booklet was written by Judith Grimm, a neonatology nurse clinician, and Glenda Cox, a mother whose daughter had a temporary ostomy during infancy. It provides information about ostomy bags, special material to protect the baby's skin, and suggested clothing and foods that might make the ostomy less intrusive.

Nutritional Problems

Doctors face two problems in trying to feed a premie: getting the nutrients into him in the first place, and trying to help him make the best use of those nutrients once he ingests them. Both tasks are made more difficult by the baby's immaturity.

A premie cannot coordinate suck and swallow until he

reaches a gestational age of 34 weeks. Many of the smallest premies, then, require another route for feeding—either an intravenous line, through which a special high-nutrition solution can be delivered, or a feeding tube (also called a "gavage") that routes milk or formula directly into the baby's digestive system.

The premie's stomach is proportionately much smaller than the stomach of a full-term newborn, but his nutritional needs are just as great—if not greater. The growth rate of a third-trimester fetus is rapid—approximately 30 grams per day by the end of pregnancy—and that's the rate that most doctors try to keep up for premies. To do so may require a continuous infusion of nutrients through the intravenous line or, if the baby is being fed through a tube, feedings as frequently as every one or two hours.

But even with the best feeding plan, a premie still might suffer nutritional deficiencies. His enzymes are still immature, so he cannot convert his carefully planned diet into the chemicals his body needs to grow and develop. That's why your baby's doctors are constantly monitoring his blood chemistry and certain enzymes, so they can correct problems before they occur.

Premies have difficulty absorbing fat from their diet, and also have trouble absorbing fat-soluble vitamins such as vitamin D. They vomit easily. Their digestive systems are sluggish, which means "residuals" from the prior feeding are often still lying in their stomachs when it's time for the next feeding. And they need large supplements of calcium and phosphorus—the two compounds needed to build bones—in order to grow properly and prevent rickets.

To prevent nutritional problems, your baby's doctor takes several precautions. He checks residuals in your baby's stomach before each feed, so he can measure the amounts still there from the last feeding. The residuals are weighed and returned to the stomach, and the next feeding is reduced by the corresponding amount. Residuals of about one-fourth of the feed are considered normal, but higher amounts, or steadily increasing amounts, might be an early sign of infection or some other problem.

The doctor also routinely measures the baby's abdomen, feeling it for areas of tenderness, to be sure the belly is not distending. He weighs the baby once or twice a day, charting his growth, and will consider increasing the baby's calories if his growth rate is too slow. If weight is a significant problem, the doctor might even administer a special calorie-rich substance, Intralipid, through an intravenous line. And some hospitals hold daily "nutrition rounds," in which neonatologists review the babies' records to see whether changes are warranted in the method of feeding, timing of feeding, or substances being fed.

PDA

One of the biggest changes from fetus to neonate occurs in the circulatory system. When a fetus is inside his mother's womb, his blood flows in a different pattern from the way it will flow after birth. In a mature system, blood flow occurs in two stages. First, the blood, colored blue because of lack of oxygen, leaves the heart through the pulmonary artery, and it heads straight for the lungs. In the lungs, the blood is enriched with oxygen, and it turns bright red. This oxygenated blood then returns, through the pulmonary vein, back to the heart for a brief stop; then it heads out again. This time the blood leaves the heart through the aorta, from which it will proceed to every organ in the body, bathing it with the oxygen needed to continue cellular function.

For a fetus, this system is short-circuited. Because the lungs don't function in a fetus, there's no need for the blood to make its first loop toward the lungs for a dose of oxygen. In a fetus, oxygen is supplied by the placenta. To avoid the useless trip to the lungs, there's a special opening just outside the fetal heart, between the pulmonary artery and the aorta. This opening is called the ductus arteriosus.

The ductus arteriosus reroutes most of the blood coming from the heart directly to the aorta, which will pump it to the rest of the body. This pattern of fetal circulation continues until the moment of birth, when some major changes occur all at once. When the baby takes his first breath, his lungs fill with air. As his lungs expand, blood flow to the lungs increases. Then another change happens: the obstetrician clamps the umbilical cord. This cuts off the placenta from the circuit, and the blood accumulating in the heart's chambers goes instead to the lungs. In response to the increased oxygen in the blood, the ductus arteriosus begins to close. If all goes well, within 72 hours the ductus has closed completely.

In a premie, this initial closing of the ductus takes longer. It might take as long as three weeks for the ductus to constrict totally in some premies. And even if the ductus arteriosus closes in the first day or two of a premie's life, it may well reopen. If the baby experiences hypoxia (a dangerously low level of oxygen in the bloodstream) or acidosis (an imbalance leaning toward the acidic rather than the alkaline end of the pH scale), the ductus may reopen. Both hypoxia and acidosis are common in premies with hyaline membrane disease. Extra fluids, which premies need for other reasons, might also help to keep the ductus open.

When the ductus arteriosus is open, the doctors call it PDA—patent (that is, open) ductus arteriosus. Approximately 20 percent of all premies will probably develop PDA, with the incidence increasing as the birthweight and gestational age decrease—up to about 75 percent among the smallest, youngest premies. The diagnosis of PDA is made on the basis of a worsening breathing problem, an abnormal pulse, heart enlargement as seen on x-ray or ultrasound, and, occasionally, a heart murmur.

Often, PDA can be left untreated. One study of premies

with PDA found that, when the affected baby survived the first month of life, the ductus closed of its own accord nearly 80 percent of the time. This is especially likely if the baby has no hyaline membrane disease, or only a mild case, because the hypoxia and acidosis of respiratory distress can exacerbate problems with PDA.

Sometimes, though, the PDA can lead to problems of its own, most commonly congestive heart failure. In congestive heart failure, babies can become lethargic and unwilling to eat, and they can experience excessive fluid buildup throughout the body, especially in the lungs. To counteract this, doctors usually will restrict the baby's fluid intake and probably will administer a diuretic to reduce water retention.

When these drugs don't help, the doctor might try a newer drug that has been found to facilitate closure of the PDA: indomethacin. Indomethacin, an anti-inflammatory drug, inhibits the release of certain body chemicals, called prostaglandins, that tend to keep the ductus open. For premies less than two weeks of age who have PDA, especially those who also have moderate to severe cases of hyaline membrane disease and congestive heart failure, indomethacin has been shown to be effective in closing at least part of the fetal blood vessel. Despite its effectiveness, though, some doctors hesitate to use indomethacin for PDA until more evidence accumulates about the long-term consequences of its use in premies.

If all else fails, and the PDA is creating severe problems in the baby—especially an inability to be weaned from the ventilator, and increases in the number of episodes of apnea—the doctor might try to close the baby's ductus surgically. The procedure is relatively simple: the baby's chest is opened, and the surgeon ties a knot around the ductus arteriosus. This is not the same as open heart surgery, because the ductus is beneath and outside of the heart, so it is not nearly as risky for the baby. But it still is surgery, with general anesthesia, so it still entails some risk for a tiny premie. Surgery for PDA, called a "ligation," usually is recommended only after less invasive treatment methods have been tried, and then only if the PDA is creating enough problems that the risk of surgery is less than the risk of continued difficulties without surgery.

RLF

RLF, which stands for retrolental fibroplasia, is a vision disorder caused by trauma to the immature retina. It can be mild, resolving itself within a year or two of diagnosis; it can be moderate, leading to nearsightedness or a tendency toward eye problems in later life; or it can be severe, causing permanent blindness. In general, the smaller the premie and the more complicated his hospital course, the more likely he is to suffer from RLF. The great majority of cases of RLF are mild or moderate, and are reversible.

RLF occurs because the retina of a premie is so immature. Before the 32nd week of gestation, the retina is poorly vascularized—that is, the tiny blood vessels that supply the retina have not yet been formed. During vascularization, which ordinarily occurs in utero, blood flow to the vessels of the eye is greater than usual because extra blood is needed to supply the rapid creation of new capillaries there.

RLF is characterized by a proliferation of abnormal blood vessels on the retina, which in turn can lead to scarring. During periods of excessive oxygen in the bloodstream, which may occur when a premie is on a ventilator or receives oxygen during resuscitation efforts, the tiny vessels in the eye react by constricting. If they constrict too much, the retina suffers a temporary loss of oxygen. This leads, in turn, to stage 1 of RLF: a dilation of retinal blood vessels, and occasionally, the development of additional, abnormal vessels and even hemorrhage. If the disease progresses, the edge of the retina, or even the entire retina, may detach.

No one knows yet the exact cause or causes of RLF. It has been related to irregularities of blood gases—specifically, high or low oxygen, high carbon dioxide, or excessive acidity—as well as to simple immaturity of the blood vessels in the eye. Premies with RLF also tend to be premies with other disorders, especially PDA, sepsis, brain bleeds, and vitamin E deficiency. At some hospitals, premies with these disorders, considered at highest risk for RLF, are given additional vitamin E, which has been shown experimentally to reduce the severity of eye problems, probably by acting as an antioxidant.

One thing is certain: the smaller the infant, the more susceptible he is to RLF. Almost all of the babies sent home with severe, permanent RLF weighed less than 1000 grams at birth.

The incidence of RLF has been shown to increase in premies who are given oxygen during their hospitalization. This is especially true of those who are given their oxygen in a particular way: either through a ventilator (an association that exists probably because these are sicker babies than those not on ventilators) or through a "bag and mask." A bag and mask is a piece of equipment used for emergency resuscitation and is needed most often in premies who experience episodes of apnea—cessation of breathing for twenty seconds or longer. Doctors do not yet know whether the premie's eyes are damaged by the apnea itself or by the physical trauma of the bag and mask.

A recent study of premies born at the Montreal Children's Hospital found that those who developed RLF (27 of the 150 babies studied, or about one-third) tended to have had particular problems during their hospital stay: septicemia (a blood infection), frequent blood transfusions, and intravenous (rather than oral) feedings for many days.

The important thing to remember is that RLF can be mild—and reversible. Doctors divide RLF into two phases: proliferative and cicatricial (pronounced "sik-a-trish'-al"), each of which is divided into five stages of increasing severity. If the disease process stops at the early proliferative phase, or even at an early grade in the cicatricial phase, it usually will, in time, correct itself. Only a small proportion of infants who are sent home with a diagnosis of RLF—about one in four, by some estimates—are likely to end up blind.

Still, RLF is a distressing problem, especially for neonatologists. It's widely acknowledged to be an "iatrogenic" disorder—that is, a disorder caused by medical care. Oxygen is needed to save very tiny babies, but oxygen also can be toxic to those babies' eyes. Each year, estimates are, nearly 550 graduates of neonatal intensive care are blinded by the very care that saves them.

Even with these sobering statistics, though, most neonatologists believe that the alternative—the risk inherent in *too little* oxygen—is even worse than the risk of *too much* oxygen. When neonatal intensive care units began holding back on oxygen in the early 1950s, soon after the cause of RLF was identified, they began experiencing higher death rates from hyaline membrane disease, and higher incidences of brain damage among surviving premies. Today, doctors regularly opt for erring on the side of too much oxygen rather than too little.

Retrolental fibroplasia usually cannot be diagnosed until the end of the baby's hospitalization. But it may take weeks or months for RLF to develop fully—or to disappear. When the baby is on a ventilator or under an oxygen hood, the diagnosis is all but impossible to make, since the oxygen leads to a constriction of the blood vessels that would mask RLF even if it did exist. RLF, if it is going to develop, cannot be diagnosed before the baby is six weeks old.

Just before your baby's discharge, he will probably be

given an eye examination to test for evidence of RLF. (This test will be described in detail in Chapter 7, which summarizes all discharge procedures.) The ten grades of RLF range from a transient blood vessel change in the retina that will have no effect on the baby's vision; to a noticeable scarring that can lead to nearsightedness, glaucoma, or a risk of retinal detachment; to partial or total blindness within five or ten years. Your doctor will discuss with you the precise meaning of your baby's grade.

If RLF is found to any degree, the hospital's ophthalmologist probably will want to see your baby again within three months. Occasionally, the more severe forms of RLF will require surgery in the years ahead. Great strides have been made in the use of lasers, a concentrated light beam, to repair the damage done to the retina by the proliferation and rupture of abnormal blood vessels. But surgery for RLF is still an experimental procedure, which has met so far with mixed success. It may be that in the years ahead, surgery will be able to reverse, or at least arrest, the process of RLF.

6: The Parents' Choices

THE BUSTLE OF THE INTENSIVE CARE nursery
seems to strip many parents of feelings of responsibility for
their own child's well-being. With doctors and nurses behaving so efficiently, making so many decisions about how
the baby should eat, sleep, and dress, how could a parent
possibly hope to speak with any authority?

But you must remember that not all decisions are the
same. There are medical decisions—the kind doctors
make—and there are caretaking decisions—the kind nurses
make. These are the choices that determine, often, whether
the child will live or die. But choices about *how* the child
will live once the crisis is passed are quite different. These
decisions, essential because they are so life-affirming, are the
responsibility—indeed, the privilege—of the parents alone.

Before your baby was born, it seemed there were dozens
of options ahead of you. Remember all the books you sifted

through looking for advice about what to name the baby, whether to breastfeed or bottle-feed, whether to use cloth diapers or paper diapers, when —and if, and how—to return to work? Each of these choices is still yours to make. They've just been complicated somewhat because they must be made in an intensive care nursery, where your proper role as a parent is a hard role to assume.

Because your baby is tiny and perhaps sick, you are likely to want to turn over all responsibility for decision making to the doctors and nurses in the unit. Don't. This is your baby, not the nurses', and you will bear the consequences of decisions about how she is treated, fed, and cared for.

Your first decision, of course, has probably already been made—the baby's name. If you haven't named the baby, do so now. A name will make the baby more real to you and to the nurses. It will help your baby establish a sense of herself, too, as she starts to hear that one word repeated more frequently than all the others. Don't hold back on naming your child because you're afraid you will lose her; you'd grieve as much for her without a name as with one. And, should your baby die, her name might give you a clearer sense that you're mourning for a real little person who really existed. The sooner you name your child, and refer to her by name, the sooner you can begin thinking of her as a being with an identity separate from yours, a being who will live or die on her own.

The Pros and Cons of Breastfeeding

Medical opinion about the proper way to feed a premie has vacillated from one extreme to the other over the past thirty years. A generation ago, most premies were not fed for the first several days, because doctors believed that any feedings would be too stressful for their immature digestive systems to handle. Fifteen years ago, doctors who noticed the extreme dehydration of some of these premies began feeding them cow's milk formula soon after birth. But instead of starving the babies, they drowned them.

Today, most neonatologists take a middle ground. They begin premies on an intravenous drip (IV) within hours of birth, supplying the baby first with sugar water and later with added electrolytes, protein, and fats. When the baby seems ready—in a bigger premie, usually by the time she is seventy-two hours old—the doctor might begin feeding her through a nasogastric tube, a tube that runs through the baby's nose and directly into her stomach. Later, usually when the child weighs at least three pounds, she begins to take her feedings by mouth.

Those early decisions about your baby's feedings—what to mix into the IV solution, how long to continue tube feedings, when to begin a bottle—are medical decisions to be made by the doctors and nurses. But the issue of what to feed the baby later—breast milk or formula—is very much yours to make. If you had decided, during your pregnancy, to breastfeed your baby, the intricacies of intravenous and tube feedings might seem to have taken that choice away from you. But, if you want to, *eventually you can nurse a premie.* All it requires is some extra motivation, some extra time, and a little bit of extra equipment.

As you wrestle over the question of whether to breastfeed, remember this: The decision *to* breastfeed is easily reversible; if nursing doesn't work for you, you can always stop. But the decision *not to* breastfeed is far more difficult to reverse. If you change your mind when your baby is three or four weeks old, it will be almost impossible to establish a sufficient supply of milk.

Most neonatologists now encourage premie mothers at least to consider providing breast milk, especially if their babies are very young and very small. But this was not always the case. Years ago, doctors tended to advocate formula feeding for premies. The question was usually cast in this way: Is breast milk rich enough to meet the premie's special needs? And when breast milk was compared to formula, it always seemed to come up short.

Breast milk, said the researchers of the 1960s and 1970s, was missing some essential compounds, especially protein, sodium, calcium, and phosphorus. And, they concluded, since the optimal growth rate for premies probably is equivalent to the very rapid growth rate of the last months in utero, breast milk just isn't rich enough.

But recent studies have shown that not all breast milk is the same. The milk of mothers of term babies—the milk usually collected in hospital milk banks and analyzed for research purposes—may indeed be insufficient for optimal growth in premies. But the milk of mothers of premies is different. Once scientists began analyzing milk *from the mothers of premies*, they found that, in many ways, preterm milk may be best suited to meet most of a premie's special needs.

The breast milk of premie mothers is richer in some of the nutrients a premie needs most: it contains more protein, fat, sodium, potassium, and chloride than a comparable amount of breast milk from mothers who gave birth at term. The only substances lacking in premie mothers' breast milk seem to be calcium and phosphorus. These compounds can easily be provided through intravenous or oral doses.

In light of this new research, many doctors now are saying that breast milk from the premie's own mother might be the ideal first food, particularly for the larger premie (over 1500 grams). Breast milk, for one thing, is easier to digest; it delivers fats and nutrients in such a way that they are used more efficiently than the nutrients found in formula. And, even more important, breast milk carries antibodies that protect the infant from the infections to which premies are especially vulnerable. Breast milk, for example, seems partially to protect the premie from NEC, an intestinal problem that occurs in up to 15 percent of premies, and is more likely to occur in those weighing under 1250 grams. (A more complete discussion of NEC can be found in Chapter 5.) Some doctors now think, though, that breast milk should be alternated with formula in order to give the best nutrition to the very small premie.

From the mother's point of view, the great advantage of breastfeeding is that it is something that she alone can do for her baby. Doctors may order drugs and perform surgery; nurses may monitor vital signs and keep the baby comfortable and clean; but only Mother can provide breast milk.

"I felt very negative about breastfeeding during my pregnancy, and I had decided to bottle-feed," recalls Ellen Thames, whose son Arthur was six weeks early. "But I was feeling guilty about that, and the night before Arthur was born I had, coincidentally, decided to nurse. I'm so glad I did. For the two weeks he was in the hospital, I was able to feel as though there was something I could do for him that no one else could. And, because Arthur still has lung problems, my breast milk is really his one chance of not catching something that could be pretty serious for him. He's six months old, and even though it was a rough winter, he's never had a cold."

There are disadvantages to breastfeeding, though—especially from the mother's point of view. Establishing a milk supply for a premie who is too young to suckle can be tiring, difficult, and often frustrating. It takes patience, hard work, and support from your mate and your baby's doctors and nurses. And patience, hard work, and support are hard to come by at a time when you are, above all else, worried about your baby's health and well-being.

What follows is a step-by-step guide to take you through the early weeks of establishing a milk supply. If you need more information, ask your nurse or your obstetrician for advice. Or contact your local chapter of La Leche League, a national self-help group of nursing mothers that provides support and assistance to women encountering special problems with breastfeeding. (Bear in mind, though, that most La Leche League members are adamantly pro-breast-feeding, and some women have complained that the members tend to place breastfeeding above such other considerations as a mother's desire to work, to sleep, or to have some time for herself.)

THE MECHANICS OF MILK PRODUCTION

When a woman gives birth to a healthy, term baby, her lactation (milk-production) process begins right on the delivery table, when she puts the newborn to her breast. As the baby suckles, the nerves of the mother's nipple send a message to the hypothalamus, an endocrine gland at the back of the brain. This stimulates another gland, the pituitary, to release two hormones—oxytocin and prolactin.

Oxytocin, the same hormone that doctors give to induce labor, stimulates contraction of the small saclike cells behind the areola (the dark area encircling the nipple). This forces the milk from the glandular tissue of the breast through the nipple and initiates the flow of milk. At the same time, prolactin, the other hormone released by the pituitary, stimulates the production of milk through its action on the milk glands in the breast.

After a time, a mother's body learns to anticipate her baby's need for milk. Even before the baby starts suckling—perhaps when the mother hears the baby cry, or even when she thinks about the baby—her lactation process is likely to begin. This is called the "letdown reflex." Many women experience the letdown as a temporary tingling in their breasts; others describe actual pain in the breasts as the milk flow begins. Letdown is a conditioned response, and it can be impeded by tension, anxiety, exhaustion, or self-consciousness.

With a little practice, a baby can learn to empty a breast in five minutes. She'll suck for longer at a feeding, though—up to 15 or 20 minutes on each breast—and the added sucking serves as further stimulation for the breasts to produce more milk. In this way, a baby and her mother operate in balance, with the supply of milk always depending on the demand from the hungry baby. On Tuesday, a baby might cry for nursings every two hours; on Wednesday, she'll only need to be nursed every three or four hours, because the stimulation her mother's breasts received the day before led to a greatly increased supply of milk.

For a successful nursing experience, then, most women need two things: a suckling baby, to help establish a milk supply; and a relaxed environment, to encourage the letdown reflex. But most premie mothers have neither.

Premies usually are either too young or too sick to suckle. As we have seen, the processes of sucking and swallowing are not coordinated until 34 weeks gestational age, so babies younger than that simply cannot nurse. In addition, many premies, especially in the early days, cannot be removed from their isolettes for nursings. They must be fed inside the isolette, which makes nursing impossible.

The intensive care nursery is far from the ideal place for a "nursing couple" to get used to one another. Privacy is all but impossible, and a sense of security and well-being so essential to successful nursing is hard for premie mothers to achieve. Concern for the baby's health seems always to get in the way of a mother's ability to relax. One study of mothers pumping their breasts to collect milk to feed their sick babies showed that the flow of milk reduced to a trickle when the topic of conversation turned to the baby's health. One woman's milk flow stopped completely when she received the mistaken impression that her child would die.

To replace the suckling baby, then, a premie mother needs a breast pump. And to replace the relaxed environment, she needs a supportive nurse, mate, or friend to smooth over the rough spots and help her think positive thoughts about her baby. Some mothers have found that a nasal spray containing oxytocin, the hormone released before the milk lets down, can stimulate milk flow artificially even when the environment is not conducive to relaxing.

USING THE BREAST PUMP

A breast pump is a device, operated either manually or electrically, that fits over the nipple and areola, just as a baby's mouth does, and, again just as with a baby, creates a constant vacuum to draw milk out of the breast and into a collecting bottle.

Electrical pumps are mobile units with powerful motors, and, although they are far from the romantic image of what nursing is all about, they are effective. Premie mothers swear by them, because they take the struggle out of a process that many consider to be tedious and debilitating. Usually, an electric pump can be rented from the hospital or from a surgical supply house. If you cannot afford the fee (it can run as high as $2 a day), you might be able to borrow an electric pump from the intensive care nursery. Also, your medical insurance might cover the cost of renting a pump if its use is prescribed by your baby's doctor.

The pump is used for two reasons: to stimulate your breasts enough to establish a milk supply and to collect milk from your breasts for feeding your baby. It might seem at first as though you're hardly getting any milk out of your breasts. Don't despair. Your baby doesn't need much milk—a typical 1500 gram premie usually will be fed about 30 cubic centimeters (that is, just one *ounce*) at a feeding when on full feeds—and the important thing is to get *some* milk. As long as your breasts are accustomed to producing milk, they will be able to step up the supply as soon as your baby's demand increases.

It will take at least two days, and might take as long as a week, before you begin getting milk out of your breasts. Before then, your breasts are producing colostrum, a thick, sticky substance rich in antibodies that protect the baby against infection. Ask your baby's doctor whether you should save the colostrum and bring it in for your baby to drink. In a recent study at the Rainbow Babies' and Children's Hospital in Cleveland, premies fed just 15 milliliters a day of human colostrum were found to have significantly fewer infections than premies not fed colostrum. Your colostrum might carry similar protection for your baby.

When pumping your breasts, try to follow these steps:

1. Wash your hands well, and sterilize, in boiling water for five or ten minutes, the bottle into which you'll be collecting milk.

2. Sit down in a quiet place. If you're at home, you might want to sit in a rocking chair in the baby's room or in a comfortable easy chair in a darkened living room. In the hospital, ask the nurse whether there's a quiet conference room you can use. Close the door, and try to relax.

3. Massage your breasts. This technique, usually used by women who want to "express" (draw out) breast milk without the use of a pump, can help set the mood for your pumping and help you condition a letdown reflex. Begin at the top of each breast, massaging your breasts with an open, flat palm in smaller and smaller circles until you finally end up rubbing your breast in a very small circle around the areola.

4. Think of your baby. It might help condition the letdown reflex if you say the baby's name to yourself, or look at a picture of her, or tell yourself something like, "My baby needs my milk. My milk will help my baby get better." Don't feel silly if you need some props to help your milk flow get started. Most mothers have their babies right there to do it for them.

5. Place the pump on one breast. If it's an electric pump,

turn it on; if it's a hand pump, get it "primed" to establish a vacuum. When your nipple and areola are pulled into the breast shield of the pump, you'll know the pump is working.

6. Consciously relax your body, especially your shoulders. And don't look at your breast or the collecting bottle—you don't want to get self-conscious about whether "enough" milk is coming out. Try to take your mind off the job at hand—but choose your distractions in such a way that you're still in touch with the "babyness" of the procedure. You might read ahead in this book, or leaf through baby magazines, or think about what you'll need to do to get your baby's room ready for her homecoming. Above all, try not to approach pumping as a dreadful chore.

7. Build up gradually. For the first day, pump each breast for only about two or three minutes each time. The next day, build up to five minutes on a side; the next day, to seven minutes on a side. As your nipples toughen, you will be able to tolerate longer and longer stretches of pumping. Work up to about fifteen to twenty minutes on each breast.

8. Disengage from the machine carefully. *First* turn the pump off, and *then* pull it from your breast. It can hurt your nipple to try to pull away from the pump while the vacuum is still established.

9. Repeat on the opposite breast. It's usually a good idea to alternate which breast you start with from one pumping to the next. In other words, pump the left breast and then the right breast at the 8:00 A.M. pumping, and at 11:00 A.M. pump the right breast first and then the left.

10. Cover the bottle of milk and refrigerate it. If you can't bring the milk to the hospital soon enough for it to be used within forty-eight hours, transfer it to a plastic container (not glass, because important antibodies in the milk can adhere to the glass when it's frozen), date it, and freeze it. The sterile plastic "bottles" made for baby nursers are good for this purpose. Frozen milk can be kept for up to three months before thawing. Fresh milk is preferable, though, because

freezing is thought to destroy some of the beneficial immunological components of breast milk.

11. Take care of your nipples. A breast pump is even more irritating to nipples than is a nursing baby, so you must take special care to avoid painful, cracked, or bleeding nipples. Let them dry in the air, and then apply some pure lanolin or a preparation such as Masse Creme to keep them soft. Don't wash your nipples with soap (that can be drying), and when you shower or bathe, toughen your nipple by rolling it between your thumb and forefinger.

12. Repeat the pumping procedure every three hours during the day. (A typical schedule might be 8:00 A.M., 11:00 A.M., 2:00 P.M., 5:00 P.M., 8:00 P.M., 11:00 P.M.) It's not necessary to wake up in the middle of the night to pump your breasts unless you're having trouble establishing a milk supply. If you're returning to work, or if you have small children at home, you might want to try a different regimen—such as every four hours during the day and once in the middle of the night. Your doctor or nurse should be able to help you decide what method is best for you.

13. Get enough sleep. The psychological stress of worrying about your baby, combined with the physical stress of commuting to visit her in the hospital and standing all day beside her isolette, can leave you bone tired; you need as much sleep as you can get. Remember, too, that excessive fatigue can interfere with your milk supply and your letdown reflex, so you're not helping anyone by running yourself into the ground.

14. Eat right. A successful milk supply depends on an adequate diet. You *must* drink at least eight glasses of liquids a day—some doctors say twelve—if you are to produce enough milk. This should include at least two glasses of milk, one glass of fruit juice (not fruit drink, which is full of sugar and of no nutritive value), and lots of water.

You'll probably need about 500 extra calories and about 20 extra grams of protein beyond your normal diet while you're nursing. This can usually be taken care of by a peanut butter sandwich on whole wheat bread and a glass of skim milk. Continue taking the prenatal vitamins you were taking throughout pregnancy. Eat lots of protein and plenty of fruits and vegetables, and try to cut out as many "empty calories" (that is, junk food) as you can. That's a tall order as you rush from vending machine to cafeteria to vending machine during your baby's hospital stay, but it's important if you want to nurse.

Try to eliminate caffeine-laden coffee, tea, and soft drinks from your diet. Don't take any drugs—including aspirin, sleeping pills, antihistamines, and other over-the-counter drugs—without first asking the neonatologist whether it will affect the baby through your breast milk. Try to give up alcohol while you're nursing—although you might find that one glass of beer or wine is helpful in relaxing you, especially just before the 5:00 P.M. pumping. If you can, stop smoking.

FEEDING ROUTINES

If you pump your breasts every three hours or so, you'll probably be collecting more milk in one day than your baby can ingest in three—even if she's relatively large and relatively healthy. Especially at first, premies are given very, very small feedings. Their stomachs are too small to hold more than a few cubic centimeters every hour, and a feeding of much more than that can prove taxing not only for the digestive system but for the respiratory and circulatory systems as well.

The nurses will show you where to store the milk you pump, and they'll probably ask you to freeze a good deal of it. Especially in the early weeks, your baby is unlikely to catch up with your supply quickly enough to use everything you pump within forty-eight hours. Your frozen milk will last for months with most—though not all—of its beneficial properties still intact.

At first, your baby probably will be fed through a naso-gastric (nose-to-stomach) tube, a long, thin plastic tube that eliminates the need to suck. A nurse will insert the tube before each feeding, and if you like you may ask to hold the small container of milk as it drips directly into the baby's stomach. During tube feedings (also called "gavage feedings"), if your baby is well enough, you might be able to hold her in your lap. This reinforces in your child the idea that feeding time, however it's implemented, is also a time for nurturance, closeness, and social interaction.

When the baby progresses to the bottle—usually when she reaches approximately 34 weeks gestational age—you might ask the nurse whether you can first offer the baby your breast. Some doctors make a point of starting the baby on bottles slowly, beginning with a special premie nipple that requires very little sucking before milk is drawn out. Others say that babies who get too accustomed to sucking on bottles, especially those with the premie nipple, become lazy and unwilling to exert the extra effort needed to get milk out of a breast. At Michael Reese Hospital in Chicago, for instance, once a baby is mature enough to suck a plastic nipple, she's considered mature enough to suck her mother's nipple. Premies there who are as small as 1250 grams are regularly—and successfully—allowed to nurse. Doctors at many other hospitals consider it unlikely that a baby can nurse successfully until she weighs 1500 grams or more. See what your doctor thinks, and ask whether you can try to nurse your baby as early as possible.

On the other hand, you don't want to nurse your baby before she's really ready. The gag reflex, which prevents a baby from choking on liquid that could go down her windpipe, is not well developed until about 32 to 34 weeks gestational age, and before then oral feedings can be difficult. Usually, a doctor or nurse is the first person to give your baby a bottle. This is done to make sure the baby is able to coordinate the complex processes of sucking and swallowing.

Before your first nursing, ask to be sure that someone has already given your baby a bottle without incident. You wouldn't want to try nursing your child—or to try giving her a bottle, for that matter—only to find that the job is too much for her and to watch her gag, or turn blue, or set off her monitors. It's hard enough for you to try nursing without having to discover that it's really too soon for the baby to suck at all. Ask a professional to pave the way for you.

The nurses will be there to show you the most comfortable way to hold the baby. Pillows often are helpful in propping the baby up, since she might be too small comfortably to reach your breast from the crook of your arm. You might want to try expressing a little milk before you begin nursing, so that the taste of milk on your nipple encourages the baby to start sucking.

Remember your letdown reflex; use whatever thoughts and images helped get you through pumping to stimulate your milk flow now that you've actually got your child at your breast. And, although it may be difficult to do in the middle of the intensive care nursery, try to relax.

Many mothers who managed, against all odds, to pump their breasts successfully for weeks or even months find their resolve crumbling once they try to nurse the baby. Don't expect nursing to be instantly successful and romantic; it rarely is even with full-term babies, and nursing a premie carries the additional problem of not quite synchronizing the mother's supply with the baby's demand. It might take some time for you and your baby to get used to one another. "The first few nursing sessions are for getting acquainted," says one neonatal nurse. A successful nursing session, this nurse says, "may consist of the baby only locating the nipple and making a few sucking movements."

If the baby is very small, the nurse might supplement

these initial breast encounters with a bottle of breast milk. If not, the baby might be placed on a demand schedule and be nursed or bottle-fed again as soon as she is hungry.

Some special devices have been designed for women experiencing particular problems with nursing or lactation. Among them are nipple shields (useful for babies who seem to prefer the bottle to the breast) and a device called a Lact-Aid. The Lact-Aid is a small plastic bag of breast milk that hangs around the mother's neck; the baby gets the milk by sucking on a thin tube that runs from the bag along the mother's chest, resting near her nipple. As the baby sucks on the tube, she's also sucking on her mother's nipple, thus stimulating her breast to produce more milk. The baby receives nourishment at the same time that she helps to build up her mother's milk supply.

Some doctors and nurses rely a great deal on devices like these. Others think they can become crutches for women who really should be able to work out their difficulties without such help. Ask your doctor and nurse for their opinion.

At home, it may be harder for a mother to accommodate her baby's needs. This is when she's all alone, afraid of damaging her fragile baby, and harried by the round-the-clock demands of a typical infant. At times like this, a mother is likely to think that the added demands of breastfeeding, especially if there's a problem with nursing, constitute an impossible burden. If she's to continue in her earlier resolve to nurse, she often needs the vigorous support of her mate, her friends, and her pediatrician.

"Charles never got the hang of nursing," says his mother, Ann Foster. "So I gave up pumping after six weeks. My obstetrician had said I should take sitz baths often for my hemorrhoids, and also should continue breastfeeding at all costs, but there was no way I could do both. I was exhausted. It seemed all I was doing was feeding Charles and pumping my breasts."

Finally, Ann switched Charles to a bottle. Breastfeeding,

says Ann, "was the last illusion to go. I'd already lost the illusion that I could have a full-term baby, and I'd lost the illusion that my baby would be easy to take care of. Now I lost the illusion that I could nurse my kid. And I cried. I cried a lot."

Sometimes, the tale ends more happily. "I pumped my breasts for three and a half months before I could nurse Matthew," says Natalie Davidson. "But now I nurse him full time. It's so important for me to nurse him, because I know he'll be my last baby and I want to do all I can for him. Breastfeeding has been a very special bond between us, maybe more so because there was so much to overcome early on."

Giving Consent to Surgery

When your child first entered the intensive care nursery, you probably were asked to sign a blanket consent form allowing doctors to proceed with "all aspects of routine care." This was done so you did not have to be approached for consent each time a doctor wanted to draw blood, or insert a peripheral intravenous line, or adjust the oxygen setting on the ventilator. But by signing this form, you did not sign away your right—indeed, your obligation—to watch your baby's progress. Even after signing a blanket consent for routine care, you still must take the time to consider, along with the doctors, whether each subsequent step in the baby's care is a step worth taking.

If your baby develops a problem that requires surgery, you will again be approached to give your consent. The term "surgery" encompasses a great many procedures, and not only those that require general anesthesia and a trip to the operating room. Surgery can include such measures as a spinal tap, a cutdown, a catheterization, or an intubation. It also includes far more dramatic, and riskier, procedures, such as an emergency operation for NEC or surgical closure of a patent ductus arteriosus.

When the neonatologist asks for your consent to surgery, you might feel confused, angry, and dumb. Any surgical procedure, however minor it might seem to the surgeon, is frightening to you. It means that something is wrong with your child. When your baby faces surgery, you're likely to feel at your worst, but you're called upon to act your best.

Giving consent to surgery is no simple matter. The long list of possible complications for any procedure, even a catheterization, can be overwhelming, and the doctor can give you only statistics as to how likely any of these complications are. He cannot tell you for certain how *your* baby will come through the operation. That uncertainty is the hardest part to bear.

"The doctors told me Jade had a 5 percent chance of even surviving the operation," recalls Lorna Jackson of her daughter's intestinal surgery for NEC. (This figure, incidentally, is unusually pessimistic because Jade weighed only 860 grams at the time, and her NEC was very far advanced.) "I guess a lot of parents would say, 'Well, then, don't bother, it's not worth taking her through all that pain.' But this was the closest we had ever come to finally having our child, and I just thought that if the doctors did all they could to save her, then I'd feel as if I had done all I could."

The typical informed consent form is an impressive document, and difficult to read through. Although it is written in plain English—a benefit of the recent move toward "consumerism" in medical care—its message is so powerful that most parents don't really focus on what the words mean. If you can, you should try to read the fine print on your informed consent form, but probably just as important is to read the faces of your doctors. Usually, you can take your cue about the pros and cons of surgery from the baby's neonatologist. He can tell you his own experience with the problem your baby has and can give you a good indication of the prospects for long-term recovery after the operation. His optimism or pessimism is probably your best measure of how much faith to place in the surgery.

The neonatologist has probably already made his determination about the risk-benefit relationship of the proposed operation. In general, if he didn't think the surgery was more useful than dangerous, he wouldn't be asking you to agree to it in the first place.

In many cases, the only professional who needs your consent for surgery will be your baby's neonatologist. He is able to do the most straightforward operations himself, such as intubations, catheterizations, and cutdowns. (In many hospitals, a signed consent form is not required for these more routine procedures.) But when the procedure involves more elaborate surgery, the neonatologist will call in a pediatric surgeon, neurosurgeon, or cardiovascular surgeon to do the operation.

It is the surgeon, then, who will ask for your consent. Most likely you'll meet him shortly before the operation, when he will outline for you its pros and cons.

Doctors are not infallible. They can be overly pessimistic regarding the fate of your child—or, sometimes, they can be overly optimistic. Cases have occurred of a doctor wanting to treat a baby aggressively for what he considered minor abnormalities, with the parents refusing to give their consent because to them the abnormalities were significant—and they did not want to prolong the life of a handicapped child. Since the parents are the ones who must live with the consequences, the parents usually have the final say. But, occasionally, doctors have successfully overriden a parent's veto in order to operate on a baby they thought could and should be saved.

Other professionals are available in the hospital to offer advice as you decide on whether to consent to your baby's operation. The neonatal social worker can offer counseling and support during this difficult time, and can often act as a useful sounding board for bouncing off the statistics and prognoses that have been bounced around to you. The hospital chaplain can provide comfort as well, since the matter of informed consent is often a deeply moral and religious one.

You might feel as though the last thing you need is another professional's opinion. If that's the case, it might be helpful to get in touch with other parents who have faced choices like yours. Often, the social worker can contact such "graduate parents" for you. A phone conversation with a mother who went through the same agonized decision making, whether she is happy or unhappy with the result, can go a long way toward helping you come to terms with your own dilemma.

For all the support and advice available to you as you try to decide whether to consent to your baby's surgery, no one else can make the decision for you. The decision is wholly yours to make. And it's a highly personal matter: One family might consider the risk of death without an operation to be far worse than the risk of damage with one; another family might see the situation in starkly different terms, concluding that even death is to be preferred to the possibility of lifetime handicap.

There is no right or wrong choice regarding surgery for a tiny baby. It is not a medical decision; it is a family decision. And the only choice that's "right" is the one that feels "right" to you and your family.

Deciding Whether to Stop Treatment

Without question, the most agonizing choice a parent can make is the decision to stop treatment. When a baby just cannot be weaned from the ventilator, or when her brain bleed seems to have done irreparable damage, or when the prematurity is complicated by certain birth defects, the neonatologist is likely to propose that the medical "heroics" be stopped. At that moment, the parents are profoundly alone.

"The decision whether to treat a severely defective infant and exert maximal efforts to save life should be the choice of the parents," the American Medical Association proclaimed in 1981. But at least some doctors think that it's cruel to leave such awesome decisions to the parents alone. These doctors make a practice of deciding *on their own* that a baby will never recover. Only *after* such a decision is made do they approach the parents with the suggestion that, should the baby need elaborate life support or resuscitation efforts, she be allowed to die.

The decision, then, is the medical team's; the parents need only give their consent. This practice, which probably occurs in the majority of intensive care nurseries, can save parents the burden of guilt that would otherwise be added to their already overpowering burden of grief.

Because neonatology is advancing in such tremendous leaps, even doctors are at a tremendous disadvantage when trying to decide which babies to treat aggressively and which to allow to die. There simply isn't enough information available with which to make informed choices. The experience gained during ten or twenty years of newborn care is relatively useless to doctors who must make decisions based on the state of the science of the 1980s. One noted bioethicist, Dr. Albert Jonsen of the University of California, San Francisco, says that, more than in any other field of medicine, decisions in neonatology are plagued by "prognostic perplexity."

In a staff paper written in 1982, the President's Commission for the Study of Ethical Problems in Medicine cited the particular hardship of making life-and-death decisions about premies and other sick newborns. "These decisions are being made on the very cutting edge of a developing technology," the commission staff wrote. "New techniques, new devices, new procedures are being developed so fast that almost insurmountable problems arise for gathering long-term data on the outcome of different types of treatment." In the absence of reliable information, doctors—and parents as well—are left to make decisions about treatment or nontreatment based on nothing more than an educated guess.

Sometimes, though, there's no decision to be made, either by the doctors *or* the parents. "When John had a severe brain bleed and they said he might be retarded, our first reaction was 'Don't do anything to prolong his life,' " recalls John's mother, Katie Lee. "The doctors assured us that he'd be functional, but we said, 'We want you to stop. The possibility of retardation or cerebral palsy is enough for us.' Still, they couldn't stop, because John never needed any help to live. He never was on a respirator, so there was nothing to turn off."

To parents, the greatest agony in making these decisions is the fact that they are, of necessity, decisions by proxy. An infant is unable to say whether she is more in dread of death or of handicap; she is unable to tell you whether her treatment is causing her pain. "Timothy went through a lot before we asked that he not be resuscitated," says George Carroll, whose son Timothy was born at 30 weeks gestation with multiple birth defects, including a hydrocephalus that had been diagnosed, and successfully treated, in a dramatic operation while he was still in utero. "But I felt," says George, "that if I had asked him, 'Do you want to go through with this?' and he had been able to answer, he always would have said, 'Yes.' " The Carrolls urged the doctors to do all they could to keep Timothy alive until it finally became clear that even all they could do would not be enough.

Some of the best minds in the country have mulled over the ethics of newborn intensive care in recent years, as the line between viable and nonviable life becomes ever fuzzier. In Chapter 13, we review some of their current thinking.

Their thoughts might help you as you try to decide for yourself how aggressively you want your baby to be treated. But they probably won't keep you from waking each morning, as Katie Lee did, "feeling as though I was choking. We had asked the doctors not to put our child on a respirator, and having said that, there was a tremendous burden of guilt. John is three years old, and the guilt is just starting to ease."

7: Preparing to Go Home

NO MATTER HOW MUCH you've prepared yourself for the fact that your baby will soon come home, the date he is discharged is likely to come as a surprise. And, incredible as it seems, you're probably not even ready—emotionally or logistically—to have your baby home just yet. You still haven't had the time, somehow, to paint the nursery or buy the crib or borrow the carriage from your sister-in-law. And you're still not quite sure that your baby is big enough, and sturdy enough, to withstand your clumsy handling at home. How could those weeks between his birth and today have slipped away so easily? Why do you still feel so unprepared?

"I spent so long badgering the doctors about when they'd discharge Charles that by the time they said OK I wasn't ready for him," says Ann Foster. "For several days, Charles weighed just a few grams less than the hospital's five-pound standard for release. I just couldn't see why they were keeping him around for the sake of those few silly grams. Finally, one Sunday morning, the nurse came up to me with a big smile on her face and said, 'Surprise! You can take Charles home today!' Well, I panicked. After all that time, I just wasn't ready yet to go home with a baby."

The fact is that you're probably much more ready than you realize to take your baby home. The nurses in the intensive care nursery have a saying: "Discharge planning begins on the day of admission." Although this is not literally true, especially for smaller and sicker premies, the basic point *is* true: your nurses have been preparing you for discharge for many weeks. Each diaper you've changed in the nursery, each feeding you've given, each bath you've orchestrated—every small chore, whether accomplished alone or with a nurse's help, has brought you a step closer toward being your baby's full-time parent, able to take care of his needs, alone, around the clock.

And even if you don't feel ready yet to have your baby home, be assured that he's not about to show up on your doorstep unannounced. His homecoming, anticipated for weeks, is heralded by several standard hospital procedures that help facilitate the move from hospital to home.

Your baby's doctor will administer certain tests, if necessary, before the baby can go home. These tests will assure both the doctor and you that the baby really is in good health and really can be treated like a normal infant who just happened to be born too soon.

The Sleep Apnea Test

If your baby encountered frequent episodes of apnea—cessation of breathing for more than fifteen seconds—during his hospitalization, he'll be given a special test for apnea before he goes home. This test, administered while the baby is asleep, is conducted to see whether the baby will need to have an apnea monitor at home with him.

Hospitals vary in the way they give the sleep apnea test. Usually, they attach the apnea and bradycardia monitor to the baby just after he's eaten and before a daytime nap, and they let him sleep for an hour or two. During this nap, the baby goes through all the cycles of sleep—the nondreaming cycle, from stage 1 (light sleep) to stage 4 (deep sleep), and the dreaming cycle of rapid eye movement (REM) sleep.

The purpose of the test is to see whether the baby can maintain even breathing patterns in all sleep stages. If he can, he's given a clean bill of health. If he can't—and the criteria for failing the sleep apnea test vary from one hospital to another—he is sent home on a monitor.

A monitor at home is very much like a monitor in the hospital. It is a small box, which plugs into an electric outlet, that measures both the baby's breathing rate and his heart rate. The parents set the alarm to go off when the pause between breaths gets too long, or the heartbeat gets too slow.

The important difference between a monitor in the hospital and a monitor at home, of course, is that when you're home and the alarm goes off, *you're* the one who must revive your baby. There are no nurses or doctors around to jiggle the baby's foot, or reattach the monitor leads, or, if need be, resuscitate the baby. That will all be your responsibility.

But don't worry. The doctors won't let you go home with your baby until you're ready to administer any first aid he might need. All parents whose babies need apnea monitors are trained, before discharge, in infant cardiopulmonary resuscitation (CPR). Your hospital probably offers an infant CPR course to anyone who might be involved in your baby's care, including grandparents, older siblings, relatives and neighbors, and babysitters. The course is not the complete Red Cross qualification course in CPR, but a short course that allows you and your baby's caretakers to feel comfortable alone with the baby, certain that you can handle emergencies with skill.

A nurse in the hospital will show you how to press on your baby's chest and breathe into his mouth in a rhythm needed to get him breathing again. If your hospital can spare it, you will probably be able to take home its special instructional doll, the "Resusci-Baby," to practice on at home. Resusci-Baby responds appropriately (yes, it actually seems to breathe!) when you correctly administer infant CPR.

Although the rules for CPR certification vary from one hospital to another, this much is common—no one may take a baby home with a monitor without proving first that he or she would be able to administer infant CPR in an emergency.

The Eye Test

All premies who have received oxygen are given an eye exam before they're sent home. This test is to check for the presence of retrolental fibroplasia (RLF), a disorder of the retina that has been associated with the use of therapeutic oxygen in newborns, especially very small premies.

A hospital ophthalmologist (an M.D. specializing in diseases of the eye) will administer the test shortly before the baby's discharge. Usually, the eye test can be given as soon as the doctors are reasonably sure the baby will not need any more supplemental oxygen. While the baby is on oxygen, the blood vessels in the eye constrict, making underlying damage all but impossible to detect.

The retina is at the back of the eyeball, serving as a screen onto which all visual images are projected. To peer into the retina (which is where RLF, if it occurs at all, takes place), the doctor will give the baby eye drops to enlarge his pupils artificially. The eye drops do not hurt the baby.

At most hospitals, the eye exam takes place in a darkened room. Occasionally, though, it can be done in the nursery, usually with the lights turned down. In either place, a nurse whom the baby knows will probably be with him at all times.

The ophthalmologist shines a tiny light into the baby's eye and looks through the enlarged pupil straight to the retina. If the blood vessel arrangement on the retina is normal, the baby's vision is considered normal. Depending on his medical history, though, the baby might need to return for a retest in about three months, because occasionally retinal changes take longer to show up.

If the blood vessel arrangement is abnormal, the ophthalmologist will describe its appearance to you (for more information about RLF, see Chapter 5). He probably will ask you to return for a second eye exam within a month or two. In the meantime, there is nothing special you should do for your baby. Just remember that the milder cases of RLF actually reverse themselves within about a year, or, if they persist, do not interfere with your baby's ability to see. And the most severe cases usually are limited to babies of very low birthweight, especially those weighing under 1000 grams at birth.

A Hospital Room of One's Own

The first night at home with a premie is endless. You'll lie awake all night listening to his breathing; you'll worry about whether he's warm enough, whether he's hungry, whether he's got a sudden fever. Will he somehow smother in the blankets? Should you wake him to change the diaper you know is dirty? The nurses in the hospital always seemed to know what to do for your baby; why do you, his own parent, feel so dumb?

One of the best ways to brace yourself for that endless

first night at home is to have your endless first night on safe ground—at the hospital. Using a "rooming-in" arrangement now common at many hospitals, you can be totally responsible for your baby's care on a trial basis, with a reassuring nurse always just around the corner. You and your baby can get used to each other gradually, calmly, without the panic that often sets in when a new parent feels suddenly, overwhelmingly alone.

If your hospital offers rooming-in, take it. The accommodations vary widely, from a cubicle just off the nursery with space for a crib and a skinny cot, to a private room on the pediatric ward where both parents can sleep, if they so choose. But rooming-in is not meant to be lavish; it's meant to be educational.

When you room-in with your baby, you'll grow accustomed to the way his breathing sounds. (The intensive care nursery is usually so busy that you probably never heard your baby breathe before!) You'll learn his signals for hunger, discomfort, overtiredness, and you'll figure out—often by trial and error—the best way to respond to each. In short, you'll begin to behave like any other parent getting used to any other new baby. The difference is that your baby is, chronologically, a little older, and you and he already have been through a lot together.

If your hospital doesn't offer rooming-in, you can provide yourself with some of the same experiences with just a little ingenuity. As you see the signs that signal impending discharge—the baby has been weaned from the ventilator, has had his eye test and sleep apnea test, and is approaching the five-pound or five-and-a-half-pound weight requirement for release—take a more active role in your baby's care. Make sure that, by the time you take your baby home, you have tried to do everything at least once: changed his diaper, given him a bath, fed him, burped him, dressed him. And if you're at all uncertain about any aspect of infant care, ask.

Getting Ready: A Shopping List

You've probably been so distracted in the past few weeks, and so busy visiting the hospital while still trying to keep your life together, that you've hardly had time to take a bath—let alone shop. But now your baby is coming home, and you must have some supplies to greet him with. Here, then, is a bare-bones list of the infant supplies that you absolutely must have.

1. A place to sleep. Eventually, your baby will need a crib to sleep in, but in the beginning you can get by on much less—a bassinet, a cradle, a carriage, even an empty dresser drawer placed on the floor and cushioned with pads. And when you do buy or borrow the crib, make sure it's safe. The crib slats should be no more than 2⅜" apart, or else the baby's head could get stuck between them; any paint on the crib should be lead-free; and the mattress should fit firmly with no gaps between the mattress and the railings.

2. Linens for the bed. These should include:

• 3 or 4 crib sheets (if you are using a bassinet or carriage, you can either fold the crib sheets to fit or use pillowcases as sheets);

• 3 or 4 mattress pads or rubber sheets;

• 3 or 4 blankets of varying weights: cotton or flannel receiving blankets, crib-sized quilts, and wool or acrylic blankets or afghans; and

• a crib bumper, especially if the crib slats are far apart or if the mattress does not fit snugly inside the crib.

Do not use pillows in the crib while your baby is small. He doesn't need a pillow to be comfortable, and it's dangerous to have a large, soft object in bed with him under which he could smother.

3. Clothes. You will need some additional warm clothes for winter babies, but in general you should be able to get by for the first three months with the following:

• 6 terrycloth "stretchies," size "small" or "3 months";

• 6 bibs (terrycloth or plastic, the larger the better);

• 10 cotton tee shirts (more if yours is a summer baby, since you'll be using the tee shirts as sleepwear, too);

• 1 hat, appropriate to the season;

• 2 sweaters, appropriate to the season;

• 1 blanket sleeper or snowsuit, appropriate to the season.

In Appendix C, we list several sources of premie-sized clothing. You might want to buy a few special outfits in an extra-small size; occasionally, you'll find, it's nice to dress up your baby in something that actually fits him! Some major department stores are now carrying premie-sized clothing, and if you're at all handy at sewing you should be able to produce at least one or two tiny outfits yourself. You might also want to consider scouring toy stores for some large doll clothes; they won't last for very long, but they might be cute enough to lift your spirits when nothing else fits.

4. Diapers. We describe diapers in more detail in the next chapter, and you'll probably want to read that section now to help you decide whether to use disposables, cloth diapers, or a diaper service.

• If you use disposable diapers or a diaper service, you'll still need 1 to 2 dozen cloth diapers for protecting the baby's bed, your shoulder, and your visitors' laps from the baby's spit-up and other accidents;

• if you use cloth diapers, you'll need 4 to 6 large diaper pins; and

• if you wash your own cloth diapers, you'll need at least 4 dozen diapers, preferably prefolded, made of either cotton gauze or bird's-eye. You'll also need 6 to 8 pairs of waterproof pants.

5. Changing area. A changing table, or a pad securely anchored to a waist-high dresser, is a must for your baby's frequent diaper changes. If you're improvising a changing table, consider building some shelves nearby that can house such essentials as:

• Baby wipes, or a jar of water and some cotton balls, for cleaning the baby's diaper area;

• cornstarch or baby powder for dusting the baby's bottom;

• ointments recommended for diaper rash, such as Desitin, A&D Ointment, or zinc oxide cream;

• a rectal thermometer, and some Vaseline for making insertion easier; and

• baby lotion, if you like to use it on the baby's skin (although it really is not necessary).

6. A car seat. Traffic accidents are the leading cause of death for children under five, and the vast majority of babies and toddlers who die on the roads were not sitting in car seats. *You must have a car seat for your baby.* It might seem like an extravagance—a good car seat costs about $50—but if you can afford a car, you can afford a car seat.

Many seats now on the market are adaptable to fit newborns and preschoolers through the age of four, but they generally will be hard to use for a baby under eight pounds. Have the car seat strapped in securely *before* you drive to the hospital to bring the baby home—many hospitals will not even let parents get in the car with their new baby unless the baby is in a car seat. Try to practice using it before the baby actually is sitting inside it, because all those straps and snaps can be tricky, especially when your baby is very small and cannot sit up unsupported. You might need to use a few folded receiving blankets on the seat to prop the baby up, so that he is high enough to reach the shoulder straps. *Use the car seat every time you get in the car, no matter how short the ride,* from now until your baby weighs forty pounds.

7. A way to get around. The collapsible umbrella-type strollers are among the most popular in use today; they fold up easily, are lightweight, and tend to cost less than more traditional strollers. Some of them even have reclining, stiff backs that babies as young as two or three months can sit in safely and comfortably. The drawbacks to an umbrella

stroller, though, are that they have no storage space, and they generally provide a bumpier ride. Whatever stroller you get, do try to get one with swivel wheels, since they make steering much easier.

Carriages are nice, but their usefulness is short-lived. If you can borrow one, or get one secondhand, you might enjoy taking your baby for walks in the park or putting him in the carriage for naptime on warm, sunny days. (Never let the baby out in direct sunlight, especially between 11:00 A.M. and 2:00 P.M.)

Front carriers and back carriers also will make it much easier for you to get around. The top-of-the-line front carrier, Snugli, makes a special version for premies, as well as a special version for twins. (The address is listed in Appendix C.) All of these carriers are useful in soothing a fussy baby, in letting you get around while still having two hands free for chores or other children, and in giving you and your baby the comforting feeling of closeness that you missed while he was hospitalized.

The Homecoming

Many premie mothers advise trying to have some help around the house in the baby's first days at home. Your nights are likely to be sleepless and your days are likely to be wrapped up in taking care of your child; if your mother, friend, or spouse can be enlisted to run the household for a while, the pressure on you will be eased considerably. And even if no one is around to help, don't try just yet to keep the house spotless and to cook a hot meal every night. Your most important job right now is taking care of your baby— and that can be a full-time responsibility.

You're sure to be surprised by how overwhelmed you feel being wholly responsible for your baby's well-being. You'll be surprised, too, by the sheer physical effort required to keep this tiny baby clean, fed, warm, and happy. At times, it might seem to be more effort than you can muster. But remember how eagerly you awaited this very experience while your baby was in the hospital.

"One clear, cold night at 3:00 A.M., I was up with Meredith," says her mother, Fran Pines. "She was crying, I was crying. Crying from frustration, at not knowing what she wanted; from fear that maybe she was ill or unhappy; from anger at Meredith, for keeping me awake; and from guilt, for being angry at my tiny baby. Then I looked up and noticed the cross-stitch sampler my sister-in-law had embroidered; it reads, 'After the storm comes the sunshine; after the rain comes the rainbow.' And I realized for the first time that we could easily have lost her, born after only 28 weeks in my uterus, and we were so lucky to have her here with us at all.

"Somehow Meredith's cries didn't seem so fretful then, but rather were the signs of a healthy, energetic infant. We've had bad nights since then, but nothing we couldn't handle."

In the next chapter, we will describe the basics of infant care. The information is brief and to the point, because in the weeks ahead you're not likely to have much time for leisurely reading. Just remember, in panicky moments like the one Fran Pines describes, how lucky you are to have your baby with you at all. And remember, too, that as your baby gets older, the job of taking care of him will get easier and easier.

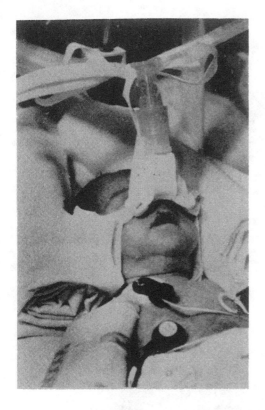

1. A baby on nasal CPAP. CPAP, which delivers air to the baby through prongs in the nostril, keeps the lungs expanded so the baby can breathe. This premie also is connected to a heart and breathing monitor through the leads visible on the baby's chest.

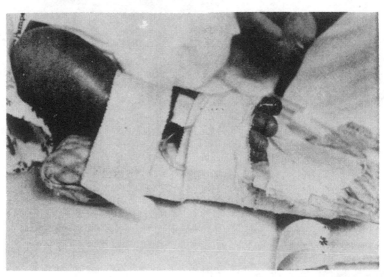

2. An intravenous line in the leg. The baby's leg is taped to a board to stabilize the line, so it cannot be dislodged if the baby moves or kicks.

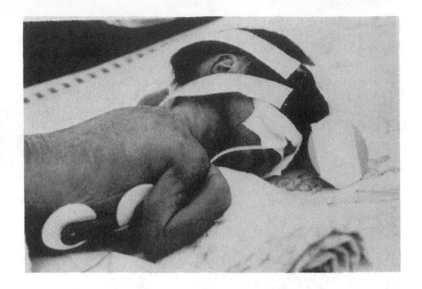

3. Eye patches typical of those used for babies under bilirubin lights. This baby also has a nasogastric tube in place, through which feedings are given. Next to the infant's head is a pacifier made from a nipple. Many hospitals allow premies to suck on pacifiers during tube feedings so they learn to associate sucking with being fed.

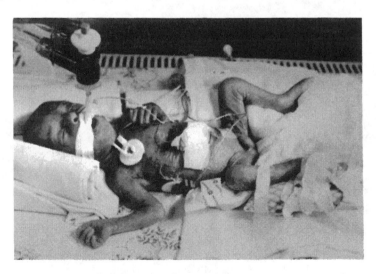

4. A baby on a ventilator. This premie has many things in place at once: a ventilator in the mouth, a nasogastric tube in the left nostril, monitor leads on the chest and side, an umbilical catheter in the belly button, and an intravenous line in the foot. He is lying on top of an open premie-sized disposable diaper. Doctors and nurses often keep a sick premie naked so they can manipulate the baby more easily, and so they can see the baby's skin color, frequently a clue to changes in functioning.

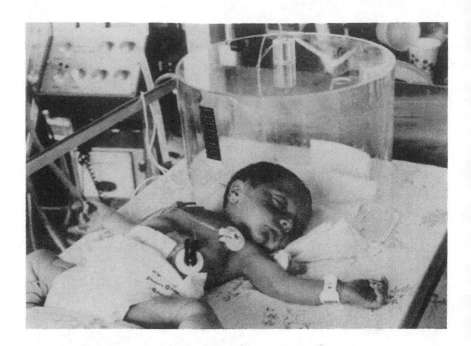

5. An oxygen hood. This baby, who is lying on an open bed under warming lights, also is attached to monitors and has an umbilical artery catheter in place.

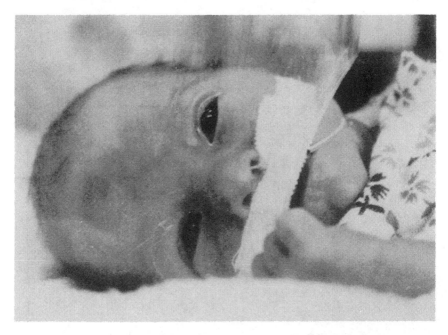

6. A nasogastric tube, probably being used for feeding.

7. An isolette can make your baby seem miles away. These parents are forced to watch their infant from outside the isolette during the time when she is under an oxygen hood and is too sick to be held.

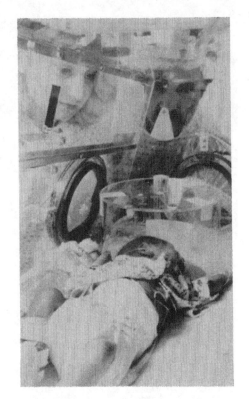

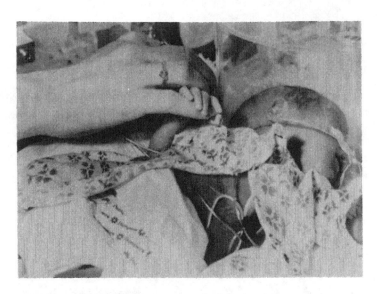

8. But even from this distance, parents can let their babies feel their presence through the magic of touch. This mother places a clean hand into her baby's isolette, strokes the baby's leg gently, and is thrilled to find that the baby grasps her pinky and holds on with surprising strength.

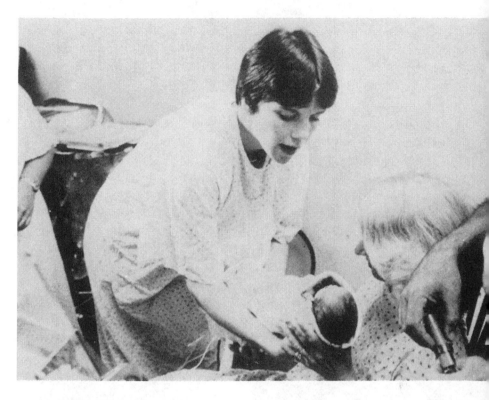

9. When the baby's condition improves, she can be held briefly by her eager parents. A nurse carefully wraps the premie, who has a nasogastric tube in place for a feeding, in a soft blanket, lifts her from the isolette, and hands her to Mother, who is seated in a comfortable rocking chair.

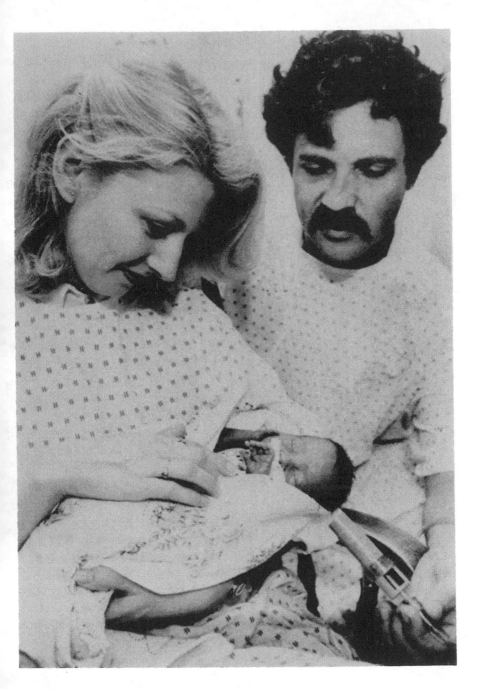

10. As Mother holds her baby for this tube feeding, Father sits nearby with an oxygen hose to supply the extra oxygen she still needs during feedings. In a few moments, the nurse will remind Father to keep the oxygen hose closer to the baby's face.

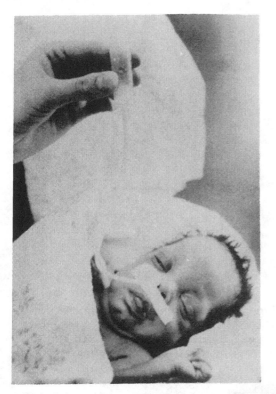

11. Two views of premie feeding: parents can help with feedings through a nasogastric tube . . .

12. . . . or through a bottle.

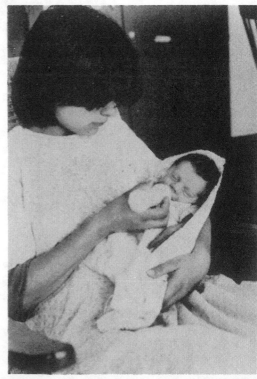

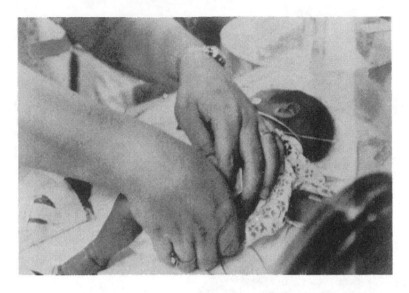

13. Not only feeding, but diapering, too, is something that parents can accomplish even while the premie is quite sick. This mother is changing her baby's diaper while he lies under an oxygen hood.

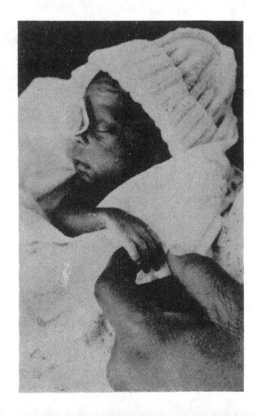

14. A father keeps his baby company during a nasogastric feeding. The baby is wearing a ski cap to prevent heat from escaping through his head.

II

Finally, Home

8: Basics of Infant Care

"OH, THAT FIRST NIGHT at home with Stephen!" says Eve Markham. "We couldn't get his monitor leads to work—we just couldn't figure out how to attach them—so I spent the night with my hand on his chest, feeling it rise and fall. All night long, Stephen and me, and I heard the cuckoo clock go off every single hour and half hour."

Most parents report similar stories of frantic fear during their babies' early days at home. "I kept taking his temperature," Ann Foster says. "I have no idea what I was looking for. But the nurses kept taking his temperature in the hospital, so I did it at home, too." Ellen Thames cut a premie-sized ski cap out of an old knee sock, and insisted that her son Arthur wear it whenever he was out of his crib. Stacy Wynn installed an intercom in Aaron's nursery so she could run down to the kitchen to make dinner without worrying about whether Aaron's apnea monitor would go off.

You're likely to feel as frantic as these mothers did when your premie first comes home. You might have thought you were prepared for full-time baby care—after all, didn't you change all your baby's diapers while you visited her, and didn't you learn weeks ago how to bathe her, feed her, and stimulate her out of an apnea attack? But once the baby's home, all your hospital-based confidence can easily wilt. "I just wished a nurse who knew my baby could come to the house and tell me he looked okay," Eve Markham says. "I needed to hear, from a professional, that I hadn't done anything yet to hurt him."

In addition to the fear, you might feel an element of disbelief that your tiny baby truly is home—and truly is yours. "We keep waiting for his parents to come pick him up," say the Rosens, whose son Claude spent his first three weeks in the intensive care nursery.

In many ways, these are the same feelings that many parents, especially first-time parents, experience when their babies first come home. But your period of adjustment is complicated by the fact that you spent such a long time feeling useless. While your baby was in the hospital, you probably tended to feel like an outsider in her day-to-day care— after all, no matter how many diapers you changed, the baby's well-being was in the hands of professionals. After such a beginning, it's difficult indeed to get used to being the one in charge.

At the same time, you'll probably be harder on *yourself* than brand-new parents are. "Why am I suddenly having so much trouble accepting myself as this baby's mother," you might ask yourself, "when I've already *been* her mother for six weeks?"

But the first thing to do to quell these fears and recriminations is: relax. If your premie has just come home from the hospital, chances are she'll do just fine if she's treated like a normal baby. By now, your baby probably has almost reached the gestational age of a full-term newborn—40 weeks—and probably weighs a reassuring five pounds at least. There's not much you can do to hurt her.

On the other hand, premies *are* different, as most premie parents find out in one way or another. Your baby, for instance, might have come home with an apnea monitor, oxygen, or a problem resulting from her time in intensive care. And even if she hasn't, she comes to you after weeks of exposure to an unnatural environment, where the lights were on round-the-clock, the noise level was high, and the stimulation was of a kind unlike that of either the womb or the home.

At its least obvious, the difference between premies and full-term babies is shown in the extra skittishness and the lack of organization in the behavior of a premie. Even at the age of two or three months, a premie is more likely to be fussy, unresponsive, and easily overstimulated than is her full-term peer. This can make the early weeks at home difficult for an unprepared parent. So forget what other people tell you about how to handle your child, and remember that, because she was premature, she'll be special for many months to come.

"My mother spent five days with us when Charles was five weeks old," Ann Foster says, "and when she left, that was the first time I really felt like Charles's mother and really felt I could take care of him. I'm the oldest of six children, so I thought I was well prepared for a kid. But I wasn't prepared for a premie. My mother was, because the first three of the six of us, including me, were premies. The most important bit of advice she gave me was this: 'I don't care what the books say—premies are different.' "

Keeping the Baby Clean

At first, your obligation toward your baby will seem rather primitive: you'll need to keep her clean, warm, and fed. As you do these chores, though, you'll also be communicating to her, both with your voice and with your touch. Think of caretaking as a gesture of love and nurturance, and it might make those piles of dirty diapers easier to bear!

About those diapers: The baby will need clean diapers regularly, sometimes as often as every hour or two. If you want to use disposable diapers, one leading brand, Pampers, is available in a special premie size to fit babies weighing less than 6 pounds. Premie Pampers can be ordered by the case only (180 diapers) directly from the manufacturer (see Appendix C). If a case seems like too many (though you'd be surprised how quickly an infant goes through diapers!), local baby supply stores or pharmacies might be able to special order premie Pampers in smaller quantities. Or see if your hospital can help put you in touch with other premie parents who might be interested in sharing a case.

Cloth diapers are easier than disposables to adjust to a premie-sized bottom. If you buy your own, you might want to cut a dozen of them in half and sew a quick hem. This will mean less fabric to twist and fold when you pin the diaper on.

It's important to wash diapers well, so that the irritating components of urine and feces are thoroughly removed. Flush any bowel movement down the toilet, and then soak the soiled and wet diapers in a diaper pail containing one teaspoon of borax per gallon of *cold* water (cold water gets out the urine better). Wash the diapers, using any good detergent (the milder the better), in hot water, and rinse them twice, adding a small amount of vinegar to the final rinse cycle. As your baby grows, you might try experimenting with bleach and fabric softeners to see if her skin can tolerate them. But for now, stick with detergent and two good rinsings.

Another idea: try a diaper service. Although diaper services are disappearing with the growing popularity of disposable diapers, most localities have at least one or two to choose from. A number of them carry diapers in a special premie size. Usually, diaper services will pick up dirty diapers once a week and replace them with a load of sixty to ninety clean diapers for the following week. They can generally get their diapers cleaner than you can yourself, and they add special "bacteriostats" to the rinse water to keep bacteria from accumulating.

A diaper service may seem like a luxury, but you might be surprised by the relatively low cost. The monthly cost of a diaper service usually is priced competitively with the cost of a month's worth of disposable diapers. In addition, a diaper service will free you from a mountain of laundry and, if it carries premie sizes, will mean that the diapers fit better than cloth diapers you buy and wash yourself.

If you have room for it in the baby's room or in your family living area, a special surface for diaper changes makes the chore much easier. Separate changing tables, made of plastic, wood, or wicker, are a nice convenience, especially those that have storage space below, but they're not really necessary. A soft pad anchored firmly to the top of a table or dresser will serve just as well.

The important thing is for the changing surface to be at a comfortable height for both parents—usually at about waist level. This will ease the strain on your back during diaper changes and will allow you to get close to your baby's face for some pleasant socializing as you work. Remember to talk to your baby when you change her, telling her what you are doing, where her knees and toes are, and how much you love her. The more words your baby hears, the sooner she'll start making sounds—and even words—of her own.

You might want to decorate the changing surface with some distracting objects that can hold your baby's attention—especially if she does not like to have her diaper changed. A nonbreakable mirror hung on the wall, or a colorful mobile dangling from a shelf overhead, can be fascinating to a small baby. Try to place these objects about a foot or so from the baby's eyes, because most young infants have trouble seeing things much closer than that or much farther away.

Lotions and powders smell nice, but they're really not necessary. In fact, some of them even cause the very rashes they're meant to prevent! When you change your baby's diaper, just wipe the genitals and buttocks with a wet washcloth or commercial "baby wipe," and let it dry for a few moments. For girls, always remember to wipe from the front to the back; otherwise, some of the bacteria from stool collecting near the rectum can invade the urethra and possibly cause an infection.

If your boy has been circumcised within the previous week or two, you'll need to take special precautions at each diaper change until the circumcision heals. Clean his penis gently and wrap it carefully in a clean gauze bandage coated in Vaseline. If your son was not circumcised, leave his foreskin alone. The foreskins of very small babies are relatively tight and cannot be retracted except with force. Retracting the foreskin for cleaning in the early months can lead to scarring and, eventually, to an inability of the foreskin to retract naturally later on.

Almost every baby eventually develops a diaper rash. Diaper rashes are caused by one thing: diapers. If babies didn't wear diapers, they wouldn't sit for long periods in their own urine and feces, and their sensitive skin would not be exposed to the potentially harmful urea there. But your baby will be in diapers for at least two more years, so the best you can hope for is fewer than your share of rashes.

Two schools of thought exist about how to prevent and treat diaper rash. One is the naturalist view, advocating three or four long, cooling baths each day to soak baby's bottom, followed by bare romps in which her bottom is exposed to the air for at least fifteen minutes. The great advantage of this technique is that it gets the baby out of the offending diapers for half an hour or more four times a day.

If you don't have the time for this, or if you're worried

about accidents on the carpet, you can try the method advocated by your mother's generation: the slather approach. Each time you change the baby, smear on plenty of Desitin, A&D Ointment, or zinc oxide cream. Then coat this with a dusting of corn starch or, if you must, baby powder. The purpose of this method is to establish an impermeable layer between the dirty diaper and the baby.

When you first watched the nurses bathe your baby, bathtime probably seemed an elaborate, mysterious ritual. But at home, it needn't be. Many products on the market today make bathing a very small baby relatively easy. And, while she is tiny, your baby can be bathed on a counter or in the kitchen sink, which is easier on your back than the bathroom tub.

Baby supply stores carry such handy items as a bath sponge, a baby-sized wedge that lies flat in the water and supports the baby's whole body; plastic tubs, just the right size for the sponge and appropriate for infants until they can sit up; and inflatable tubs, which have built-in support that serves as sponge and tub in one. With this equipment, you really don't need three or four hands to bathe a baby safely!

Make sure there are no drafts in the room where your baby will be bathed; the worst thing you can do for her is to expose her wet, naked body to a sudden chill. Assemble all your essentials ahead of time, including a washcloth and, most important, a big dry towel. Try to have her clean diaper and clothes handy, too, so you can dress her right away.

Soap is unnecessary. It only makes the baby slippery, dries out her skin, and presents one more item for you to keep track of. Instead of using soap, drop one or two drops of baby oil (or the cheaper equivalent, mineral oil) into the bath water and use a washcloth to wet the baby all over. If you prefer to use soap, use a mild baby soap, either liquid or bar, and apply some baby lotion after the bath. Don't use Vaseline on a small baby's sensitive skin; it tends to clog the sweat pores, and the skin needs to "breathe."

One of the easiest, and most pleasant, ways to bathe your baby is to get in the big tub with her. This requires some co-ordination, but it can be done—and it can be relaxing for both of you. Make sure you have all the baby's needs and a few big towels in the bathroom with you. Leave the towels on the floor near the tub, where they're easily at hand. After the bath, don't try to get out of the slippery tub while holding the baby. Just reach out for a towel, dry the baby quickly, wrap her up, and lay her gently on the floor while you dry yourself off. Then you can step out of the tub alone, tie on a robe, and finish drying and dressing the baby.

Tandem bathing can work wonders for a busy mother's schedule. "During those long afternoons when Charles wouldn't stop crying, I was being told to take sitz baths for my hemorrhoids," says Ann Foster. "But I couldn't do everything, and it seemed that Charles needed me to hold him sixteen hours a day. Finally, I hit on a plan: I would try to do two things at once by bathing with Charles. Well, while Charles was screaming, I ran the bath, and when we got in together he settled down instantly. Now I find that a warm bath is the only sure-fire way to make him happy."

Keeping the Baby Warm

You might need to take some extra precautions in the early days at home to make sure your baby stays warm. If she's big enough to be home, of course, she's big enough to regulate her own body temperature, but it's always wise to be a little cautious at first.

Your baby is still thinner than most newborns, which means she hasn't the "padding" most babies have to trap body heat. In addition, she's longer, proportionally, than she is wide, and her extra skin surface means that heat is easily lost.

If your baby is fussy, consider the possibility that she's

uncomfortably cold. One easy way to keep her warm is to have her wear a hat, even indoors. Up to half the heat lost from the body is lost through the head. Other time-honored methods of baby warming are also useful: dress her in layers (an undershirt, shirt, long-legged "stretchie," and sweater), or wrap her in swaddling. If you can afford it, turn the thermostat in the house up to 72 to 76 degrees, or at least turn on a space heater in the room where the baby is.

And if you have time, you might try the most enjoyable way of all to keep your baby warm: cuddle up with her under a big blanket, and use your body's heat to help warm hers.

Eventually, you won't need to go out of your way to keep your baby warm. Standard advice of pediatricians for two-month-olds is usually, "If you're comfortable, the baby will be comfortable dressed in the same way." Ask your doctor how soon this rule of thumb will apply to your baby.

Keeping the Baby Fed

For a while, it might seem as though all you're doing is feeding the baby. If you're nursing, this can be especially stressful. Your child's frequent cries of hunger make you wonder whether she really is able to get all the milk she needs from you. And for all parents, nursing or not, the emotional and physical strain of being always "on call" to cater to a hungry infant can be enormous.

But if your baby seems to be squalling constantly for more and more food, it's not because you're doing anything wrong. It's because premies tend to be hungrier than full-term babies. Premies' stomachs are still quite small, and they can't hold enough to carry them for much more than three hours at a time. That means that premies typically will need to be fed every two or three hours. Many premies also are sluggish eaters, taking as long as an hour to empty a four-ounce bottle. In those early weeks, this means that you really will have little time for anything else.

There's one benefit to this pattern, though. In general, the more frequently a baby eats during the day, the longer she is able to go between feedings at night.

Breastfeeding a premie creates a special problem. After weeks or perhaps months of pumping your breasts and giving your baby breast milk in a bottle, followed by nursing in the fishbowl of the intensive care nursery, you've finally got your baby home. You are eager to continue the nursing experience, at last, in comfort and privacy. But you might find that the uncertainty of breastfeeding can be overwhelming. You can never see the milk actually go into the baby; you can never measure exactly how much she took at a feeding. With weight gain always a crucial issue for your child, you might feel frightened at the possibility of "not having enough milk." What if your baby starves at the breast?

"I guess I could have nursed Meredith round-the-clock to build up my milk supply," says her mother, Fran Pines. "But I just didn't have the energy. We had been through so much with Meredith—she had had a grade IV bleed, PDA, and a pneumothorax while she was in the hospital—that I didn't want to take any chances. So I nursed her when she was hungry, and then I'd supplement that with the breast milk I had pumped and frozen when Meredith was so sick."

Many breastfeeding advocates would be appalled at Fran's supplementary bottles. Indeed, Fran's quickness to turn to a bottle *might* have interfered with her establishment of an adequate milk supply. The more a baby suckles, the more milk a mother's breasts produce. This delicate balance between supply and demand is interrupted when bottles are introduced.

But breastfeeding dogma during Meredith's first weeks at home would have done Fran little good. What she needed then was a way to feed her baby adequately, happily, with a minimum of stress or guilt. And, luckily, she stumbled on such a way—and just when she most needed it.

"The night the frozen milk ran out, I panicked," Fran recalls. "My husband, Eddie, and my father were standing over me, saying, 'You have to decide. How are you going to feed this child?' and I said 'Okay! Give her formula!' I still nurse her when she's hungry, but then Eddie or someone else gives her a bottle of formula. I'm glad I'm doing it this way; Meredith still gets some of the benefits of my breast milk, I still get the experience of nursing, and we both still have time together for other things."

Fran's attitude toward infant feeding is one worth remembering: get the baby the food she needs, no matter how it's done, and try not to let battles over feeding dominate your relationship.

If you're bottle-feeding your baby, there are several kinds of formulas now on the market, one of which is sure to meet your baby's special needs. Your pediatrician will discuss with you which brands he likes best. Your baby probably no longer needs the special premie formula she might have received in the hospital; indeed, if she eats heartily and is growing well, she'll probably do fine on the cheapest formula, in the most convenient form, that you can find. But she might need a milk-free or corn-free formula, especially if allergies run in the family, or a special predigested formula if she experiences digestive problems. Your doctor will look for clues of her need to change formula, including listlessness, excessive spitting up, failure to gain weight, or general fussiness.

For at least the next few months, you will need to sterilize your baby's bottles and probably her formula as well. Pediatricians differ in their opinions as to how long sterilization should continue. Some doctors say you need never sterilize your baby's bottles; others suggest you continue sterilization for three or four months. Because your baby was premature, and therefore at a slightly higher risk of infection in the first year, you'll probably want to exercise extra caution in keeping her feeding supplies clean.

Automatic dishwashers usually do a satisfactory job of sterilizing bottles. If you have a dishwasher, you can wash your baby's bottles there; then you need only boil the nipples (which should not go into a dishwasher) and the water you use to mix the baby's formula. Some salt rubbed into the nipple before washing will keep the hole from clogging.

If you have no dishwasher, it's easiest to sterilize your bottles and formula en masse, in a large pot with a tight-fitting lid. Scrub the bottles in warm soapy water, rinse well, fill them with formula—mixed *exactly* according to package directions—place an inverted nipple on each bottle, and screw on the bottle caps (loosely, so steam can escape). Then place the bottles in a pot half-filled with water, bring the water to a boil, and boil for about twenty-five minutes. Afterward, leave the pot, with the lid on, to cool for two hours—the slow cooling prevents a skin from forming on the milk—and then tighten the caps and refrigerate the bottles you won't be using right away. Sterilized bottles can stay in the refrigerator for up to forty-eight hours.

The amount of formula your baby needs is difficult to gauge. In general, a baby should be drinking about three ounces of formula for each pound of body weight per twenty-four hours. This usually allows a baby to grow at the rate of six to eight ounces a week. When your baby weighs six pounds, then, she should be drinking eighteen ounces of formula a day, usually over the course of five or six feedings. When you make up your bottles, add an extra one-half to one ounce more than you expect the baby to take, just in case she's especially hungry at any particular feeding. Don't calculate her needs so precisely that you don't allow her to take more than you think she should. As child psychologist Penelope Leach writes in her best-selling *Your Baby and Child*, "Regularly emptied bottles are a reproach, not a cause for congratulations. If the bottle is emptied, how can you be sure that the baby would not have liked another ounce or two?" Especially when your baby is small, it's better to err on the side of too much formula in the bottle than too little. And if your baby doesn't drain the bottle, don't force her to; just throw the remainder away.

Keeping the Baby Happy

It might seem as though your days are so filled with the details of child care that you never have time to interact with your child. You're so busy changing diapers, preparing bottles, and doing the laundry that the notion of actually *playing* with your baby seems almost laughable.

But it doesn't take much time to make a small infant happy. All it takes is ingenuity. And, with premies, it probably takes more ingenuity than usual.

There will be times—and even whole days or weeks—when nothing you do seems to settle the baby. Some babies, for instance, simply have crying spells every day (usually around 4:00 to 6:00 P.M., the period that new mothers learn to call "the arsenic hours"). At times like this, no amount of holding or cooing or rocking can calm your baby. After you've tried all the obvious tricks—you've fed her, you've changed her diaper, you've put on a record and danced—there's only one thing to do. Place her down in a crib or bassinet, and let her cry. (If you can't stand listening, try going somewhere where you can't hear the baby. A shower is great for muffling sounds.) Crying for about fifteen minutes or so won't hurt the baby. If she cries for longer than that, and still can't be comforted, call your pediatrician.

But—and this might be hard to believe during these awful afternoons—your baby won't *always* be inconsolable. There will be times when she's quiet and alert and willing to engage in some sort of interaction. These periods, which grow longer and more frequent as your baby gets older, are the golden moments of parenting.

Because your baby was a premie, these moments take on a special meaning—and must be treated with special care. Your baby is fragile during these quiet, alert periods because she is not yet as "organized" in her behavior as a full-term baby her age. Scientists who have compared the behavior of premies with the behavior of full-term infants have found that, even when corrected for gestational age, premies tend to be behind in their ability to focus on objects, interact with people, and learn from new situations. So you have to go slowly with your baby, and take your cues from her.

Many premies are easily overstimulated. They take longer than term babies do to focus their attention on a particular stimulus; when they do finally focus, they take longer to disconnect themselves from it and move on to something else. Psychologists describe infants who were born prematurely with words like "irritable" and "restless."

Part of the reason why premies tend to act so disorganized is that they aren't yet in control of their bodies. They exhibit a great deal of "motility"—that is, spontaneous movement of the arms and legs—which can interfere with their ability to focus on an external stimulus.

"Evidence is accumulating," notes Dr. Anneliese Korner, a psychiatrist at the Stanford University School of Medicine, "that any means that restrain the infant's erratic motility will also increase, at least temporarily, the maturity of [her] functioning." According to Dr. Korner, the baby can function and respond more effectively if she is swaddled, if she sucks on a pacifier, or if she is put down to sleep on her belly instead of her back. All these measures, says Dr. Korner, reduce the premie's movements, lead to lowered heart rates and improved oxygenation, and heighten visual attentiveness.

You can use these findings to your own benefit when it's time to play with your baby. To help your baby reach a

quiet, alert state, in which she is most receptive to interaction and to learning, try swaddling her gently and placing
her in an infant seat. (An upright, as opposed to a horizon-
tal, position also heightens a baby's alertness.) As she sits,
show her an object that will catch her attention—a brightly
colored ball, a picture of a face with an exaggerated expres-
sion, a bell, a rattle, your gloved hand. Move the object from
one side to the other, slowly, so the baby can follow it with
her eyes and, later, with her head.

Now try some gentle socializing. Move your face into the
baby's visual field—about a foot away from her eyes—and
talk to her. Use simple words, a loving voice, and smile! A
smile is recognized by babies as a gesture of happiness, and
it will make you happier, too, as you talk to your baby.
Many babies show more interest in a moving face than a still
one, so you might try nodding or shaking your head a little
as you talk.

If the baby shows interest in what you're doing, pay attention to the *way* in which she shows interest. If she starts
gurgling and cooing, stop your own speech for a while and
let her have her say. Then, when she stops, talk back to her
in her own language, repeating—as well as you can—some
of the sweet sounds she has made. She'll be flattered by the
imitation, and soon she'll start again.

If the baby doesn't show interest, don't strain to continue
the conversation. Just gaze at her, quietly, for a while, or
maybe even look away. Babies respond *most* actively to parents who are *least* active; when a parent tries too hard to be
interesting to a young baby, the baby quickly turns off altogether. If, even by waiting patiently, you still can't get your
baby's attention, give her a toy or picture to look at or hold
and try again later.

Your social interactions, once you both get the hang of it,
will make your baby extremely happy—and extremely excited. You might find that after a very few moments of conversation with you, your baby starts to lose control. She

might begin kicking her legs in a happy bicycling movement, waving her arms, arching her back. These are signs of happiness, yes, but for the disorganized premie they can also be the beginning of a crying spell. If you see your baby getting overexcited, stop talking and help her settle herself. Swaddle her more tightly, give her a pacifier to suck on, pick her up and quietly carry her around the room.

Your job as a parent, now and forever, has finally begun in earnest: to show your child how much fun it can be to interact with people who love her, and at the same time to protect her from the stormy emotions that are an inevitable part of human relationships.

9: The Premie's Special Needs

BASIC BABY CARE is just not enough for most premies. For many months, there'll always be something that's special about your baby because he was born too soon. In this chapter, we outline for you some of the special situations you're likely to encounter as a premie parent and offer suggestions about how to survive them. Remember—no one ever said parenthood was easy! As a premie parent, your tasks might be a little bit harder, but your rewards will be the sweeter for it.

Feeding

Once you've made your decision about breast or bottle, and gotten accustomed to the routine either of pumping your breast and nursing your baby or of washing out bottles and preparing formula, you might think the major hurdles of feeding are behind you. But that's not necessarily true. With premies, feeding often gets harder, not easier, once the baby is at home and growing quickly. The feeding schedules and feeding habits of premies tend to differ slightly from those of full-term babies, and it might take some time for you to adjust yourself to your baby's unusual demands.

As we have seen, premies have smaller stomachs, and therefore need to be fed more frequently, than full-term babies. This can mean feedings as often as every two or three hours during the day and once or twice at night—an exhausting schedule for any new parent. And because weight gain continues to be so important for your baby, you will—and should—hesitate to try to wean him of his night feedings for many months.

The premie's feeding schedule can be even more maddening if mealtime is a chore—and, for many premies, it is. Premies are more likely to have trouble swallowing, to spit up frequently, to suck more slowly, and to resist feeding than are babies born at term. And when premies complain, their cries are usually interpreted as far more distressing than are the cries of term babies. Some studies have found that adults' heartbeats actually increase more in response to a premie's cry than in response to a term baby's cry. When your baby is screaming and your heart is racing, mealtime can quickly degenerate into a battle.

One way out of this battle is through compromise. There is no one right way to feed a premie, just as there is no one right way to feed any baby. You must experiment with many different combinations until you hit on the one that's right for your child.

Feeding is the one thing you do for your baby every day, yet it is the topic that new parents call their pediatricians about most frequently. Parents are afraid to try different formulas, or to start a baby on solid foods, or to stop sterilizing bottles without the doctor's okay. In general, this caution is a wise policy, especially for feeding a premie who has been sick. But try not to let caution overwhelm you so that you're afraid to do anything for your child on your own. After all, you'll be making his breakfasts, packing his lunches, and cooking his dinners for many years to come.

A catchall explanation for feeding difficulties is that a baby has "colic." This commonly refers to a digestive problem that causes abdominal cramps, excess gas, and a good deal of crying. If your baby has colic, he will draw up his legs to his abdomen after meals—or sometimes right in the middle of a feeding—and scream. He might scream unconsolably for hours.

Premies, if they are going to develop colic, usually show signs of it by about four to eight weeks of age, and outgrow it by about four or five months. There are few ways to soothe a colicky baby. Sometimes carrying the baby helps, or rubbing his belly gently. More often, however, nothing helps. Ask an unflappable friend or relative to spend a few hours carrying the baby to give you an occasional afternoon out, and remember that the best "cure" for colic is time.

Colic is more rare in breastfed babies, but breastfeeding is no guarantee against colic. If your colicky baby is bottle-fed, you might want to consider switching brands of formula or giving it to him at a different temperature—heat up his bottles if he has been getting them cold, or keep them cold if you have been heating them up. You might want to try different nipples, too; sometimes the baby takes in too much air with one kind of nipple and will have fewer problems with a different nipple.

Doctors do not put much faith in the value of feeding changes, but some parents have managed to reduce colic significantly in this way. In general, switching formulas will only work for a few days unless your baby's problem is a milk allergy—which affects less than 5 percent of infants. Your pediatrician will be able to advise you about whether the formula really needs to be changed.

The best way to hold a baby with colic is upright, so the air can rise to the top of the milk in his stomach, making it easier to burp it out. As you hold the baby over your shoulder, try singing, try dancing, try rocking in a rocking chair—try anything that will calm down the baby and you.

The most reasonable attitude toward colic is one that Dr. Penelope Leach, author of *Your Baby and Child*, calls "constructive resignation." Since there's little you can do to help the baby, Dr. Leach says, parents who must live with colic should "concentrate on trying to stay sane, supporting each other and believing that there is nothing the matter with your child. He is physically perfect. It is just that he is still very immature and his nervous system and his digestion are showing their immaturity in this particularly stressful way." Occasionally, extreme family conflict can create severe colic that a baby might not outgrow, and that is why all bad cases of colic should be brought to a physician's attention. But in general, if the infant is gaining weight, there is probably nothing terribly wrong—and, eventually, the colic will disappear.

Other digestive or feeding problems might arise in your premie that are not related to colic. Be alert to clues of difficulty—listlessness, failure to gain weight, frequent spitting up or vomiting—so you can let your doctor know that something seems to be wrong. A premie who behaves atypically should first be suspected of having a particular, physical problem. Only after a physical problem has been ruled out should the unusual pattern be ascribed to an immature system, colic, or some other vague nondiagnosis.

Stephen Markham, for example, spit up excessively during his first month home from the hospital. His mother, Eve, hesitated to bring it to the attention of Stephen's pediatrician. When she did, the doctor simply said, "Is he spitting up a lot, or just the usual amount? If it's just the usual amount, he'll grow out of it." As Eve recalls, "I just would smile weakly at the doctor, thank him, and then go home and wring my hands." Finally, when Eve insisted that Stephen's behavior was indeed very unusual, the baby was hospitalized. It turned out he was still having breathing difficulties and needed supplementary oxygen. With oxygen, he was able to keep his feedings down, and at last he started to grow.

When Charles Foster had the same symptoms—excessive spitting up—his mother, Ann, told Charles's doctor about it right away. The doctor considered every possibility, including milk allergy (they tried a milk-free formula; it didn't help), corn allergy (they tried a corn syrup-free formula; it still didn't help), and colic. Finally, the doctor concluded that Charles had an immaturely formed esophagus that failed to close off completely at the entrance to his stomach after his feedings, creating a condition known as reflux. At the doctor's suggestion, Ann began thickening the baby's formula with rice cereal and propping him in an infant seat to help his feedings stay down. And she sewed two dozen pretty bibs to protect Charles's clothes while she waited for his esophagus to mature.

Because feeding problems can signal so many difficulties, you must not be shy about bringing them to your doctor's attention. When it comes to feeding your child, you and your doctor are full partners. Feeding choices are lifestyle decisions as much as they are medical decisions, and you must be an observant, concerned member of the health care team if your baby is to thrive and grow.

If you are concerned about your baby's feeding habits, keep a diary of what he eats, when he eats, and how much he eats. Try to record, too, your baby's behavior between meals—is he sleeping, awake and happy, fussing? does he spit up a lot? does he seem to be uncomfortable?—and his bowel movements. With a diary like this, you will be better equipped to tell your doctor exactly how your baby is behaving, and you and your doctor will better be able to see any patterns that might be related to food.

Susceptibility to Infections

Many premies, especially those of very low birthweight or with bronchopulmonary dysplasia (BPD), are highly susceptible to infection. This might mean you have to rearrange your life somewhat to keep the baby away from crowds, away from visitors—and, most important and most difficult, away from children with colds.

Ellen Thames, for instance, was told to take all precautions in trying to prevent infection in her son Arthur during his first year. Arthur was six weeks premature, and since he had hyaline membrane disease and BPD he was susceptible to infections of the upper respiratory tract. Not only was he more likely to catch something, but if he did catch something the infection was likely to go straight to his lungs.

Ellen did all she could to prevent Arthur's exposure to other people's infections. "When I went back to work part-time, I had to hire a babysitter to come to the house instead of bringing Arthur to a sitter's house where there would be other children," Ellen says. "In fact, the main reason I went back to work at all is that I had to keep Arthur isolated. If I'd been able to do the things other mothers can do—enroll him in classes at the Y, take him shopping and to the park, visit friends—I wouldn't have felt the need to go back to work."

Ellen nursed Arthur exclusively, even though she had decided during her pregnancy not to breastfeed, because breast milk contains some protective antibodies that improve the baby's immune system. "And I became phobic about germs," she says. "I would spray the house with Lysol after visitors had left, especially visitors with children. I was a wreck at Halloween!"

Such precautions are difficult, but to a certain extent necessary, for a premie with lung problems. If your baby has BPD, resign yourself to staying at home a good deal of the time, especially if it's wintertime and colds and flu are in the air. Try to avoid department stores, museums, shopping malls, restaurants—anyplace where large groups of people assemble in an enclosed area. Invite guests over one at a time and screen them carefully for illnesses of their own. If your visitor has a cold, ask her politely but firmly to come back another time. Don't be afraid of losing friends by being cautious; your true friends will understand.

It is not unusual for premies, especially those with lung complications, to be hospitalized one or two more times within the first year of life for treatment of infections. One recent study found that nearly one-fifth of babies who weighed less than 2500 grams at birth, and nearly 40 percent of those weighing less than 1500 grams, were rehospitalized in the first year of life. This compared to a rehospitalization rate of less than 10 percent for babies who were born at term.

Although the prospect of rehospitalization is worrisome, be assured that it will probably never be as stressful—for you or for the baby—as was his first hospitalization in his early days of life.

By the time your baby is about a year old, your doctor will probably tell you that the danger of infection has passed. Then you can slowly start to introduce your baby to the wondrous sights, sounds, smells, and germs of the world at large. You can't protect him from infection forever—nor should you try to. By one year of age, your baby will need interaction with other people more than he'll need isolation from them. But be prepared for more than your share of illnesses during the next few years. Depending on how severe

his lung problems are, a child with BPD will probably continue to remain susceptible to infection for at least two or
three more years.

Monitoring the Monitors

If your baby has a positive sleep apnea test when he is
discharged from the hospital, the doctors will send him
home with an apnea and bradycardia monitor. Most babies
need to be attached to the monitor at all times; others need it
only, or especially, while they are asleep. The purpose of the
monitor at home is the same as it was in the hospital—to
measure the baby's rates of breathing and heartbeat and to
sound an alarm when either rate drops below the limits that
are set.

Premies are at higher-than-normal risk of sudden infant
death syndrome (SIDS), which has been associated with
episodes of sleep apnea. SIDS is just what its dreadful name
implies: an apparently healthy infant dies, suddenly, in his
sleep. It occurs most frequently in male babies, between the
ages of one and seven months, when the baby has a slight
cold or upper respiratory tract infection. It is to prevent
SIDS that doctors prescribe home monitors for premies with
sleep apnea.

What will it mean to have your baby at home on a monitor? It will mean, for one thing, that you're somewhat more
housebound than you would have been otherwise. Although
a baby on a monitor can go outdoors, you will want to keep
the monitor attached whenever the baby is either asleep or
unattended. And since the monitor needs a wall outlet to
work, the baby—and you—might be spending a lot more
time at home than you had anticipated.

It also might be harder for you to find people willing to
babysit for your baby if they see he's on a monitor. Few potential sitters, especially teenagers, are willing to learn infant

CPR and take on the responsibility of resuscitating a baby should he need it. This makes an occasional evening out, not to mention employment outside the home, difficult or even impossible. If you have trouble finding a sitter, ask the nurses in the intensive care nursery whether they know anyone who might be willing to sit for your baby. Occasionally, a former nurse, who quit a full-time job to be with her own young children, might want a babysitting job because of its flexible hours.

If you travel, you'll have to take the monitor with you. And your mode of travel might be constrained by the monitor. If the baby is in transit, he's not on his monitor. That means you must monitor him yourself, constantly keeping a watchful eye on him so you'll know if he stops breathing.

Nurses suggest that you not drive alone in a car with your baby. Either wait until someone else can drive with you (so you or your friend can sit in the back seat alongside the baby) or take buses and trains (so you can have the baby with you on your lap).

Nurses suggest, too, that you learn the route to the nearest hospital emergency room—just in case. Call the emergency room when you get home, as well as your local fire department, rescue squad, or ambulance service. Let them know there's an infant in the area who is using an apnea monitor, and give them your address. You never know when this preparation will pay off.

Most parents whose babies are on monitors willingly put up with its minor inconveniences for the peace of mind a monitor can afford. But remember—a monitor is not foolproof. If the monitor alarm is sounding but the baby seems fine, or if the baby seems in trouble but you don't hear an alarm, trust your instincts. Look at the baby, not the machine, for an indication of how well he is doing.

You'll probably be told to keep a diary of your baby's apneic episodes—when they occurred, how long they lasted, and what you needed to do to get the baby breathing again.

This diary will help the baby's doctor decide whether to change the amount of apnea medicine he's taking and, most important, will help the hospital know when the baby can be taken off the monitor altogether.

By the time your child reaches the age of six to nine months, he should experience longer and longer stretches of normal breathing. When he has gone for a month or two without setting off the monitor alarm, he'll return to the hospital for another sleep apnea test. Once again, the baby will nap in the hospital for about an hour, and doctors will record the rise and fall of his breathing and heart rates, noting the way these rates relate to the different stages of sleep. In all likelihood, this retest will show that your child has outgrown his apnea problem and no longer needs to be hooked up to a machine to tell you whether or not he's breathing.

Parenting for Twins

Twins occur just once in every ninety births, but they're far more common among premies, accounting for some 15 percent (one out of seven) of babies born weighing under 2500 grams. Twins tend to be born prematurely for several reasons. During the third trimester of pregnancy, the placenta is unable to meet the increasing nutritional needs of more than one fetus. In addition, the added weight of two fetuses bearing down on the cervix can hasten dilation and the onset of labor.

Many twin pregnancies are diagnosed some time before delivery. Usually, the presence of twins is suspected if the mother's weight gain is unusually rapid or if she secretes an excessive amount (usually twice the normal amount) of a fetal substance called alpha fetoprotein (AFP) in her urine or blood. If there's a reason to suspect twins, the obstetrician will order an ultrasound scan. This will allow him to see the shadows of more than one fetus on the screen.

For a woman carrying twins, obstetricians often advise partial or complete bed rest, even if she is not experiencing labor pains. This preventive bed rest has been shown to increase significantly the birthweight of twins when compared to the birthweight of twins born to mothers who walked around throughout their pregnancies.

Even though ultrasound provides a safe and foolproof way to "see" twins in the uterus, some twin pregnancies are not diagnosed until delivery. When a twin birth is a surprise, it is usually because the pregnancy offered no signs to the mother or her doctor that there was a need to do an ultrasound scan for twins. Premature labor often is the first clue that more than one baby will be born.

Twin parents usually experience an overwhelming crush of emotions in the intensive care nursery as they learn to love two tiny infants. Their emotions are especially complex if one of the twins is much sicker than the other, or if one twin dies. But now that you've got your twins home, all the bittersweet emotions of the hospitalization are behind you. Now you have a new set of feelings to deal with—confusion, panic, and unbelievable exhaustion.

"During the early months, you know you see two babies, but it may seem you are only caring for one baby who keeps you totally busy," writes Karen Kerkhoff Gromada in the recent publication *Mothering Multiples* (available from La Leche League International, 9616 Minneapolis Avenue, Franklin Park, Illinois 60130). This paradox, she admits, "is difficult to explain, and only another twin mother can understand." But it can have a dizzying effect on a new parent, who feels constantly on call to cater to the needs of one or the other baby.

Gromada, who is a nurse and the mother of twins, recommends coordinating baby care as much as possible. Feed

them together, change them together, put them to sleep together whenever you can. This will make it more likely that
you'll be able to grab five minutes of quiet for yourself before the next round of demands begins.

Even the simplest outing, like grocery shopping or a doctor's appointment, is complicated with twins. Many twin
parents enlist the aid of grandparents, spouses, friends, or
mother's helpers to help tote the two babies. If you must go
out alone, there are several pieces of equipment—tandem
strollers, back packs for use with a single stroller, even a
special twin front carrier made by the Snugli company—
that make the process a little less complicated. But it will
never be easy, at least not as long as two babies must be carried from crib to car seat to stroller and back.

You might find yourself constantly thinking of your
babies as a unit, "The Twins." Try not to. They are two individuals with individual needs, and each one needs your love
and attention in his own right. In her pamphlet Gromada
offers hints for helping to foster each baby's individuality:

• Beware of cute "twinnie" names, the kind that rhyme or
begin with the same letter or sound similar. These names
can increase confusion, especially if the twins are hard to tell
apart, and might cause the twins in later years to feel as
though each is really only one-half of a whole.

• Don't label the babies' personalities. It's not fair to
either of them to categorize Sam as the friendly one and
Emma as the shy one, or to say Julia is aggressive while Lori
is passive. And if you label them too quickly, you might miss
an important surprise—that twins often alternate personality traits.

• If you're on an outing with one twin and a stranger
comments on what a cute child you have, resist the urge to
say, "Thank you, and he's got a twin brother at home who's
just as cute." According to Gromada, "This is more difficult
than it sounds. . . . You become a celebrity by default, simply
by giving birth to twins. This might tempt you to reinforce

the idea of them as a unit." Although such an urge is normal, she says, it can have a negative effect on each child's self-image. "Always announcing his twinness might make him feel his twinness has more value to you than his uniqueness."

• When you take pictures of the twins together, take a few pictures of each baby separately as well.

• Don't refer to them as "the twins," especially in their presence. And never let them hear you admitting to anyone that you have trouble telling them apart! (As Gromada says, "Can you imagine how you would feel if your parents weren't sure who *you* were?")

• If you really *can't* tell them apart at first, polish the fingernail or toenail of one baby or initial the soles of their feet with a nontoxic marker. Then begin to look for differences—a slightly fuller face, a birthmark, slightly more rounded eyes—to serve as more permanent clues as to who is who.

It's easy, when parenting twins, to feel guilty for attending to one at the expense of the other. One baby will generally be more vocal in his demands and will be the one you cater to more frequently. This might make you worry that your quiet, easy baby will suffer from a lack of cuddling. How will the quiet twin know how much you love him? Will he grow up feeling jealous of his more demanding sidekick?

Gromada's response is simple: "Stop and think, 'If these children were a year apart, would I be so worried about treating them exactly the same at all times?' " You can't be a simultaneous parent to each twin any more than you can be a simultaneous parent to any two siblings—and there's no reason to expect yourself to be. Twins just have to learn, earlier than other babies, the value of sharing and of patience.

The Follow-up Clinic

By the time he's a year old, your baby probably will have experienced more than his share of interaction with the health care delivery system. Not only was his initial hospitalization long, and not only does he run a higher-than-normal risk of needing hospitalization again sometime in his first twelve months, but even if he's never really "sick" again your premie will be followed more closely than other babies.

First there are the well-baby visits to the pediatrician—usually at one, two, three, four, six, nine, and twelve months chronological age. Like all babies, yours will be examined during these visits for physical and psychological growth. He'll also receive routine innoculations against diphtheria, pertussis, and tetanus (the DPT shot); measles, mumps, and rubella (the MMR shot); and polio.

For babies born weighing less than 1500 grams, there probably will be another kind of well-baby visit, too—visits to the follow-up clinic at the hospital where your baby was first treated. Many intensive care nurseries are now engaging in long-term follow-up studies of their "graduates" to see whether unforeseen complications are developing that can be ascribed either to prematurity or to the effects of intensive care.

The follow-up clinic is run by a neonatologist or psychologist affiliated with the intensive care nursery. If your baby was of very low birthweight, you probably will be asked to return to the clinic every four to six months during the baby's first two years, and then annually up to the age of about five, for a comprehensive medical and psychological examination.

The follow-up clinic is wholly voluntary. It's often hard to try to fit clinic appointments into your busy schedule, already crammed with other doctors' appointments and with the myriad chores involved in caring for one or more small children. Each visit to the clinic can be a day's affair, with lots of professionals to see and lots of time spent in waiting rooms. But, if you can spare the time and effort involved in getting to the clinic, you'll find it's well worth the added hassle. For one thing, your cooperation will add to physicians' body of knowledge about how best to treat premature infants—a body of knowledge that contributed to the miracle of your own baby's life today. And, even more relevant, your cooperation will enable you to detect possible problems in your baby early enough to treat them. Nowhere else can your baby get such comprehensive attention from such well-trained experts, attention specifically geared to his needs as a premie. Usually, this expert care is available free of charge, or on a sliding fee scale with charges made according to what the parents can pay or what their insurance plans will cover.

The tests done at your follow-up clinic visits will depend on the specific conditions for which your baby is considered at risk, and the specific studies being conducted at your baby's hospital. A typical visit will usually consist of a physical examination from a pediatrician; a developmental examination from a psychologist; a hearing and speech examination, when needed, from an audiologist; and a test of the baby's motor skills from a physiatrist, an expert in physical medicine. Each of these experts will then make recommendations about further courses of evaluation and treatment, as necessary, and will discuss plans at length with you and with your baby's primary care pediatrician.

10: The Next Twelve Months: Surprises and Solutions

ONCE YOU GET YOUR BABY HOME, chances are you can put your hospital experience behind you and get on with the business of raising your child. Your baby's prematurity will soon fade into the background, becoming less and less important as you find yourself facing the everyday issues of baby care. In time, the hospitalization will become little more than a medical curiosity that you can tell your child about in five or ten years. "Yes, you weighed only three pounds when you were born," you'll say, showing her pictures of her first days of life. And she will say, delightedly, "Was I really that small?"

For the great majority of premies, especially bigger premies who weighed between 1500 and 2500 grams at birth, the long-term effects of prematurity may disappear within months. If your baby was a bigger premie with an uncomplicated hospitalization, you'll soon be treating her just like a normal baby.

This is not to say that your premie will be as easy as any other infant. Even with a relatively healthy premie, the year ahead is likely to include some special occurrences—and even some setbacks—related to her prematurity. You might need to watch, for instance, for signs of the "premie personality" we describe in this chapter. And you might need to brace yourself for a more frequent than average association with the medical profession.

For most premies, the only time you'll be reminded of their prematurity is when you make some simple adjustments for gestational age. By the time your premie is two or three years old, she'll have caught up in every way with other children born on her birth date. In terms of height, weight, intelligence, physical skill, emotional development, she'll be everything she would have been if she had been born at term. That's the "catch-up" that your doctors probably have mentioned to you.

In the meantime, though, there *is* a difference between your baby and other babies born at the same time. Chronologically, your baby might be four months old, but if she was eight weeks premature you simply cannot expect her to behave like a four-month-old. To be fair to her, you must subtract those two months of growth she missed in the womb, and expect her to behave like a two-month-old. This is called "correcting for gestational age."

Obviously, the more premature your baby was, the more you will subtract from her chronological age to get her corrected age. Opinion varies about how long you continue figuring corrected age. At most hospitals, psychologists in the premie follow-up programs stop correcting ages sometime around the baby's second birthday. By then, the toddler is presumed to have caught up sufficiently for her no longer to need the "handicap" of a corrected age when her developmental progress is evaluated.

A quick way to figure your baby's corrected age is to count the time that has elapsed since your baby's *due date*. Another way is to compute how many *months* early your baby was born (a premie born at 34 weeks, for instance, is one and a half months short of the 40-week term) and subtract those months from the baby's actual chronological age.

Except for this extra step, you should expect your premie to behave much like any other baby. Like all babies, she will roll over before she can crawl, and crawl before she can walk. She will at first forget objects once they're hidden from her sight, and only later will she think to look for them. She will respond to people indiscriminately at first, and only later will she come to prefer her parents to others.

Appendix D is a chart that describes the developmental milestones of a baby's first year. Although we hesitate to get too specific about what is "normal" at each stage—since there's really no such thing as an "average" baby—we present this information for one important reason: so you can spot trouble early. Premies, especially those of very low birthweight (less than 1500 grams), are considered to be "at risk" for certain developmental problems. That doesn't mean they *will* encounter problems. All it means is that you and your baby's doctor should be on the lookout for symptoms of problems that *might* turn up.

An early sign of problems is a significant delay in achieving certain basic milestones during the first year. If your child is extremely slow (that is, at least three or four months behind her corrected age) in learning to roll over, crawl, sit up, respond to your voice, track an object, or discover her hands, you might want to consider taking her for some professional evaluation. Often, this kind of evaluation is available to you as part of your hospital's follow-up clinic, where specialists in physical medicine, hearing, and speech routinely see all premies. If your baby has a problem, it might be related to her prematurity, or to the side effects of intensive care, or it might be a problem she would have encountered even if she had been born at term.

As you read through Appendix D, consider setting up your own record system to chart how your baby measures up. Buy a small notebook in which you can record some of your baby's biggest accomplishments. It will be an interesting diary to return to in later years—and, perhaps more important, it will be an invaluable diagnostic tool if there are problems later on. Every Saturday morning, or any regular time when you can get half an hour to yourself, write down what your baby did that week—especially what she did for the first time. Every month or so, compare the diary to the growth chart in Appendix D. If your baby is progressing within a month or two of her corrected age, you can put the books away for another week and get on with the essential business of parenting—enjoying your baby.

The Special Children

Most babies who weighed under 2500 grams at birth grow up to be normal children. By the age of about two, they'll carry with them no reminders of their early starts in life. But a significant minority—some 10 to 20 percent, by most estimates—will carry scars of their prematurity far beyond the age of two. These are the children we will describe in this chapter.

The scars of prematurity might be mild—muscular difficulties, learning disabilities, poor socialization—or they might be severe—cerebral palsy, blindness, deafness, or mental retardation. In general, babies most likely to suffer problems are those in the "very low birthweight" group— that is, babies who weighed less than 1500 grams at birth. But birthweight itself is not the only predictor of subsequent problems. Other factors have been found to be even more important than birthweight, including the conditions of the baby's birth, the complications that developed during her hospitalization, and the surroundings in which she is raised.

The aim of this chapter is to give you license to feel concerned if there's something unusual about your baby's growth and development. *Don't be afraid of seeming overanxious if you think there's something wrong with your baby.* And don't let your doctor shrug off your baby's worrisome symptoms with a casual statement like "She'll grow out of it." If you're concerned, let your doctor know and insist on referral to a professional who can evaluate your baby and can detect problems while there's still time to correct them.

"Practicing physicians tend to postpone the referral of damaged infants to intervention programs," notes Dr. T. Berry Brazelton, a pediatrics professor at Harvard and one of the nation's top experts in child development. "The United Cerebral Palsy Foundation, which has been instituting early intervention programs in various parts of the country, reports a disturbing statistic: if one waits for a pediatrician to refer a cerebrally damaged infant, the mean age at referral is 14 months; if parents self-refer, infants arrive by 4 months of age."

The moral of this statement: Don't wait for your pediatrician to tell you your baby has a problem. If a problem exists, you'll probably be the first one to sense it. No one, not even your baby's doctor, knows your child as well as you do. You cannot assume the pediatrician will inevitably spot any problem, nor can you take his failure to spot one as a reassuring sign that the baby must be all right.

From the parent's point of view, it's far better to have a doctor give you a name for the baby's problem—and, presumably, a reasonable course of action based on the diagnosis—than it is to suffer privately with the vague feeling that something isn't right. And from the baby's point of view, too, early diagnosis is preferred. A program of therapy instituted during the baby's first year can go a long way toward minimizing the baby's disabilities and helping her learn to compensate for those disabilities that remain.

Cerebral Palsy

One of the most common long-term effects of prematurity is cerebral palsy. This is a broad term and refers only to the source of the problem—brain damage that leads to poor muscle control—and not to the extent of the disability. Cerebral palsy is nonprogressive—it does not get more serious with time—and it need not be crippling. The term "CP" often conjures up images of tiny crutches, braces, wheelchairs, and worse, but a child with cerebral palsy might suffer no more than a slight dragging of one foot, or a tremor in one arm and leg. And even these symptoms might be helped enormously by a conscientious course of physical therapy.

There are four kinds of cerebral palsy:

• spastic, in which the child's movements are stiff and difficult;

• flaccid, in which the range and amount of the child's movements are decreased;

• athetotic, in which involuntary movements interfere with the child's voluntary movements; and

• ataxic, in which the child's disturbed sense of balance and depth perception interfere with her movements.

The muscle disorder most frequently affects either two limbs on the same side of the body (hemiplegia), all four limbs (quadriplegia), or all limbs with a concentration in either both arms or both legs (diplegia). Rarely, CP can affect only the lower half of the body (paraplegia) or only one limb (monoplegia).

Approximately three hundred thousand children in the United States have cerebral palsy; more than one-third of them weighed less than 2500 grams at birth. In one form of

CP, spastic diplegia, half of the children affected had low birthweights. CP generally results from lack of oxygen to the brain just before, during, or after delivery. More rarely, CP can be a complication of untreated hyperbilirubinemia (jaundice).

The diagnosis of CP can be difficult to make. The first clue that a baby might have CP occurs when the primitive reflexes of the newborn period persist beyond three or four months corrected age. Typically, CP children, especially those with spastic diplegia, maintain the grasp and tonic neck reflexes of early infancy (described in Appendix D). When you hold the baby upright, her back arches, her legs stiffen, and her hips rotate inward. Some parents have reported with pride that their babies "can't wait to walk; she looks like she's trying to stand all alone when I hold her on my lap!" They don't know that this rigidity can be an early sign of CP.

What makes diagnosis especially difficult, says Dr. Lawrence Taft of the Rutgers Medical School in New Jersey, is that "the symptoms of cerebral palsy in infancy can be changeable." Dr. Taft says that during the first months of life, an infant with CP might exhibit "hypertonia"—that is, rigidity and exaggerated reflexes, such as the apparent desire to walk right off a parent's lap. But within months, this hypertonia may gradually subside, so that by about five or six months corrected age the baby's body might behave much like a healthy baby's body.

Gradually, though, the decline in muscle tone continues and becomes dangerously low, falling into the category of hypotonia. Hypotonic, or "floppy," babies have no strength in their backs or limbs and so cannot begin the motions that are essential to crawling, sitting, and walking. The first sign of hypotonia might not appear until about ten months, when the child exhibits a "raking" grasp instead of the normal "pincer grasp" between the thumb and forefinger. In another six months or a year, though, this same baby might again be hypertonic, and the classic writhing movements of athetotic CP might begin.

If your pediatrician suspects your child has cerebral palsy, there are a few tests he can perform to confirm the diagnosis. In general, the tests are done to rule out other disorders that often cause the same symptoms as CP. The doctor might want to do a blood test (to measure the level of certain enzymes that are elevated in muscular dystrophy but not in CP), a family history (because family clustering can occur in some muscle disorders but not in CP), or, in rare instances, a spinal tap (to measure spinal fluid pressure, which is elevated in certain brain diseases but again not in CP).

Once a positive diagnosis of CP is made, the doctor probably will refer you to a physical therapist for weekly or even daily treatment. In mild cases of CP, physical therapy can mean the difference between walking poorly—or sometimes not at all—and walking well. And even in severe cases, though physical therapy probably will not train the child to walk, the therapy sessions can be a blessing. For the child with CP, physical therapy can serve as emotional therapy as well. It can mean an improved relationship between the child and her parents, an improved self-image for the child, and an increase in her ability to compensate for the physical handicap and find her way independently in the world.

Many communities now offer infant stimulation programs, usually at no charge, to babies under the age of two. These programs meet weekly, twice weekly, or even more frequently to combine physical therapy, occupational (or "play") therapy, and some more directed experiences such as moving to music, fingerpainting, and exploring new environments with hands, feet, and mouths. Similar programs usually are available for toddlers and preschoolers as well.

The physical therapy your baby receives in an infant stimulation program, or from a therapist who makes regular visits to your home, must be continued during the rest of the week—by you. This does not mean you need to set aside a half hour each day for directed exercises, although such a practice, if you have the time and temperament for it, is probably helpful as well. More important, you should incorporate the lessons learned during formal physical therapy into your everyday interactions with your child. You should position her in ways that encourage her to move her body independently, hold her in ways that stretch the limbs that don't want to stretch, and encourage her to explore her environment (an environment you've made both safe and interesting) by bold, inquisitive motion.

Such goals are not really as awesome as they sound. After some training in the theories of physical therapy, and some practice with its techniques, you will be able to position your baby in therapeutic ways without even thinking about it. Appropriate handling of your baby will become almost second nature to you, and exercises will become a vehicle for play, fun, and exploration.

Many clues to achieving this natural approach to physical therapy are presented in a comprehensive book, *Handling the Young Cerebral Palsied Child at Home*, by Nancie R. Finnie (E.P. Dutton & Company: New York, 1975). Finnie, a London physical therapist with long experience working with children with CP, provides illustrated suggestions about the best way to lift, carry, bathe, feed, dress, and toilet train an affected child. She recommends, for instance, that if the child habitually turns her head only to the right, then her bed should be positioned in such a way that all the interesting things in the room are to her left. Similarly, she shows the importance of handing a child toys head-on, so that her already uneven balance is not further compromised. And she shows that unusual ways of carrying the child—with the child facing out, her legs either bent together or straddling your hips (depending on the extent and location of the disability)—not only make the job easier for the parent but also allow the baby to practice strengthening some of her weakest muscles.

A comprehensive program of physical therapy, then, includes not only the exercises you do with your child but every aspect of the way you care for her and play with her. "I'm working with Matthew all the time," says Natalie Davidson. Natalie's son experienced a Grade IV brain bleed in the hospital and was found to have "high muscle tone"—one of the many euphemisms for cerebral palsy—when he returned for his three-month follow-up visit. "He keeps his body tight, and I play with him every morning—hide and seek, playing with toys—to increase his range of movement. When I change his diapers, I flex his legs and try to uncurl his toes. When I'm just holding him, I massage his back to make it more stretchable. And we go to a county program every week for babies considered high-risk for developmental problems.

"Why do I work so hard with Matthew? Because everything he learns to do now will have a direct impact on what he can do in the future. The region of the brain involved in crawling is the same region involved in reading, and if he doesn't crawl properly I worry that he won't read properly. If parts of his body are tight and remain tight, he won't be able to crawl in anything but the 'commando crawl' he's using now.

"I don't expect Matthew to fail. He's made such rapid progress in the past year, and I see no bounds to it. By the time he is a teenager, I think he'll be just like any other teenager."

Inguinal Hernia

At least 25 percent of premies are born with hernias or develop them within the first six months of life. The type of hernia most common in premies is an inguinal hernia (the "inguen" is the groin), an opening of the abdominal wall that allows some of the contents of the abdomen to protrude.

Hernias occur because of an interruption in the development of the abdominal cavity during gestation. They are most commonly seen in boys, although about 10 percent of hernias in infancy occur in girls. In utero, a boy's testicles, which are formed within the abdominal cavity, do not descend permanently into the scrotum until approximately the 36th week of gestation. At this time, a pouch is formed from the membrane within the abdominal cavity to protect the testicles during their descent.

Ordinarily, part of this pouch remains as a covering for the testicles, and the rest of it closes off and eventually disappears. (A similar process occurs in the formation of external genitals in girls.) But if the pouch remains open, this sac can serve as a pathway between the abdominal cavity and the outer wall of the abdomen—and an inguinal hernia can develop.

A hernia (the word literally means "rupture") appears as a bulge in the scrotum whenever the baby strains—when he cries, when he has a bowel movement, even when he is placed in a standing position. Usually, the contents of the abdomen can be pushed back to where they belong by gently pressing on the hernia sac until the scrotum is flat again—or by having the baby lie on his back and relax with a bottle or pacifier.

Sometimes, though, the abdominal contents cannot be pushed back. They become "incarcerated," to use the doctors' term, in the region between the interior abdominal cavity and the exterior abdominal wall. An incarcerated hernia must be operated on, because the bowel contents trapped there cannot function properly. In addition, incarceration can lead to a more serious complication: "strangulation," with a cut off of blood flow to the herniated bowel.

Surgeons consider operations for hernias rather routine

and of minimal risk. But the parents of babies who need them usually worry nonetheless. "I saw Matthew's hernia right after he came home from the hospital at three and a half months," says Natalie Davidson. "At first, it was easy just to push it back in, but soon it started staying out more often and I had trouble getting it back in. The pediatric surgeon wanted to wait to schedule the surgery until Matthew was five months old. He felt he was too vulnerable. In truth, *I* was too vulnerable."

To repair an inguinal hernia, the surgeon will make an incision in the crease of the groin, locate the hernia sac, and tie off the sac so the bowel cannot protrude into it anymore. Recuperation usually is complete within a week.

Seizures

Most premies do not develop seizures during the initial hospitalization. For all the brain insult that can occur during or just after a premature birth, premies seem relatively immune at first to the seizure disorders that can develop after some damage to the brain. When a seizure (also called a convulsion) does occur in a premie, especially when she is home and apparently healthy, it can be frightening.

Seizures are caused by a sudden burst of electrical activity in the brain. They are usually, but not always, the result of scarring or damage in the brain tissue. The abnormal electrical activity leads to abnormal movements of the body, which is the first sign of a seizure disorder. (Seizure disorders were formerly called epilepsy, but doctors today try to avoid that term because of the negative stereotype associated with it.)

In full-term infants, the most common seizures are characterized by alternating contraction and relaxation of the entire body (what doctors call "tonic-clonic seizures"). But the seizures of premies are different. They tend to be local-

ized to one area of the body, and are called "focal seizures."
They can range in severity from tiny twitches to severe
shaking.

Most seizures seen shortly after birth are caused by perinatal asphyxia or, in premies, brain bleeds. But the seizures
that develop later, in the first or second year of life, often
have causes that cannot be found. Among full-term, healthy
babies who later develop seizures, doctors can find the cause
in only about one-half the cases. For premies, perhaps more
of the causes can be traced. If a premie with seizures also
had a low Apgar score (see glossary), a brain bleed just after
birth, episodes of asphyxia or hypoxia (see glossary), or any
combination of these, it's likely that events of her first days
of life led to the brain damage that results in seizures.

Seizures are relatively harmless, especially if they cause
small jerks or twitches that do not in themselves endanger
the child. Still, there is some evidence that continued seizures, however small, can do some permanent damage to the
brain. For this reason, your doctor will want to diagnose
your baby's condition as soon as possible and begin administration of anticonvulsant drugs.

The electroencephalogram (EEG), a machine that records
the rise and fall of electrical rhythms of the brain, is used to
make the diagnosis of seizure disorder. The EEG works
through electrodes attached to the scalp with a jelly and a
sticky substance called collodian. Collodian can be removed
afterward with acetone. The test itself is painless.

In newborn premies, the EEG often is difficult to interpret, because there are no good models available of what a
normal EEG pattern looks like for an infant who still should
be in the womb. An EEG might look normal even in a baby
who has seizures; similarly, a baby who is seizure-free might
have an EEG pattern that looks abnormal. When the brain
has matured, normal and abnormal EEGs are easier to differentiate—although the normal patterns of infants and
children are different from those of adults.

The problem of seizures in premies is that they can arise just when parents thought the worst was over. Because only mature, well-insulated brain cells are capable of creating the electricity needed for a seizure, convulsions usually occur between the ages of one and two, when the brain has become more mature and when earlier injuries have resulted in scar tissue in the brain.

"We were so afraid of seizures while John was in the hospital," Katie Lee says. "Every time he twitched, I thought he'd had a seizure. I begged John's doctor to do an EEG, and the test came back normal.

"Then, when we began at last to fall into a pattern at home—John was two years old, going to school, doing well—he had a bad seizure. We had thought that, with all John's other problems, at least he wouldn't have that one. But he does."

The diagnosis of a seizure disorder does not mean the condition is permanent. Often, the seizures can be successfully treated with anticonvulsant drugs; eventually, the drugs might even be stopped. The most popular anticonvulsants used in infants are phenobarbital and Dilantin. Diazepam (Valium) might be used to control a seizure initially. Your doctor will recommend one of these drugs and will adjust the dosage up or down, depending on the drug level in the blood, the recurrence of seizures, and the effect of the drug on your child's behavior. When your child has been seizure-free for a year and the EEG appears normal, your doctor might try weaning your child from the drug.

John Lee's treatment began immediately, and he hasn't had a seizure since. It took him more than a month to get used to the phenobarbital he took to control his convulsions—"he slept all the time," says his mother—and it took his parents a while to get used to the idea that their son had a seizure disorder. But now all the Lees have adjusted to the problem, and the seizures are a thing of the past.

Slow Mental Development

In the first year of life, it's difficult to predict which baby will grow up normal and which will suffer from developmental delay, learning disability, or mental retardation. Most tests administered to babies under the age of two have been shown to have little value in predicting which babies will have difficulties later on. A poor performance on an intelligence test at twelve months of age does not necessarily mean that the baby will test as mentally "slow" at age five.

But parents often have an uncanny second sense about whether their babies are developing normally. They can, with a certain reliability, detect either a "brightness" or a "dullness" in their premie's eyes; either a fire of curiosity or a listlessness in her explorations; either a drive to examine objects thoroughly or an inability to stay interested in one object for long enough to learn anything about it. Especially if they are experienced parents, comparing their premie's progress with that of their older children, their concerns about their premie's intellectual development might indeed be well-founded.

Some pediatricians take these parents' concerns seriously, and are quick to refer their babies for intelligence testing or special education programs. But most pediatricians hesitate to confirm parents' darkest fears. They don't want to label a baby as "retarded" if she is not. "Each child is different," your doctor is likely to tell you if you inform him of your concern. "Don't compare the baby to her brothers and sisters. She's simply developing at her own rate, and she'll probably grow out of her slowness."

The odds are that, even if your baby does show a "developmental lag," she will indeed outgrow it. (Developmental lag generally is defined as progress that is 25 to 50 percent behind the average for her corrected age, as charted in Appendix D.) "Most high-risk, low-birth-weight infants show transient abnormal central nervous system signs between 4 and 12 months, which then resolve so that the infants appear to be growing up normally," says Dr. Eric Denhoff, a pediatrician at Brown University in Providence, Rhode Island. "Only 10 to 20 percent of infants weighing less than 2500 grams at birth develop obvious neurological problems, assuming they receive sophisticated care."

Although most experts agree on this 10 to 20 percent figure, the number represents a wide range of problems, from mild learning disabilities to such serious neurological disorders as cerebral palsy, blindness, and deafness. To become more precise in their prediction of just *which* babies will experience developmental delay, neonatologists are conducting long-term studies to follow the "graduates" of the intensive care nursery for at least five years after they leave the hospital. Their findings, they hope, will provide a better method of assessing how grave the risk of long-term disability truly is, and perhaps of identifying affected babies earlier in an effort to correct their disabilities.

Currently, no such information exists—for two reasons. First, long-term follow-up studies now being reported are looking at children who were born six to sixteen years ago, when neonatology was in its infancy. The care your premie is receiving in the 1980s is far superior to what was available in the 1970s—and, therefore, the odds of your baby recovering *completely* from her early birth are much greater today than they were for the youngsters now being studied.

Second, some of the more simple comparisons between premies and nonpremies fail to account for the fact that premies are more likely to be drawn from disadvantaged backgrounds—a factor known to lead to poorer performance on intelligence tests. Children born to mothers of low educational attainment, young age, and low income are more likely to be born prematurely. This same group of children, whether they're premature or not, are also more likely to receive low scores on the tests used in these studies.

Still, even with the odds on your side, your baby might experience some intellectual problems. If you think that is the case, you will probably want to have her tested. Although intelligence tests for babies are not 100 percent predictive, they are of some use. They can tell you whether your child needs some intensive stimulation, or whether she can be treated like a normal but slow-to-warm-up baby.

Several intelligence tests have been devised recently specifically for use with young, preverbal infants. These tests measure such clues to intelligence as the baby's visual attentiveness, ability to manipulate objects, memory, and powers of interpretation—all mental skills that even very young babies have. If he sees the need, your doctor will refer you to a child development center in your area that can administer one or several of these tests to your baby to measure her development to date. But since infant development is such a dynamic and fast-paced event, this one test score usually will not be enough to tell the psychologists or doctors anything about your baby's future. Your baby probably will have to be tested at least once more, and perhaps several more times, to see whether any previously noted lag persists.

Infant stimulation programs have been shown to be effective in boosting the test performance of babies at high risk for intellectual delay. These programs, similar to those available for children with physical handicaps, emphasize stimulation of all the senses through music, dance, exercise, manipulation, and exploration. Check to see whether your community offers such a program, and ask the official in charge, or your pediatrician, whether your child qualifies for enrollment.

Slow Social Development

Ask any premie mother: there definitely is a "premie personality." The definition of this personality varies from one family to the next, but there seems to be a consensus that *something* during the first year of a premie's life sets her apart from other infants her age.

What sets her apart, in essence, is her general unwillingness to socialize. The reasons for this lack of sociability, observed over and over again in psychological experiments on premies, are still unclear. The explanations that have been offered range from the biological, to the sociological, to the psychological.

Some experts, for instance, blame the premie's inability to socialize on her immature nervous system. Her brain cells, they say, take longer to form the neural circuitry needed to transmit the complex impulses involved in human interaction.

Others think her lack of sociability relates to the premie's earliest experiences in the intensive care nursery. In the nursery, according to this theory, she learned the value of shutting out sights and sounds that threatened to overwhelm her.

And still others believe the difficulty premies sometimes have in socializing is, ironically, a result of "burnout" on the part of mothers and fathers who spend the first months of their babies' lives trying to respond *for* the baby. This last theory is perhaps the most intriguing—and the most useful for premie parents to understand. If there's some truth to it, then maybe an awareness of the mistakes most often made by other premie parents will help you avoid them in your own family.

Dr. Kathryn Barnard, a professor of neonatal nursing at the University of Washington in Seattle, recently studied mother-premie pairs at two points during the baby's first year—at four months and eight months of age. (Dr. Barnard, by the way, does not correct for gestational age in her behavioral studies, because, she says, actual age is closer to the way the parents *experience* their babies. "It is difficult in a dynamic interaction to be constantly correcting for gestational age," she says. "The parent reacts to the 'here-and-now' of the child.")

What Dr. Barnard found was this: At four months of age, the premies behaved quite differently from their full-term peers. Premies "provided less clear cues and [were] less responsive to the parents. . . . [They] did less vocalizing or smiling in response to the parents' vocalization, and they explored or reached out to parents less often than did term infants."

But the premie mothers after four months seemed undaunted by their babies' withdrawn behavior. Even though their babies were generally less responsive—and therefore less rewarding—premie mothers talked to, cuddled, and comforted their babies in the same way that full-term mothers did.

But by eight months, this picture had changed. Eight-month-old premies had begun at last to behave like their full-term peers (although they were still, in general, somewhat less responsive). But their mothers had begun to behave less and less like mothers of full-term babies. By eight months, premie mothers smiled less at their babies, praised their babies less often, and laughed less than did the mothers of full-term infants. Dr. Barnard's explanation: After months of exuding cheer and sensitivity with little reward, these premie mothers might have exhausted their supply of unilateral goodwill.

It seems a vicious cycle, and one that can be stopped only by parents who know ahead of time that premies tend to be less responsive. Don't try too hard to be a playmate—or a teacher—to an unresponsive baby. You might wear yourself out doing so, and then you'd be too tired and offended to relate to the baby in later months, when she's ready and eager for your games.

If your baby averts her eyes when you try to engage her in a game, stop trying. If she stares blankly at the ceiling, or begins to move her body in a way that seems to signal distress, when you gurgle and coo at her, she might just be asking you—in the most polite way she knows—to let her lie quietly for a while.

Of course, it's difficult to practice self-control with a baby you've waited so long to hold and to play with. In the weeks when your baby was in the hospital, you might have longed for the time when you could nuzzle your nose in her belly to her delighted squeals. Even now, you might be spending long, lonely hours simply waiting, since in the first months of life premies typically sleep more than full-term babies do. (Premies' sleep patterns are significant in regard to their sociability, as well. Studies have shown, for example, that the longer a baby sleeps, the longer her mother takes to feel "attached" to her child.)

"When the parents have been deprived of caring for their child for so long, they get him home and want him to show his babyness," says Dr. Juarlyn Gaiter, the neonatal psychologist at Children's Hospital National Medical Center in Washington, D.C. "But these babies [often] are not visually alert; they have low levels of irritability. They can't cue their parents about what they want, and some even avoid eye contact." The result: a poor fit between parents' expectations and baby's behavior.

You must find a happy medium between allowing your baby her privacy and leaving her alone altogether. Whether they know it or not, babies thrive on the love of other people, especially their parents. Even if your baby is unresponsive or unsociable, she still needs human contact.

Your infant might seem withdrawn today, but you don't want to encourage her to be a hermit for life. Babies surrounded by the sights, sounds, and feelings of people grow up happier, more self-confident, more able to relate to people in the future.

Most babies love people, love to please people, love to perform, and the only encouragement they need is the laughter and appreciation that come naturally from an adoring adult audience. But your baby is different. She needs you to draw her out of her shell.

If you want to socialize with your baby, you must prepare her, emotionally and physically, for interaction. You might find it helpful to swaddle the baby in a soft blanket or in some other way to restrict the movements of her arms and legs. Psychologists have found that premies tend to wave their arms and legs more when they are excited. And if the baby's limbs, and therefore her entire body, get out of control, the sensation might become overwhelming. Eventually, the revved-up baby will begin to fight the whole overstimulating experience and may simply break down and cry.

When your baby is awake, alert, quiet, fed, and dry (a tall order, especially in the early weeks at home!), she's probably ready for some gentle socializing. Place the swaddled baby in an infant seat or prop her in the corner of a sofa, and seat yourself about a foot away so she can see you clearly. Now's the time for some friendly conversation.

And conversation it is, as Dr. Tiffany Martini Field, a psychologist at the University of Miami and a leader in the study of high-risk infants, has pointed out. Dr. Field analyzed videotapes of healthy mother-infant pairs to see what makes their playtimes so rewarding. Typically, she says, these mothers use such conversational techniques as "slowing down, exaggerating and repeating their behaviors, . . . imitating or highlighting the infant's behavior, taking turns or not interrupting, and respecting the infant's need for an occasional break." When premie mothers are urged to try these techniques as well, says Dr. Field, the infants invariably squirm and cry less, avert their gaze less often, and become more attentive.

Dr. Field's recipe for healthy conversation with a premie: imitate the infant's behavior, repeat phrases, allow your baby a turn at initiating interaction, and give her breaks when she seems to get too worked up. One of the most important ingredients, she says, is sensitivity.

"Generally," Dr. Field says, "it seems as though [these] instructions encourage a greater attentiveness on the part of the mother so that she not only becomes less active, but also becomes more sensitive to her infant's signals. . . . Her behaviors seem to become more 'infantized' and, particularly during her imitation of her infant's behaviors, her own behaviors become more similar to those behaviors already in her infant's repertoire. As such, they might be more readily assimilated by the infant."

Visual or Hearing Problems

It should be so easy to spot an infant who can't see or hear. After all, infants respond to the world almost exclusively through sight and sound, at least until they gain control of their bodies. How can an observant parent miss the signs of a baby who's not responding properly?

The fact is that it's easy. Even doctors specializing in vision (ophthalmologists) and hearing (otolaryngologists) can miss the signs of visual or hearing problems in a very young baby. You can't ask a baby if she's seeing or hearing well, so you have to be especially attuned to her to be able to tell that she's not.

The experiences of intensive care, combined with her prematurity, place your baby at risk of visual or hearing problems. Oxygen required to keep small babies alive can be damaging to the premie's fragile, immature eyes; there's no way of knowing whether damage has occurred, or to what extent, until long after the need for oxygen has passed.

Similarly, the environment of the intensive care nursery can be damaging to a premie's immature ears. From the inside of a premie's isolette, the hum of the motor can carry up to 70 or 80 decibels of sound—about as much noise as a busy street corner or factory. This continual noise—combined with such other risk factors as excessive highs and lows of oxygen in the bloodstream, high levels of bilirubin in the bloodstream, and the use of drugs, such as antibiotics, that can have an adverse effect on hearing—can lead to temporary or permanent hearing loss in some babies. Dr. Robert Galambos, a neuroscientist at the University of California, San Diego, has estimated that the incidence of hearing impairment among premies ranges from one in fifteen for premies considered at high risk (because of complications during hospitalization) to one in fifty for all premies. By comparison, the proportion of serious hearing impairment among all newborns is one in two thousand.

How can you tell if your baby has a problem seeing or hearing? The D.C. Society for Crippled Children of Washington, D.C., has published a list of important "early warning signs" of sensory problems, for which you can be alert.

Seeing might be a problem if your baby

• cannot focus on objects or does not respond to bright light;

• sometimes or always crosses one or both eyes;

• is often unable to locate and pick up small objects within reach;

• frequently rubs her eyes or indicates that her eyes hurt;

• holds her head in a strained or awkward position (tilting it to either side or thrusting it forward or backward) when trying to look at a particular object; or

• has reddened, watering, or encrusted eyelids.

Hearing might be a problem if your baby

• makes no attempt at vocalization by three months of age;

• does not turn to face the source of strange sounds or voices by six months of age;

• turns the same ear toward a sound she wishes to hear;

• talks in a very loud or very soft voice;

• does not respond when you call from another room; or

• has frequent earaches or running ears.

But even the most observant of parents can miss the signs

of sensory damage in their premies. "I was convinced that John was stone deaf," says his mother, Katie Lee. "The slam of a car door, his older brother's shouts, any sudden noise created no response in him. He was like a dead duck that ate and slept."

But Katie was so busy worrying about John's hearing—which turned out to be perfectly normal—that she missed the fact that he was going blind. The blindness, not deafness, accounted in large part for his lack of responsiveness and for the nameless other oddities Katie had noticed in her son's behavior.

The earlier your child's sensory losses can be detected, the better it is for her. As soon as you know your child has a problem, you can begin to help her compensate for the senses she's lacking by enriching her experiences through the senses she still has.

John Lee changed dramatically once his blindness was diagnosed, at about three months, when he embarked on a program of infant stimulation. A social worker came to the house once a week to teach Katie how to expand John's sightless world. "I tied bells to his feet so when he kicked his feet he heard something," Katie recalls. "I strung noisemaking toys and tactile toys on a string and hung it so that if he moved at all he had to hit something. I filled a cloth bag with bottle caps for him to touch and jingle, I gave him rattles to hold and shake, I rigged up his infant seat so he could sit at the piano and bang on it. And within two weeks, John changed from a lump to a human being."

Infants as young as three months of age can be fitted for eyeglasses or hearing aids and can be shown how to explore the world through touch or motion rather than sight or sound. Formal programs for babies this young exist in many communities to help deaf or blind infants develop roughly according to schedule.

If you suspect your baby has a hearing or vision problem, tell your pediatrician. Several tests now exist to measure a baby's brainwave or heartbeat changes in response to sights and sounds, an indirect way of testing whether the baby is able to see and hear. These tests are reliable, and many university medical centers are equipped to administer them. You might also want to contact a local chapter of a charity organization, such as the March of Dimes or the Lions Club, to see what testing locations they can recommend. Also, check the resources listed in Appendix C for some national organizations geared specifically for testing and education of the visually and hearing impaired child.

11: How Protective Is Too Protective?

EVE MARKHAM SAYS she'll always think of Stephen as a special child who needs an extra dose of protection. "We went through so much with Stephen during his first year, when he had severe lung problems and constantly needed extra oxygen, that I don't think we can ever forget it," she says. Her "special" feelings about her son were crystallized one winter evening when Stephen was about two and a half. Driving home alone, Eve noticed that an ambulance was headed in the same direction as she. She turned left; the ambulance turned left. She turned right; it turned right. Finally, it turned down her street. Eve was sure it was coming for Stephen and that Stephen had died.

"I don't think I'll ever get over this fatalistic sense that he's frailer than other children, that someday something dreadful will happen to him," Eve says. That night, when

Eve told her husband Tom about her premonition, he admitted that he'd often felt the same way—worrying, almost expecting, that Stephen will always have more illnesses and accidents than his big sister or any other child. (The ambulance, it turned out, was for a neighbor.)

As memories of Stephen's year-long illness fade, Eve and Tom are finally beginning to let go. When Stephen was three, he fell on his head—he'd been climbing on the furniture—and had a concussion. But he recovered, and the experience proved to his parents that Stephen is not made of glass.

Most premie parents go through a process of letting go that is much like the Markhams'. Over time, they begin to think of their child less as a fragile bundle and more as a normal kid—a kid who can experiment, and even hurt himself, and still bounce back. But there might remain in the background a nagging fear that something about this child is different, that he needs a little more protection, a little more guidance, to keep him safe in this big, dangerous world.

Some lucky parents can begin to relax almost as soon as they get their baby home—if the baby is healthy and thriving. "If anyone had told me when Arthur was born that he would weigh sixteen pounds—four times his birthweight!—within four months, and that he'd be big and happy and perfectly normal, I wouldn't have believed them," Ellen Thames says in awe. "He seems so big and healthy that I'm already starting to think of him as a normal baby who happened to have been born early."

But some premie parents never relax. This is especially true of parents whose babies were extremely sick in the intensive care nursery or whose prematurity has created permanent problems. And it is true of parents who derive satisfaction, consciously or unconsciously, from having a "special" child to whom they can devote their time, attention, concern, and intelligence.

When Protection Is a Way of Life

Pat Anders, for instance, still thinks of her son Ben as a premie, even though he was born in 1976. In part, this is because Ben was so sick in his infancy that he is indeed a little frail. But in part—and even Pat will admit this—it is because protecting Ben has become Pat's lifestyle, her occupation, her way to deal with her still-present feelings of guilt and trepidation about Ben's perilous start in life.

Ben was thirteen weeks premature and weighed 1280 grams (2 pounds 13 ounces) at birth. He experienced severe lung problems and spent his first four and a half months in an intensive care nursery, where he brushed death several times. Five months after he was sent home, Ben was rehospitalized for respiratory complications. It was then the doctors told Pat that Ben probably would die. But Pat wouldn't settle for a diagnosis of gloom. She found another doctor, halfway across the country, who aggressively treated Ben's lung problems—and Ben recovered. Today, the child who didn't smile until the age of ten months, who didn't walk until nineteen months or talk until he was past two, is "a dynamo of energy," as one psychologist put it. He is a sweet-tempered boy who is fond of "bouncing on the couch, crawling under the table, playing little games . . . with engaging good humor." This psychologist calls Ben "a very bright, curious little boy who is well aware of his environment and is learning from it." What more can a mother ask?

Somehow, it's not enough for Pat. She knows that Ben has come as far as he has only because she threw herself into his recovery—following the best doctors from Chicago to Los Angeles, taking voluminous notes on his development, filing all his medical charts and psychological evaluations. Although Ben's problems now are relatively minor—he moves stiffly, speaks with a lisp, and cannot grasp a pencil—Pat worries that these might foreshadow more serious problems in school later on. So she drives Ben thirty miles a day to the best nursery school she could find, and she takes him to lung specialists, physical therapists, occupational therapists, and psychologists for periodic evaluations. She's always searching out something new that might help her son.

"People think I'm overzealous in what I will do for Ben," Pat admits. "My sisters, my mother-in-law, even my husband think I've made Ben's development too much of a crusade. But I'm determined to do anything for him—take him to the best doctors, send him to the best schools, go through the weirdest games and exercises with him. I look at it as insurance. Rolling on a huge beach ball may be the dumbest thing we can do together—but, on the other hand, it just might unlock some door."

Like other premie parents, though, Pat worries about being "overprotective." She worries, too, about focusing on Ben so much that she ignores his two younger sisters (both of whom were born at term). "I'm starting, now, to let go a little," says Pat. "Ben is going to day camp, and he loves it, but I worry about athlete's foot and roughhousing in the locker room. I let him go not because I want to but because it's time."

How do you know when your natural, and healthy, concern for your child's welfare has gone too far? When does your dedication to your child become less a necessary commitment than a habit, a way of defining your value and elevating your status as a teacher-parent? When does your attention to your child threaten the health and stability of your marriage and family? How and where do you draw the line between protective and overprotective?

When Protection Makes Sense

With a premie, especially during the first year, you'd have to go to great lengths to be considered overprotective. Right now, your premie needs all the protection you can give him.

He doesn't know right from wrong, safe from dangerous, yes from no, so you must set up limits and barriers for him. All parents must do this, of course, but you will take on this chore with an added fervor. In the back of your mind is the thought that your baby hasn't come this far, against such odds, simply to be damaged by an accident that could have been prevented.

Indeed, some of the dangers that all parents fear—infection, injury, underfeeding, overstimulation—*are* more of a threat to a premie than to a baby born at term. For this reason, you can follow your instincts with your premie. If he behaves recklessly, or if he seems especially prone to infection, or if he gets overexcited easily, then go ahead and guard him from some of the tough knocks he's bound to encounter.

But don't guard him from everything. Tough knocks— and the experience of recovering from them—are an important part of growing up. Your baby will never learn to fall if he's never fallen before, and he'll never learn to run if he's afraid to fall. It might be safer for your premie to spend his days in a playpen or crib, away from other children with their dangerous germs and their tendency to push and poke, close to you and far from stairs, ladders, swings, and slides. But absolute safety won't teach him anything. Your baby needs some freedom if he's ever to grow up. A padded cell might be sterile and safe, but it's no place to raise a baby.

The Vulnerable Child Syndrome

In a classic paper on overprotectiveness, Dr. Morris Green of Indiana University and Dr. Albert J. Solnit of Yale University presented twenty-five case studies of what they called the "vulnerable child syndrome." All the children described in this paper had, at one point in their lives, been very sick; all the parents had, during the illness, been told that their child would die. Although the children all recovered completely, the parents never got over the trauma of almost losing them. They developed misplaced fears and anxieties that led to disciplinary, learning, and psychological problems for the children as long as fourteen years after the initial illness.

The symptoms of overprotectiveness, as outlined by Drs. Green and Solnit, were as follows:

• inability of the parent and child to separate;
• inability of the parent to set disciplinary limits;
• feeding problems;
• sleeping problems;
• hypochondriacal concerns about the child's health; and
• slow psychosocial development and underachievement in school.

Especially damaging to the child was the tendency of overprotective parents to "infantilize" their children—that is, to treat them like babies even though they had long outgrown babyhood. Both parent and child suffer in this situation, Drs. Green and Solnit point out: "The parent is overprotective, overly indulgent, and oversolicitous while the child is overly dependent, disobedient, irritable, argumentative, and uncooperative.... Some of these children are physically and publicly abusive to the mother, e.g., hitting, biting, or scratching her. Although resentful and embarrassed by this behavior, the mother cannot control the child. It is common for such mothers, however, to restrict the child's physical activity, e.g., by keeping him in a playpen excessively, confining him in a fenced yard beyond the usual age for such precaution and forbidding bicycling and contact sports."

Three-year-old Jerry A. and his mother were two victims of the vulnerable child syndrome who came to the attention of Drs. Green and Solnit. Jerry, his mother said, had not slept since he was born—and, therefore, neither had she. "I can't continue to get along without sleep," Mrs. A. moaned in desperation. Jerry's case is described as follows:

> The child was physically well, active and developing normally in other respects. In the interviews the mother eventually made it clear to the pediatrician that at the time of birth she had expected to lose her only son because of a placenta previa and prematurity. Over a period of two months, in five interviews, she discussed and remembered the details of the birth that had threatened her life and that of her baby. She vividly described the obstetrician's concern, and his decision, "I may have to choose between you and the baby, so don't be surprised if the baby doesn't live."
>
> With this as a background, the pediatrician's questions tactfully but specifically evoked a description of the mother being unable to sleep at night unless she felt the baby was safe and sound. It became apparent that she unwittingly kept the baby awake each night through a series of visual, auditory, and tactile stimuli which conveyed her insistence that the baby not fall asleep, probably because of her fear that she would again feel the baby was dead. The pediatrician did not attempt to interpret the mother's reactions, but after each interview he gave advice about reduction of stimuli at bedtime for child and mother, always with the realistic reassurance that the child was safe. Within a month the mother and child were sleeping, and the mother began to refer to the past exhaustion and sleep disturbance as a bad dream.

Overprotectiveness: Causes and Guises

According to the noted pediatrician, Dr. Benjamin Spock, overprotectiveness is caused in part by some of the noblest instincts of parenthood. "Overprotective feelings occur mostly in very devoted, tenderhearted parents who are too inclined to feel guilty when there is no realistic need for it," he writes in *Baby and Child Care*. But overprotectiveness can have its darker motives, too. As Dr. Spock writes, "In a majority of cases, [overprotectiveness comes from] the parent's inability to admit that she or he is sometimes resentful or angry toward the child."

Overprotective parents, says Dr. Spock, can't admit that occasionally—and naturally—they wish their children harm. These parents "have to imagine instead that all the dangers in the world come from somewhere else, and grossly exaggerate them. . . . A mother, for instance, may suppress her occasional mean thoughts and exaggerate the dangers of kidnappers or whooping cough or home accidents or inadequate diet. She has to stay close to the child to make sure the dangers don't strike."

Sometimes, a parent's protective feelings toward a premie are complicated by earlier feelings of revulsion, or even rejection, shortly after the baby's birth. "I didn't really feel close to Stephen during the first year, when he was so sick," Eve Markham says. "I didn't think he even knew who I was at that point—he had a closer bond to Tom than to me. So if anything, I was *under*protective; I just didn't worry that much about him. And because everyone had told me I'd be *over*protective, I felt terribly guilty."

Katie Lee had a similar experience when she brought her son John home, after she and her husband had asked the doctors not to do anything heroic to save their baby's life. "In a way, we had given up on John in the hospital," Katie says. "But once he was home, and alive, and ours, I surprised myself by becoming absolutely obsessed with John's development. Because John is totally blind and probably retarded, it took all my time and attention just to get him to do anything physically or mentally. Now that I've found a school for him, I'm beginning to get my life back together. I do what I have to do with John, but I do other things, too."

After John came home, Katie changed her attitude not only toward John, but toward John's older brother Christopher. "Now I think that nothing, no one, is safe," she says. "I make Christopher sit in the middle of the back seat of the car, the safest place in case of an accident. I hover over him much more than I used to—maybe because I feel sorry about all the attention John takes away from him, maybe because now I know he'll be the only healthy child we have."

Overprotectiveness can take many forms. Mark, an overprotective father, shields his baby from any interaction with babies her own age, fearful that his child will suffer by the comparison. He orders neighborhood children out of the house, refusing to allow them to touch the baby for fear of spreading germs.

Mark's behavior is easy to recognize as overprotectiveness. But sometimes an overprotective instinct can create behavior that looks like something quite different. For instance, Tiffany, an overprotective mother, does not hover at all: she leaves her baby with relatives at every opportunity. Tiffany might look like a careless, disinterested parent, but that's not the case. In fact, she longs to be alone with her baby, but she is afraid to allow herself that luxury. Tiffany is insecure in her mothering role, and she is fearful that, if she's left alone with her baby, she will somehow hurt the child.

Overprotective instincts might also cause parents to exacerbate friction between the baby and his older sibling. This could happen if parents devote excessive attention to the new baby or—just as damaging—if they forsake the new baby for the safety and familiarity of the firstborn. A parent who frequently tells the older child, "Stay away from the baby, you'll hurt him," is inviting trouble between the children in the years ahead.

Overprotectiveness can cause a parent to guard the baby not only from physical harm but from emotional and intellectual harm as well. Dr. Juarlyn Gaiter, neonatal psychologist at Children's Hospital in Washington, D.C., regularly administers psychological exams to premies at the hospital's follow-up clinic. She has often seen mothers who actually complete test items for the child. "It's perfectly understandable for the mother to want her baby to do well, and it's understandable for her to want to protect her child after all he's been through," Dr. Gaiter says. "But if the mother's behavior continues too long it can be really debilitating. It can kill the child's motivation completely, creating an expectancy on the child's part for all problems to be solved by his mother."

When it takes this extreme form, overprotectiveness can interfere with your baby's intellectual development. If you react to his cries immediately, if you never allow him to be frustrated in a task, he won't have a chance to learn patience, trial and error, and perseverance. Just because your baby was born prematurely is no reason to prevent him from experiencing the normal emotions of babyhood: frustration, anger, loneliness, fear. You don't want him to experience any of these feelings for too long—just as you don't want a full-term baby to be lonely if there's no reason for him to be—but you do want him to learn that he can ease himself out of troublesome situations and doesn't always need Mother or Father to set things right.

How to Avoid the Overprotectiveness Trap

Katie Lee had to learn to censor her own first instincts in her interactions with both her sons. "I had to bite my tongue whenever I saw my older son playing with John," she recalls. "He was so rough with him! I kept wanting to cry out, 'Oh, Christopher, be careful with the baby! He's blind, and small, and you might hurt him.' But my husband held me back—and he was right. Christopher had learned that, because of John's blindness, the only way to interact with him was physically. All that wrestling and tumbling was necessary for John to develop an intimate relationship with his brother." Had Katie followed her overprotective instincts, she would have interfered with the establishment of the very special closeness that John and Chris now share.

You, too, must try to get beyond your overprotective instincts, not only for your premie's sake but for your own sake as well. If you are to have a life of your own, and if you are to maintain a healthy relationship with your mate, there must be times when you can get away from the baby, both separately and together. Overprotective parents often cannot break away even for an evening. They might complain that they can't see a movie together because the baby doesn't like babysitters, but often the problem is far deeper than that. Often, it's the *parents* who don't like babysitters—because they don't believe (or they don't want to find out) that someone else can give their child the special care and attention he needs.

If you can break the habit of overprotectiveness now, while your baby is still small, you will be a better parent. You will allow your child the freedom to move and explore on his own, to take a few lumps, and to learn from his mistakes. And you will give yourself, and your mate, the freedom to stop being parents every now and again, and to enjoy yourselves as adults with your own fair share of independence.

III

The Outlook

12: Future Pregnancies

ANN FOSTER is eager to get pregnant again. "I want to see if I can carry a baby to term," says Ann, whose first baby was born six weeks early. "I stand a better chance next time, because I know so much more, and because my doctors know I'm at high risk of delivering prematurely. And I think that caring for the next baby will be easier, too, even if it is a premie, because now I know all the ways that premies are different."

Many mothers of premies feel like Ann. But many others feel quite differently. With the outcome so uncertain, they hesitate to get pregnant again. They don't think it would be fair—either to their premie or to her unborn sibling—to bring another premie into the world. And they don't think they have the emotional or physical stamina to go through premie parenthood a second time.

"I won't have another baby," says Katie Lee three years

after her son John's premature birth. "John's birth crashed all my illusions, destroyed the feeling I had had that I was lucky or somehow immune from problems. I don't trust life anymore—and to get pregnant again would be an act of trust."

Another premie mother echoes Katie's concerns. "Martha was a difficult baby," says Sue Evans. "Even now, when she's nearly three, caring for her is more than a full-time job. I held her round-the-clock till she was nine months old; I nursed her every hour or so; I slept with her and catered to her and never let her out of my sight. I don't want another child because I just don't think I could go through three years like that again."

If you do decide to have another baby, your next pregnancy will probably be quite different from your last. Because you have had one premie, you are considered at high risk of having another. This means that you will be followed more closely during your pregnancy to detect the early warning signs of premature labor—and, if any of those signs should arise, you might be ordered to stop working, stay in bed, refrain from sex, and take medications. If the situation warrants it, your obstetrician might even admit you to a hospital for prolonged bedrest, intravenous medication, and perhaps minor surgery to keep your womb intact.

Your pregnancy will be considered less a healthy, natural part of the life cycle than a medical condition requiring medical intervention. But with this careful attention, you stand a very good chance of having a full-term baby next time around.

Women who have had one premie, for whatever reason, run a one in four chance of having another premie. This compares to a one in ten risk of prematurity among the pregnant population at large. If the first prematurity is due to an abnormality of the uterus or cervix, the woman's chance of having another premie might be even higher than one in four. Luckily, great strides have been made recently in the new field of perinatology—the care of mother and fetus, both before and after birth—and the outlook for high-risk pregnant women is improving all the time.

As a high-risk patient, you will have unique needs during this pregnancy. You might need to find a different obstetrician, and you should be counting on a different kind of medical care to extend your pregnancy as close to term as possible. In addition, because you now have at least one other child at home, you might need some additional help with cooking, cleaning, and child care, especially if your doctor tells you that you need to stay in bed. Your mate, friends, relatives, and neighbors might need to pitch in with the chores to allow you to rest. And you'll have to learn to accept their help, realizing that bedrest is not an idle luxury but a treatment that might mean the difference between health and illness for your growing fetus.

Choosing an Obstetrician

When you were pregnant with your premie, you probably wanted an obstetrician who was friendly, sympathetic, and convenient, who delivered at a clean, pleasant hospital near your home, and who had the same ideas you had about drugs during childbirth, your mate's participation, and other details of labor and delivery.

But the next time, you will need an obstetrician with different credentials. You will want your doctor to be affiliated with a major medical center where your next baby can, if necessary, receive sophisticated neonatal care. You will want the doctor to be abreast of the latest methods of delaying premature labor, including bedrest, drugs, stitches in the cervix, and the like. And if you had a Cesarean when your first premie was born (as 20 percent of premature mothers do), you might want to consider choosing a doctor who is willing to do vaginal deliveries on mothers who have had

Cesareans. If you do have a Cesarean next time, which is always more likely for women who already have had one, then the matter of your doctor's feelings about childbirth drugs and episiotomies—so important when you chose your last obstetrician—is likely to be moot.

One issue that's as important as it ever was in your choice of an obstetrician is the issue of convenience. During your high-risk pregnancy, you will be going in for check-ups once a week beginning around the 24th week—often with a small child in tow. But if you can find a top-flight obstetrician only by traveling an extra ten or twenty miles, you'd do well to choose credentials over convenience.

A good obstetrician will examine his high-risk pregnant patient weekly for changes in her cervix. He is looking especially for signs that the cervix is softening, thinning out (effacing), or opening up (dilating). In addition, a good obstetrician will work with you in trying to recognize some of the earliest signs of labor—signs that occur when labor is still so early that bedrest and medicine can be effective in stopping it altogether.

Early Labor: The Warning Signs

Dr. Robert Creasy, an obstetrician at the University of California, San Francisco, has developed a numerical rating system for identifying women at high risk of going into premature labor. He scores women according to the following criteria:

- socioeconomic status;
- past pregnancy history;
- daily habits during this pregnancy; and
- medical events during this pregnancy.

Dr. Creasy then assigns points according to how much more likely premature labor becomes with any one habit or event. For instance, a woman who works outside the home is given 1 point; if her work is physically tiring, or if it involves a long, difficult commute (an hour or more of continuous riding, five days a week), she is given 3 more points. And if she had a premature delivery in a previous pregnancy, for whatever reason, she is given 10 points.

According to Dr. Creasy's criteria, outlined in Table 12-1, any woman who can accumulate 10 points is considered a high-risk patient. That means that, just by having had one premature birth, you would automatically be considered high-risk in Dr. Creasy's clinic. Some obstetricians think this is a little overcautious. But by using his exacting standards, Dr. Creasy says he has been able to decrease the incidence of premature births at the University of California, San Francisco, by an impressive 50 percent a year for the past two years.

Women who are identified as high-risk are taught to recognize the very first signs of labor—signs that indicate labor is in its earliest, and most stoppable, stages. Since, as the mother of a premie, you would be considered high-risk, you would do well to be alert to these signs as well. Call your doctor or clinic whenever you notice a change in the character or amount of any one of the following symptoms:

• menstrual-like cramps;
• dull, low backache;
• pressure in the lower abdomen, back, or thighs, sometimes described as a heaviness in the pelvis;
• vaginal discharge, especially if it is mucusy, watery, or bloody; or
• diarrhea or indigestion.

High-risk women in Dr. Creasy's program are also taught how to feel (in doctors' words, "palpate") their own uteruses. This allows them to feel from the outside a sensation so subtle they can't feel it from the inside—the mild clenching and unclenching of the uterus in the earliest stages of labor.

The following guide for self-palpation for uterine contractions was compiled by Marie Herron and Susan Krow-

TABLE 12-1   RISK OF PRETERM DELIVERY*

Adapted from "Prevention of Preterm Birth" by Robert K. Creasy and Marie A. Herron, *Seminars in Perinatology*, vol. 5, no. 3, 1981, p. 297. Used with permission.

	SOCIAL FACTORS	PAST HISTORY	MOTHER'S DAILY HABITS	CURRENT PREGNANCY
1	2 children at home Moderately low socioeconomic status	1 first-trimester abortion Less than one year since last birth	Work outside home	Unusual fatigue
2	Mother's age 18 to 20 years Mother's age more than 40 years Low socioeconomic status Single parent	2 first-trimester abortions	More than ten cigarettes per day	Weight gain under 5 kg. (12 lb) by 32 weeks Albuminuria Bacteriuria Hypertension (usually higher than 140/90)
3	Mother less than 5 feet tall Mother less than 100 pounds pre-pregnancy Very low socioeconomic status	3 first-trimester abortions	Heavy work Long, tiring commute	Fibroids of the uterus Weight loss of 2 kg. (5 lb) Illness with fever Breech position at 32 weeks Baby's head engaged at 32-34 weeks

4	Mother's age less than 18 years	Repeated urinary tract infections		Uterine bleeding after 12 weeks Cervix effaced more than 40% Cervix dilated Uterine irritability
5		Cone biopsy Uterine anomaly 1 second-trimester abortion DES exposure in utero		Placenta previa Hydramnios (too much or too little amniotic fluid)
10		Previous premature labor Previous premature delivery 2 second-trimester abortions		Twins Abdominal surgery after 12 weeks

SCORE: ☐ 0–5 ☐ 6–9 ☐ 10 or more

*Score is computed by addition of the number of points given any item.

ley, nurses in the preterm labor program run by Dr. Creasy. Ask your obstetrician whether he thinks there is value in self-palpation. If he recommends it, use this technique:

1. While lying on your back in bed or on the sofa, place your fingertips on the top of your uterus.

2. Contractions usually begin at the top of your uterus. They are best described as a "tension" or "hardening" of your uterus, feeling as hard as, or even harder than, the tip of your nose. If your uterus is contracting, you will actually feel your abdomen get tight or hard and then relax (soften). You may even see it move up slightly in your abdomen. The tightness will increase, reaching a peak, and then slowly decrease.

3. If your uterus is tightening and relaxing, note the time each "tightening" starts, how long it lasts, and how often it occurs. These tightenings are really silent contractions. Time the contractions for an hour, from the beginning of one contraction to the beginning of the next contraction.

4. If you are experiencing uterine contractions at regular intervals and any of the warning signs and symptoms of preterm labor are also present, do the following:
• Lie down.
• Tilt yourself toward your left side, placing a pillow behind your back for support.
• Drink two or three cups of juice or water.
• Continue to check for uterine contractions and/or other signs and symptoms of preterm labor.

5. If the uterine contractions or other signs and symptoms continue for an hour on bedrest, call your doctor, clinic, or delivery room. *Do not wait for the symptoms to disappear.* They might not disappear, and waiting might cause your baby to be born too early.

Palpate your uterus twice a day, every day, whether or not you are experiencing symptoms of premature labor. The value of regular palpation is that it can detect contractions that might be occurring without your feeling them. If you wait for the "silent contractions" to become strong enough to bother you, they might already have caused your cervix to dilate enough to make it difficult or impossible to forestall full-blown labor.

Early Labor: The Ways to Stop It

If you experience any of the warning signs of premature labor—cramps, backache, diarrhea, pelvic pressure, discharge—or if you can detect some silent contractions by palpating your uterus, you might be in early labor. If you are, your doctor will begin steps to try to stop the labor from progressing. The steps he recommends will depend on how far the labor has already progressed, based on such factors as the intensity of your symptoms, the history of your pregnancy, and the appearance of your cervix.

The first step in treating early labor is bedrest. You will be told to lie down for several additional hours every day, on your left side. (You may roll over onto your right side occasionally, but avoid lying on your back; it inhibits blood flow to the uterus.) The conditions of bedrest vary: some women are allowed to walk around for much of the day, some can leave the bed only for trips to the bathroom or the doctor's office, others cannot leave the bed at all. (Women in this last group usually are hospitalized for bedrest and often receive antilabor drugs at the same time.)

Ten years ago, the standard treatment for premature labor was for the woman to go to bed and drink enough wine or liquor to keep her slightly drunk. If that didn't work, she'd be hospitalized for intravenous administration of pure alcohol. Alcohol relaxes the muscles of the uterus and inhibits their contraction. But the technique was abandoned, because it worked only occasionally, caused unpleasant side effects of drunkenness in the mother, and was potentially hazardous for the baby.

For mild contractions, though, doctors still suggest that you go to bed early each evening with one glass of wine. One glass of wine contains enough alcohol to relax not only the uterus but the mother as well and probably is a small enough dose to be relatively safe for the fetus. (The most damage done by alcohol during pregnancy occurs in the first trimester.)

Despite your doctor's prescriptions of bed and wine, he is not suggesting a romantic interlude for you and your mate. In fact, he might prohibit sex altogether. The physical changes of orgasm are associated with uterine contractions, and sexual excitement therefore could hasten the early labor you are trying to stop. If your doctor tells you to refrain from sex, he means sex in all forms, including masturbation. It is the orgasm, not the intercourse itself, that is potentially hazardous in this situation.

If bedrest and wine don't help the contractions, your doctor might try administering antilabor drugs. The most popular of these drugs, known collectively as beta-adrenergic drugs, is called Ritodrine, although similar drugs are known by other brand names (Albuteral, Bricanyl, Partusisten, Vasodilan). They work best if begun early—before the cervix has opened to 3 or 4 centimeters, and before the amniotic sac has ruptured.

Ritodrine given early enough can be quite effective in stopping premature labor. At first, it is administered intravenously, in the hospital. Once the contractions stop (usually in a matter of days), your doctor will switch you to an oral dose and send you home—although even at home you might have to stay in bed.

The drug has its share of side effects in the mother, including elevations of blood pressure and heart rate, lightheadedness, nasal congestion, nausea, and tremors. And because Ritodrine has been used as an antilabor drug for only a few years, its long-term effect on the fetus is not known. Most doctors consider it far safer, from the fetus's point of view, to be able to spend a few added weeks in the womb— even though that means exposure to beta-adrenergic drugs—than to be born weeks or months before its time.

Occasionally, the cause of your first premature birth can

give your doctor a clue about how to prevent another one. This is especially true if the prematurity was due to an "incompetent cervix." This refers to a cervix that opens up spontaneously during the second trimester, in response to the pressure of the growing womb and fetus. True cervical incompetence is a rare condition, affecting a very small proportion of women with a history of miscarriages or premature births. It is generally applied as a description more than a diagnosis, since a woman who goes into advanced labor too soon must, almost by definition, have a cervix that cannot stay closed throughout gestation.

Today, an operation is available to correct carefully diagnosed cervical incompetence. Your obstetrician can sew your cervix shut using a special surgical stitch called a cerclage. The cerclage serves as a drawstring to hold the O-shaped cervix closed. When it is time for delivery, the doctor can simply pull out the stitch and open the drawstring. Cervical suturing is a simple procedure, done in the hospital under local anesthesia and posing little risk to the fetus. But so far it has not been tested rigorously to see whether it really does add significantly to the length of gestation in a high-risk pregnancy. One thing is certain, however: cerclage does not guarantee a term pregnancy. Often, mothers go into premature labor even with the stitches in place, and the doctors are forced to cut the stitches early in order to deliver the baby.

Experience: A Mixed Blessing

If you do get pregnant after having had a premature baby, you can expect your earlier birth experience to have both a positive and a negative effect. Because you've had one premie, you know enough to seek treatment as a high-risk obstetrical patient. This in itself is positive effect enough— especially if it helps to prevent the birth of a second premie, or at least to give your second premie a longer time in the womb.

You know enough, too, to be able to handle another pre-mie with relative ease, thanks to your experience with your first. "I was at such a loss with Charles," Ann Foster says. "I didn't know the first thing about how to calm a premie, how to dress him, how to take care of him. But if our next baby is premature, I'll know plenty."

Ann has compiled a list that she calls "Things I will do differently next time." Her resolutions are testimony to the value of experience in helping you, your mate, and your next baby through the crisis of an early birth.

What will Ann Foster do differently next time?

1. I will have a private room and pay for TV and radio.

2. I will stay away from full-term babies and their mothers more at first.

3. I will ask the doctor to allow me to stay in the hospital longer, especially if I have a long commute.

4. I will spend more time in the intensive care nursery at night while I'm in the hospital.

5. I will take an alarm clock to the hospital with me to en-sure that I get up for the night feedings (since the nurses didn't always wake me).

6. I will rent an electric breast pump immediately.

7. I will remember to ask these questions at the hospital:

   • What are the visiting hours for intensive care nurs-ery babies? (Family and friends might be able to visit the baby at different hours than the visiting hours al-lowed for term babies.)

   • What are the chances of having close relatives (for example, the baby's grandparents) scrub and come in to see the baby?

   • Do the baby's parents need an ID bracelet to enter the hospital after visiting hours?

8. I will explore the possibility of leaving a tape recording of our voices to play in the baby's isolette.

9. I will ask to bring our own receiving blankets to wrap the baby in when we take him out of the isolette.

10. I will go to the hospital with change for the vending machines!

11. I will buy doll clothes to bring the baby home in and will have something at home—more doll clothes, handmade clothes, or special premie clothes—for the child to wear that fits.

12. I will get a mother's helper as soon as the baby is born—at first to do the laundry and help clean up, later to help with child care.

13. I will find out where I can get premie Pampers.

14. I will have someone here (my mother, my mother-in-law) the day the baby comes home.

15. I will have someone go with me to the first few doctor's appointments.

The advantage of your experience is that you know what to expect. But that can be a disadvantage, too. If your first premie was very sick, or if you encountered very sick premies during your stay in the intensive care nursery, you know that babies born too soon can have many problems. This might make you more worried about premature delivery than you would have been without this experience. Your nightmares are more vivid, and more personal, because you have been there once before.

In the end, no one can decide for you whether you want another child. No two pregnancies are alike, and no two children are alike. The fact that you had one premie is no reason to think you are fated to have another. Indeed, an argument can be made that a family with a premie is an ideal family to expand. Today, you shower all your attention and concern on your premie, the youngest and most fragile-seeming member of the family. But the glare of life in the spotlight can get overpowering, even for a small child. If your premie had a little brother or sister to share that spotlight, he might really thrive. And you might thrive, too. You might learn to think of your premie more casually, as a part of a larger whole, if there's another baby around.

13: The Legacy of Prematurity

"I was a premie." Millions of Americans make that statement every day—most of them speaking with a mixture of pride and astonishment. To hear a big, burly man, or a bright young woman in medical school, or a pair of athletic twins utter those words—"I was a premie"—is to feel the awesome power of the primitive will to live. Infants born before their time, especially those born a generation or so ago, did a lot of fighting in order to survive. And they fought bravely, instinctively, with a strength far greater than anything their elders could summon.

As the parent of a premie, you have probably been told the story of a cousin or neighbor born in the 1920s who was so small they put her in the oven to keep her warm. You have probably been told, too, about someone born in the 1950s who was blinded by the high oxygen level used in the incubator. But these premie stories are different from that of your child, whose medical care has been refined to the point where the intensive care nursery really does, in many ways, mimic the essential functions of the womb. And because your child was lucky enough to be born in the 1980s, the outcome of your story will be different from the outcome of the stories you've been hearing. Your baby's story is likely to end far more happily.

Premies born thirty or fifty or seventy years ago are now living out the legacy of their prematurity. For many of them, that legacy is a painful reminder of a painful time. But the legacy of prematurity can also be triumphant. Legend has it that some of the world's most remarkable men were premature. From their sickly, scrawny beginnings, some premies from the past went on to become important world leaders in politics—Churchill, Napoleon, Rousseau—in the arts—Victor Hugo, Renoir, Mark Twain—and in science—Charles Darwin, Albert Einstein, and Isaac Newton.

These men, of course, were the exception. They were born prematurely, and survived unharmed, during a time when the majority of premies died or were damaged shortly after birth. For premies born in the 1980s, thanks to dramatic improvements in neonatal intensive care, a triumphant legacy will be less the exception than the rule.

A Brief History of Premie Care

The special care of premature infants was brought to the United States in 1902 by Dr. Martin Couney, a French physician who toured the country exhibiting premies in their incubators. Dr. Couney's "child hatchery" was a major attraction of every fair he attended, from the Pan American Exposition in Buffalo in 1902 to the New York World's Fair in 1940. His premies were so popular that they brought in more customers at the Chicago World's Fair than any other exhibit except for Sally Rand, the famous "fan dancer."

Dr. Couney's exhibition employed state-of-the-art techniques in premie care. He learned those techniques in Paris under his mentor, Dr. Pierre Budin, who is recognized as the first modern neonatologist. Dr. Couney raised more than five thousand premies in temperature-controlled incubators, and he fed them breast milk.

But although Dr. Couney paid close attention to his patients' physical needs, he seriously neglected their social and emotional needs. The babies' parents were excluded from the child hatchery (although Dr. Couney gave them free passes to the exhibit!) and they frustrated the doctor by frequently rejecting their babies when they were "saved" and were sent home.

During Dr. Couney's successful American tour, hospitals across the country opened their own special-care nurseries, beginning in 1923 with the Sarah Morris Hospital in Chicago. Most of these fledgling nurseries adopted Dr. Couney's methods—including the use of incubators, the use of breast milk, and, unfortunately, the exclusion from the nurseries of the babies' parents.

These were the days before antibiotics and pasteurization, so hospitals were compelled to maintain strict rules against parents touching, or even visiting, their premies in order to prevent epidemics of infection. But such policies took their toll. In large numbers, the parents whose premies were saved by these nurseries began treating their babies like strangers—or, worse, like intruders—when they returned home. Many of these babies were given up for adoption.

We have come a long way since the early days of newborn special care. The technological advances have been dizzying, leading to a sophistication undreamed of in Dr. Couney's time. And the social and psychological advances, while far less dramatic—and of far more recent vintage—have been impressive, too.

As recently as 15 years ago, parents were still excluded from the intensive care nursery. "My son was born in 1969," says one premie mother. "The eleven days he was in the hospital were the loneliest, loneliest days of my life. They wouldn't let me near my baby. They wouldn't let me nurse him. I just went to the hospital every day and stood outside the nursery, looking at him. During that time, my baby and I were always separated by two layers of glass—the glass of his incubator and the glass of the nursery window."

In 1970, a survey of intensive care nurseries showed that less than one-third of hospitals even allowed parents into the intensive care nursery; of these, less than half let the parents touch their premies in the first days of life. Such practices led to a disturbing trend—the greater incidence of so-called "disorders of mothering" among babies born prematurely than among term babies. In the mid-1970s, nearly 20 percent of the victims of child abuse were found to have been premature—even though premies made up no more than 5 percent of the childhood population.

Such dismal statistics began to change in 1975, when neonatology was formally recognized as a subspecialty of pediatrics. At about the same time, psychological research began to reveal that premies who were touched and talked to actually gained weight faster, and recovered better, than premies whose surroundings were sterile and purely medical. Gradually, then, parents were granted entry into the intensive care nursery. Today, parents are allowed unlimited visiting privileges—and, within reason, touching privileges—at almost all of the nation's intensive care nurseries.

The Scars of Prematurity

In the 1950s and 1960s, follow-up studies of "very low birthweight" premies were almost uniformly pessimistic. One typical study in those days found that 83 percent of infants weighing less than 1250 grams at birth were abnormal at follow-up. Since that time, follow-up statistics have been turned on their heads. Today, instead of seeing about 80 percent of very low birthweight infants ending up *abnormal*, we find about 80 percent of very low birthweight infants ending up *normal*. And the odds are even better for larger premies (with birthweights above 1500 grams), premies with nontraumatic births, premies with good Apgar scores (see Chapter 1), and premies who never experienced lung or heart problems in the nursery.

Of the 10 to 20 percent of premies who do bear some scars of prematurity, about one-half experience problems that are minor—and even reversible. This "mild to moderate" category includes learning disabilities, slight developmental lag, nearsightedness, short stature, and physical awkwardness. And, despite improvements in nursery policies toward parents' visits, premies also still remain at slightly increased risk of "disorders of mothering." These disorders generally are related to prolonged mother-infant separation shortly after birth and can include problems ranging from maternal anxiety and overprotectiveness, to "failure to thrive" (an unexplained lack of physical and intellectual growth during infancy or childhood), to such extremes as neglect, physical violence, child abuse, or even abandonment.

Most of the problems associated with prematurity are related to slowness in catching up to where the baby should be, based on his chronological (birth) age. These lags, both physical and developmental, usually disappear within the first twelve to eighteen months of life. In 1975, when neonatal care was far less sophisticated than the care available today, a Canadian pediatrician published a follow-up study of sixty-seven premies born before 33 weeks gestation. By the time they reached twelve months corrected age, all the boys in the study had caught up in size to the boys in a control group of babies born at term. The girls had caught up in most ways to the girls in the control group, although their rate of weight gain was significantly slower. And, developmentally, both girls and boys in the study scored as well on the tests they were given as did the one-year-olds in the control group.

According to a report, "The Costs and Effectiveness of Neonatal Intensive Care," issued to the U.S. Congress in 1980, nearly nineteen thousand very low birthweight infants are sent home from intensive care nurseries each year who are happy, healthy, and normal. Twenty years ago, before the advent of modern neonatology, sixteen thousand of those nineteen thousand babies would have died.

These survival statistics are nothing short of astounding. Who would have believed, twenty years ago, that so many three-pound babies would be going home to live perfectly normal lives? But even with this impressive record, neonatologists are also sending home a disturbing minority of handicapped children who, twenty years ago, might not have gone home at all.

The 1980 report to Congress concluded that, for a group of very low birthweight premies given optimal intensive care immediately after birth, about 10 percent of the survivors would have severe neurological damage (significant cerebral palsy or major seizure disorders); 10 percent would be severely retarded (IQs below 70); 5 percent would have severe vision problems, including total blindness, from retrolental fibroplasia; and another 10 percent would suffer mild or moderate intellectual or neurological damage (including such problems as sensory, behavioral, language, and learning disorders).

Each year, estimates are, approximately three thousand graduates of intensive care nurseries leave the hospital with major problems—and another four thousand or so leave with some of these same problems to a lesser degree. Many of these seven thousand children cease being the neonatologists' burden only to become, instead, a burden to their parents and, ultimately, to society.

Who are these seven thousand damaged children? Will your premie be among them? Generally, the babies with the most severe damage are the ones with the most catastrophic hospital stays, the babies who weighed 1250 grams or less at birth, who had very low Apgar scores, who suffered massive bleeds in the hospital, or who spent prolonged periods under high concentrations of oxygen. If your baby is going to develop any of the severe complications of prematurity, you've probably already had clues, either during the baby's hospital stay or in the first few months at home. These complications usually come, if they come at all, as no surprise.

The milder problems, though, might be harder to detect in the early months. If your baby's prematurity is destined to have some effect on later intelligence, behavior, or school performance, you probably won't know about it for years to come. Indeed, it might be hard for you ever directly to ascribe certain difficulties—such as nearsightedness, physical awkwardness, or learning disabilities—to the fact that your child was born too soon. How can you be sure she wouldn't have had those problems anyway?

The possibility of a normal, healthy outcome for even the sickest and tiniest of premies is an uplifting one, but it also can be maddening. It might lead you to work regularly with your child to overcome mental or physical lags; to cart him to the best infant stimulation programs; and, hardest of all, to wait to see how well he develops. If your baby is at high risk for some of the more serious problems of prematurity, you and your pediatrician will probably watch him closely in the months ahead. But "at risk" does not mean "destined," and you're likely to spend much time and energy in trying to beat your baby's odds.

In prospect, such a task seems formidable, and you might wonder whether you are equal to it. But parents who go home with a child they know is damaged, or whom they know is likely to have problems in the years ahead, often exhibit a strength and dedication that astonishes even them.

"If you had told me a year ago that I would have a retarded baby or one with a physical handicap, I would have been devastated," says Fran Pines. "But Meredith is Meredith, and her beautiful blue eyes and loving smile overcome most of the fear and worry." Meredith, who was born at 28 weeks gestation, suffered a Grade IV brain bleed at two days of age, and she might someday develop mental or physical problems as a result. "Of course," Fran says, "we are still afraid she will have an impairment that will cause her discomfort or embarrassment in later life. But each of her achievements is priceless. When she first reached for a rattle, when she giggled, when she smiled at Grandpa—somehow we see her accomplishments as more precious than we would if she had been a 'regular,' full-term infant."

The Ethics of Neonatal Intensive Care

When neonatology came of age in the 1970s, some observers worried that the dramatic salvaging of very tiny premies might in fact be doing more harm than good. They worried, to put it bluntly, that the miracles of modern medicine might be saving some premies who would have been better off dead.

Indeed, based on the track record of the 1950s and 1960s, these critics had good cause to worry. With great fanfare and heroics, many premies of a generation ago were salvaged by newborn intensive care only to become children with damaged brains and bodies. Sometimes, as was the case with oxygen-induced blindness, the damage was a result of the intensive care itself. Sometimes, as was the case with some forms of mental retardation, it was a result of the profound immaturity of the premie's delicate organs—organs that were simply too fragile for life outside the uterus.

Today, neonatologists ask themselves difficult questions about what they are doing. Is it worth expending great effort, for instance, toward saving a premie weighing 750 grams—since he has about a 50–50 chance of living and, if he lives, about a one in five chance of suffering severe and permanent damage? Who is to decide which babies are worth saving and which babies should be allowed to die?

Such questions are especially difficult to answer because the outcome of neonatal intensive care is often impossible to predict in advance. Some babies who seem doomed at birth, based on birthweight and gestational age, somehow breathe well on their own right from the start and never encounter difficulties during their hospital stays. These are the babies who, despite the odds, will go home healthy, happy—and normal. Other babies, though, who might have been given better odds at birth because of their size and maturity, suffer from asphyxia, or bad hyaline membrane disease, or a bleed in the brain; they survive, if they survive at all, with numerous permanent complications.

Dr. Albert Jonsen, professor of bioethics at the University of California, San Francisco, provides a case study to highlight what he calls the "prognostic perplexity" facing doctors and parents who must decide how aggressively to treat a premie. Dr. Jonsen tells the story of two premies born, after 28 weeks gestation, in the early 1970s—a time when 28-weekers rarely survived intact. While the mothers were still in labor, each family asked that the baby not be resuscitated at birth. They based their requests, says Dr. Jonsen, "on the grounds that prematurely born infants are likely to end up retarded or otherwise markedly handicapped. In both cases, the attending physicians argued in favor of providing intensive care, and won the consent of the parents to this line of action."

Both babies, whom we will call Richard and Mary, were vigorously resuscitated, and both did well in the early weeks of life. But their outcomes were completely different—something their doctors could not have predicted when they first made the decision to treat the babies aggressively. At the age of four, Richard was of normal size, stature, and intelligence. But, at four, Mary was severely retarded and was probably autistic as well.

If doctors knew from the beginning which babies would thrive, like Richard, and which would suffer irreversible damage, like Mary, they might at least have clear-cut choices to make: this intact baby versus this damaged baby. But with premies, it's very hard to predict anything with certainty. Doctors know the statistical probabilities that a particular problem will lead to a particular outcome—they know, for instance, that premies with very severe bleeds are statistically more likely than other premies to suffer mental or physical problems—but a probability is not a prognosis. How can any doctor, or any parent, use statistics to determine whether an individual baby's life will be a life worth living?

When little Matthew Davidson suffered a Grade IV bleed, for instance, doctors had little to go on when they told Will and Natalie Davidson the probable fate of their son. They told them that most premies with massive bleeds encounter serious problems later. But that's all they could say for sure. Despite the likelihood of severe developmental problems for Matthew, the Davidsons urged the doctors to continue whatever treatment was necessary to correct the many complications that arose during Matthew's long hospital stay. Many other parents, based on the slim chance of an "intact outcome" for their child, would long since have given up.

Will and Natalie's faith paid off. One year later, Matthew's mental and motor development were almost on a par with his age level, despite his massive bleed. Matthew surprised his doctors—and, in truth, even his parents—by doing so well. No one can predict how many other babies with Grade IV bleeds might also surprise their doctors, if given the chance.

Parents usually are the final arbiters of the life-and-death decisions made in behalf of premies. Acting as their baby's proxies, they must decide whether the baby's probable handicaps are so severe, so painful, and so inevitable that death is to be preferred.

Parents, of course, must deal with the same "prognostic perplexity" as doctors do. They search for any information that will give them a clue about how their baby will turn out. But, because each premie is so different, nothing can predict precisely what will face their child in five or ten more years. In addition, each family's emotional and economic resources are unique, as are its views toward handicap, normalcy, and the right to life. What might be an unbearable burden for one family might simply be a fact of life for another.

"I badgered the doctors with questions about John's future and the nature and extent of his disabilities," recalls Katie Lee about the days shortly after her son's Grade III bleed. "I begged the social workers at the hospital to put me in touch with parents of older children who had similar bleeds. But, wisely, they refrained. I know now that it is easier to slide gently into the knowledge of your child's limitations than to be confronted with an image of what he may or may not be twenty years from now."

Like many other important philosophical questions of our time, the question of which premie is worth saving sometimes comes down, in part, to a matter of money. Neonatologists make their decisions based on science; parents make their decisions based on emotions; but bioethicists and political decision makers talk a good deal about money. In a society of scarce resources, policy makers often ask which baby is "worth" the great expense of neonatal intensive care. In a society that supports its handicapped, they ask whether we can "afford" to create several thousand children a year who will need lifelong assistance.

Caring for a sick newborn is extraordinarily expensive, and society usually foots the bill through Medicaid, Blue Cross, or other insurance plans. Neonatal intensive care was found, in one recent study, to average about $9,000 in 1978 dollars for each baby saved. Other studies have placed the average cost of care as high as $20,000 per baby—comparable to kidney dialysis and coronary bypass surgery, the two most expensive forms of treatment for adults. Unfortunately, when such a high price tag is attached to the service, doctors and biomedical philosophers occasionally find themselves wondering: "Will it really be worth $20,000 to save this child?"

Doctors tend to make decisions on a case-by-case basis when determining which premies to treat. They usually give any premie the benefit of a doubt, beginning aggressive medical therapy as soon as they can no matter how small the baby is. This is especially true if the baby, despite his prematurity, seems to have had a relatively good start in life.

Most neonatologists believe they are better off trying to save a baby than not trying at all. In general, when they're uncertain about whether a baby will make it, they usually at least try resuscitating the baby at birth, in the hopes of avoiding complications that could result from prolonged birth asphyxia (see glossary). If it turns out that the baby has suffered irreparable damage, the physician, in consultation with the baby's parents, will usually have an opportunity later on to call a halt to the medical heroics.

After weeks or months in the intensive care nursery, after every effort has been made to save the baby, doctors and parents can reassess the probable outcome for that particular child. They can begin asking each other whether the child will in fact ever be able to live a full, meaningful life —and they can decide precisely what they mean by such words as "full" and "meaningful." In most cases, parents need not make these profound decisions suddenly—nor need they make them alone. In consultation with neonatologists, social workers, and counselors, the parents can devote to this decision all the careful, reasoned thinking that it demands.

The Joys of Your Premie

Premies are special. That's a truth that premie parents come to know gradually, and only after they've acquired the confidence and calm to love their babies for themselves and not for what they can or cannot become. "Once I threw out my child development charts and began to compare Charles's progress only with Charles," says his mother, Ann Foster, "I became thrilled with the strides he has made and continues to make almost daily. In many ways, he *is* slower than a term baby or than his gestational age would indicate. I am learning, however, that his slowness is compensated for by his magnificent determination—and his stubbornness."

Each special joy of premie parenthood occurs in small and quiet ways. It might happen when your baby douses the bathroom floor with water in a burst of bathtime discovery—and you remember, before you yell, how unlikely *any* exploration had seemed when he was in the intensive care nursery. It might come when the baby's height and weight have finally increased enough to allow the doctor to plot a position for him on a normal infant growth curve. It might come when you hear your premie and his older brother squealing together in a secret game, or when he and his father kick a soccer ball around the backyard, or when he sings to himself in his crib when he first awakens. All the moments of parenthood in which you fall in love with your baby, again and again, are more deep and more poignant for premie parents. You and your baby have traveled so long and hard to get to those moments that you relish them all the more.

"Premies are special," Ann Foster says, "and because they are, we parents are, too. Our emotional involvement is undoubtedly higher than that of term babies' parents. Before we were ready, we were asked to make some difficult decisions, and to love and care for our 'scared little animals,' as my husband once called them. We've had fears that other parents haven't had; we've had to find a strength within ourselves that we might not have even suspected was there.

"And as I hold Charles in my arms trying to coax him to sleep, or listen to him blowing bubbles in his car seat, I realize that this child has wormed his way into my heart more deeply than I think a 'normal' baby could have. The bonding was slower than it would have been otherwise, but we are bound now by steel cables."

Appendices

APPENDIX A
METRIC CONVERSION CHART: GRAMS TO POUNDS

Pounds ↓ / Ounces →	0	1	2	3	4	5	6	7	8	9	10	11	12	13	14	15
0	Grams →	28	57	85	113	142	170	198	207	225	284	312	340	369	387	425
1	454	482	510	539	567	595	624	652	680	709	737	765	794	822	850	879
2	907	936	964	992	1021	1049	1097	1106	1134	1162	1191	1219	1247	1276	1309	1332
3	1361	1389	1418	1446	1474	1501	1531	1559	1588	1616	1644	1673	1701	1729	1758	1786
4	1814	1843	1871	1898	1928	1956	1984	2013	2041	2070	2098	2126	2155	2183	2211	2240
5	2268	2296	2325	2353	2382	2410	2438	2461	2495	2523	2552	2580	2608	2637	2665	2690
6	2722	2750	2778	2807	2835	2863	2892	2920	2948	2977	3005	3034	3062	3090	3119	3145
7	3175	3204	3232	3260	3289	3317	3343	3374	3402	3430	3459	3487	3516	3544	3572	3601
8	3629	3657	3686	3714	3742	3771	3799	3827	3856	3884	3912	3941	3969	3997	4025	4059
9	4082	4111	4139	4168	4196	4224	4253	4281	4309	4338	4366	4394	4423	4451	4479	4508
10	4536	4564	4593	4621	4640	4678	4706	4735	4763	4791	4820	4848	4876	4905	4933	4961

Appendix B
Glossary of Medical Terms

alveolus: The small terminal air sac in the lung which is the site where blood in the lungs can exchange carbon dioxide for oxygen. The alveoli of the lungs begin development between the 26th and 28th weeks of gestation.

aminophylline: A medication used commonly in the treatment of apnea and bradycardia. It has a direct effect on the breathing center of the brain.

amniocentesis: A prenatal test, usually performed between the 16th and 18th weeks of gestation, in which a long needle is inserted through the mother's abdomen into the fluid contained in the uterus. The fluid (called amniotic fluid) is then removed so physicians can look for certain inherited diseases or chromosomal abnormalities. Amniocentesis is also performed on some women in premature labor to measure the L/S ratio of the fluid. *See also* **L/S ratio.**

anemia: A blood condition that exists in many premature

infants in which the numbers of red blood cells are decreased in relation to the total volume of blood.

antibiotic: A drug that fights bacterial infection and may be used singly or in combination with other antibiotics. The most commonly known antibiotic is penicillin.

aorta: The major artery coming from the heart, which supplies all the organs of the body with oxygen-rich blood.

Apgar score: A ranking system for newborn infants, named after Dr. Virginia Apgar (1909–74), based on five items: respiration, heart rate, muscle tone, color, and reflexes. A perfect Apgar score is 10. Low scores (under 3) have been shown to correlate with problems later in childhood.

apnea: A short period of no breathing, seen commonly in small premature infants. An abnormal period of no breathing is usually defined as greater than ten to fifteen seconds. It frequently occurs with bradycardia. Apnea can be treated with drugs and with the use of a monitor to record when breathing has stopped. An episode of apnea is called an apneic episode. *See also* **bradycardia.**

artery: One of the many divisions of the major vessel, the aorta, which carries oxygen to all organs of the body. *See also* **aorta.**

asphyxia: A period of time in which an inadequate supply of oxygen is being supplied to the body organs. Asphyxia may occur in the uterus, during delivery, or any time after birth. Depending on the length and degree of oxygen deprivation, it may be associated with organ damage.

bag and mask: Two items available at delivery, or at bedside in the intensive care nursery, for resuscitation of the premature infant. The mask fits over the infant's nose and mouth and is attached to a plastic or rubber bag with a supply of oxygen. A nurse or physician can use this equipment to get oxygen into the infant during a period of apnea. *See also* **apnea.**

bilirubin: A pigment that comes from the breakdown of red blood cells, the presence of which causes the skin to become yellow. Bilirubin can come from old, unneeded red blood cells, or it can accumulate because of the abnormal breakdown of the cells. *See also* **jaundice, phototherapy.**

blood chemistries: Laboratory tests routinely performed on an infant's blood when the baby is admitted to the intensive care nursery. The tests may include measurements of the levels of sodium, potassium, chloride, bicarbonate, blood sugar, and bilirubin in the blood.

blood gases: The levels in the bloodstream of oxygen, carbon dioxide, and acidity (pH), which are measured to help doctors in treating infants with respiratory distress.

bradycardia: A slowing of the heart rate below 100 beats/minute. Unless prolonged, it may be normal in a premature infant. Bradycardia often occurs a few seconds after the onset of an episode of apnea.

breech birth: An abnormality of positioning of the fetus in the uterus just before delivery, so that the first part to emerge is the buttocks or leg rather than the head.

bronchopulmonary dysplasia (BPD): A chronic lung disease, usually produced in infants with severe, acute disease of any origin whose treatment required the use of ventilators and high levels of oxygen. It usually begins to develop after four to six days of treatment in the intensive care nursery.

brown fat: A layer of fat cells in the fetus, deposited in the last weeks in utero, that serves as a source of energy and heat regulation in the baby's first weeks of life. Premature infants usually have no brown fat deposits.

capillary: The smallest blood vessel going to or coming from an organ in the body, through which oxygen and carbon dioxide can pass between the blood inside the vessel and the surrounding tissue.

catheter: A small tube, usually made of plastic, which can be placed into a blood vessel and through which fluids may be given. A catheter may be placed in the umbilicus to obtain blood gases, into a large artery or vein to measure blood pressures, into a vein to give total nutrition, or into a small vein to give fluids with or without nutrients.

cerebral palsy: A disorder of muscular control caused by damage to the brain, most often due to asphyxia sometime immediately before or after birth. Cerebral palsy occurs in four forms—spastic (stiff and difficult movements), flaccid (decreased movements), athetotic (excessive involuntary movements), and ataxic (improper balance and depth perception)—and can affect one limb, two limbs, or four limbs.

Cesarean birth: Delivery of a baby through a surgical incision in the mother's abdomen, rather than through the mother's vagina. A Cesarean birth requires either local anesthesia (an epidural) or general anesthesia. It is named for Julius Caesar, who is thought to have been one of the first babies to be delivered surgically.

conceptional age: The age of the infant starting from fertilization of the egg by the sperm. A full-term infant is born at a conceptional age of 38 weeks. *See also* **gestational age.**

concrete lung: Another term for bronchopulmonary dysplasia.

congestive heart failure: An inability of the heart to pump enough blood to all the organs of the body. Congestive heart failure, which can occur for many reasons, is characterized by the accumulation of excess fluid in the body. *See also* **edema, patent ductus arteriosus.**

constriction: A clamping down or tightening of a blood vessel, either an artery, vein, or capillary.

corrected age: The age a premature baby would have been if he had been born on his due date, at 40 weeks gestational age. In assessing growth and development, experts usually calculate the corrected age for the first two years of a premie's life.

CPAP: Continuous positive airway pressure applied at the end of expiration, either in an infant who is able to breathe on his own or in an infant on a ventilator. CPAP, which is also called PEEP (positive end expiratory pressure), helps to keep the lung expanded.

CT scan: A specialized form of x-ray that allows the brain or other parts of the body to be viewed at many levels, giving a computerized cross-sectional image on a screen. In infants, the CT scan is usually used to look for brain bleeds. It involves no more radiation exposure than would a series of skull x-rays. The initials stand for "computerized tomography."

cutdown: A small incision made through the skin to expose a vein or artery to facilitate placement of a catheter. Catheter placement does not always require a cutdown.

dilation: An expansion of a blood vessel, either an artery, vein, or capillary.

diplegia: A form of cerebral palsy in which both arms or both legs are affected; the lower limbs are usually affected more severely. *See also* **cerebral palsy.**

edema: An excessive accumulation of fluid in the body tissues.

electrolytes: Substances in the blood that have positive or negative electrical charges which are capable of combining chemically to carry out essential body functions. Electrolytes include potassium (K^+), chloride (Cl^-), calcium (Ca^{++}), and magnesium (Mg^{++}).

endotracheal tube: A tube placed through the mouth into the trachea (windpipe) that allows the infant to be attached to a ventilator.

exchange transfusion: The repeated process of taking small volumes of blood out of an infant and putting new blood in (usually in volumes of 5 to 20 cubic centimeters) when an infant's bilirubin level becomes too high. *See also* **bilirubin.**

feeding tube: Another term for nasogastric tube.

gavage feeding: Feeding an infant through a nasogastric tube. Also called tube feeding. *See also* **nasogastric tube.**

gestational age: The number of weeks the infant remains

in the uterus, usually computed from the date of the mother's last menstrual period (LMP). A premature infant's gestational age is determined shortly after birth based on the mother's LMP, the date the fetus's heartbeat was first heard, and the infant's reflexes. Doctors continue to refer to the baby's gestational age until it reaches 40 weeks, the age of a newborn infant born at term. *See also* **conceptional age.**

hemiplegia: A form of cerebral palsy in which the arm and leg on only one side of the body are affected. *See also* **cerebral palsy.**

hyaline membrane disease: A breathing disorder commonly seen in premature infants characterized by a collapse of the air spaces in the lungs. Common symptoms include rapid respirations, heaving of the chest, and grunting. "Hyaline" refers to the pink, glassy membrane in the air sac that can be seen under a microscope. The disorder is also called respiratory distress syndrome.

hydrocephalus: A condition characterized by an abnormal collection of cerebrospinal fluid in the spaces (ventricles) of the brain. It is commonly referred to as "water on the brain." Hydrocephalus can be caused by many things, including a severe brain bleed. *See also* **intraventricular hemorrhage.**

hyperalimentation: The giving of all of an infant's nutritional requirements intravenously. In hyperalimentation, also called total parenteral nutrition, the infant receives a solution of protein, sugar, fat, minerals, and vitamins through a tube inserted in the vein.

hypertension: An abnormal elevation of the blood pressure.

hypotension: An abnormal lowering of the blood pressure. If untreated, it can eventually lead to shock (loss of consciousness).

hypovolemia: A decrease in the total blood volume. This can have several causes, including loss of blood just before or during delivery, a hurried clamping of the umbilical cord after an infant's birth, or frequent withdrawal of the infant's blood for laboratory analysis.

hypoxia: A decrease in the pO_2 (partial pressure of oxygen) in the blood.

iatrogenic: A problem caused by medical intervention meant to treat a different problem. Iatrogenic diseases may be unavoidable, or they may be the result of medical error.

indomethacin: A drug used with some success to close the ductus arteriosus, a vessel outside the heart that sometimes remains open in premature infants. Indomethacin is also used to treat many other disorders. *See also* **patent ductus arteriosus.**

intravenous line: A needle or catheter placed into a vein, through which fluids are given. It is commonly called an IV.

intraventricular hemorrhage: Bleeding into the fluid-filled spaces (ventricles) or nearby regions of the brain, seen commonly in premature infants. Also called brain bleeds, they occur in nearly one-half of premies weighing under 1500 grams at birth, and they are graded according to the extent of the bleeding.

intubation: The process of placing an endotracheal tube. *See also* **endotracheal tube.**

jaundice: A symptom of liver problems or immaturity of the liver, characterized by a yellow color in the skin and blood because of the accumulation of bilirubin. It is usually treated with fluorescent lights, or, in more severe cases, with exchange transfusions. *See also* **bilirubin, exchange transfusion, phototherapy.**

lanugo: Fine, furlike hair seen on the body surfaces of the premature infant, especially on the back and shoulders, which disappears with age.

ligation: The tying off of a vessel so that nothing may pass through it. Ligation is the surgery used to treat patent ductus arteriosus. *See also* **patent ductus arteriosus.**

line: An intravenous or intra-arterial line.

L/S ratio: The relative proportions of two substances

present in the amniotic fluid before birth or in the fluids coming from the trachea at the time of birth. L (lecithin) and S (sphingomyelin) are both components of the lung compound surfactant. The more L there is in relation to S, the more mature the lungs, since L rises after 35 weeks of gestation. *See also* **surfactant.**

metabolic acidosis: An excess of acidity in the bloodstream because of respiratory problems, which occurs when the pH falls below 7.3.

nasogastric tube: A tube passed through the nose and into the stomach, which can be used either to drain material from the stomach or for feeding. The tube is also called a feeding tube or N/G tube.

nasotracheal tube: A tube placed through the nose into the trachea (windpipe) that allows the infant to be attached to a ventilator.

necrotizing enterocolitis (NEC): A disorder of the bowel that occurs most often in premature infants of very low birthweight who have suffered from periods of low oxygen or low blood pressure. NEC usually occurs sometime after feeding has begun. In NEC, the lining of the bowel or parts of it may die and then must regrow. Treatment includes antibiotics, cessation of oral feedings, and, often, surgery.

NPO: A doctor's order meaning nothing by mouth ("nil per os"), which means the infant can be fed only intravenously.

ostomy: A suffix referring to any operation in which an artificial opening is made to the skin surface. An opening from the trachea is a tracheostomy; an opening from the small bowel is an ileostomy; an opening from the large bowel is a colostomy; an opening from the stomach is a gastrostomy. When used by itself, the suffix ostomy most commonly is used as shorthand for an ileostomy or colostomy.

paraplegia: A form of cerebral palsy affecting only the lower half of the body. *See also* **cerebral palsy.**

patent ductus arteriosus (PDA): The ductus arteriosus is the fetal vessel that connects the pulmonary artery to the aorta. This vessel, which is open (patent) in the uterus to divert blood from the inactive lungs to the rest of the body, should close when the infant is born. If it does not, the PDA may cause difficulty, including congestive heart failure. Usually, a PDA that fails to close is treated with medication or surgery. *See also* **indomethacin, ligation.**

PEEP: *See* CPAP.

persistent fetal circulation: A condition in which the blood pressure remains higher in the pulmonary (lung) circulation than in the systemic (body) circulation. This condition, also called persistent pulmonary hypertension, means blood cannot get into the lungs to receive oxygen. Persistent fetal circulation is often seen in babies who experienced birth asphyxia.

pH: A term that reflects the level of acidity in a solution, usually blood. The pH measures the concentration of hydrogen ions (H^+). Normal blood pH ranges from 7.35 to 7.45. A pH below 7.35 is too acidic and is called acidosis; a pH above 7.45 is too basic, or alkaline, and is called alkalosis.

phototherapy: Treatment of jaundice by exposure to light. *See also* **jaundice.**

pneumothorax: A collection of air or gas in the chest cavity, resulting from perforation of the chest wall or lung. Treatment includes removal of the air through a tube inserted in the baby's chest (a chest tube).

pulmonary: Relating to the lungs.

pulmonary artery: The major vessel going from the right side of the heart to the lungs. It carries unoxygenated (low-oxygen) blood.

respirator: *See* **ventilator.**

respirator lung: Another term for bronchopulmonary dysplasia.

respiratory acidosis: A condition that occurs when carbon dioxide (CO_2) cannot be removed properly from the lungs. Thus, the level of CO_2 in the bloodstream rises, and the pH falls below normal.

respiratory distress syndrome (RDS): *See* hyaline membrane disease.

resuscitation: The process of reviving an infant, either at birth or in the nursery, by means of oxygen administration, bag and mask breathing, or intubation and drugs.

retrolental fibroplasia (RLF): A disorder of the eyes, characterized by abnormal blood vessels on the retina, seen most commonly in very low birthweight infants. RLF, also known as retinopathy of prematurity, may improve with time or may worsen and lead to blindness. There are many proposed causes of RLF, including immaturity of the eye and prolonged use of supplemental oxygen.

rickets: A disorder of growing bones caused by inadequate calcium, phosphorus, or vitamin D in the diet. This condition can be corrected with nutritional supplements.

Ritodrine: Brand name for one of a class of drugs, called the beta-adrenergics, shown effective in stopping premature labor if administered before the cervix has dilated to 3 or 4 centimeters.

sepsis: An infection in the blood caused by bacteria.

shock: Low blood pressure leading to pallor or an ashen gray color of the skin and occasionally to sweating and loss of consciousness. It can be a result of infection, failure of the heart to pump blood normally, severe hypoxia, or decreased blood volume (hypovolemia).

shunt: The redirection of a substance either through an existing structure or by the artificial creation of a new structure. The PDA, for example, may act as a shunt for blood from the lung to the body. An artificial shunt may be used to treat hydrocephalus, in which case the shunt is inserted into the brain to drain cerebrospinal fluid away from the head and into the abdomen.

spinal tap: The insertion of a needle through the spinal column to remove cerebrospinal fluid for analysis.

staph: Shorthand for staphylococcus, a form of bacteria that may cause infection in premature infants.

streptococcus type B: One of the most common forms of bacteria to cause infection in the newborn. It is usually transmitted from mother to baby as the infant passes through the birth canal.

sudden infant death syndrome (SIDS): A condition, also called crib death, in which an apparently healthy infant, or one with only a cold, dies unexpectedly while sleeping. The cause of SIDS is unknown, but it has been shown to occur more frequently in males between the ages of one and seven months, in low birthweight infants, in infants with colds, and in infants who experience apnea. Premature infants who have sleep apnea wear monitors to prevent the occurrence of SIDS.

surfactant: The material secreted by the lung cells into the air spaces of the lung which serves as a lining layer to help keep the lung from collapsing at the end of each expiration. This substance, which is not manufactured in sufficient quantities until the end of gestation, may be deficient in premature infants. The absence of surfactant is thought to cause hyaline membrane disease. *See also* **hyaline membrane disease, L/S ratio.**

syphilis: A venereal (sexually transmitted) disease caused by an organism called a spirochete which has been increasing in the general population. Syphilis can be passed on to ⸱tus after the first twelve weeks of pregnancy and pro- ⸱ disease in the infant. If the mother is treated ade- ly for syphilis during her pregnancy, this will usually ⸱nt disease in the newborn.

⸱ypnea: Rapid breathing.

⸱phylline (aminophylline): A medication used com- ⸱ in the treatment of apnea and bradycardia. It has a effect on the breathing center of the brain.

⸱r: A unit of pressure necessary to support 1 millimeter of mercury. Oxygen and carbon dioxide measurements are usually expressed as Torr.

toxoplasmosis: An infection caused by a parasite that can cause disease in the newborn infant when the mother has minimal or no symptoms. It is transmitted through raw meat or the feces of cats and dogs. It cannot be passed from one person to another except through the placenta.

transfusion: The giving of blood through an intravenous line. This may be a simple transfusion, such as to replace the blood withdrawn for laboratory tests, or an exchange transfusion. *See also* **exchange transfusion.**

ultrasound: High-frequency sound waves used in the process of ultrasonography to look at deep structures of the body (brain, heart, abdomen). As sound waves are passed through an area, the density of tissue, blood, or air will send back echoes of different wavelengths to form a picture. Ultrasound is thought to be harmless.

Appendix C
Resources for Parents of Premies

Self-Help Groups

CALIFORNIA

Parent-to-Parent
26392 Via Juanita
Mission Viejo, California 92691
Offers counseling to new parents of premies or other special-care infants at the Children's Hospital of Orange County. Counseling provided by graduate parents of babies with similar medical histories. Contact: Dottie Andrews, 714-581-4519.

Parent Support Group
Salinas Valley Memorial Hospital
232 Hawthorne Steeet
Salinas, California 93901

Phone and personal consultations between experienced premie parents and new premie parents; educational meetings; loans of books, tapes, and clothing; glossary of medical terms. Contact: Susan Tucker, 408-757-1817.

Parent Support Group
Moffitt Hospital
A-203 University of California at San Francisco
San Francisco, California 94143

Telephone support from other parents of premies, newsletter, breastfeeding counseling, glossary of medical terms, referral to community resources for high-risk infants. Contact: Nancy McCabe, 415-666-4575.

COLORADO
Parent-to-Parent Program
The Children's Hospital
1056 East 19th Avenue
Denver, Colorado 80218

Offers one-to-one support from graduate parents to parents of babies in the hospital's intensive care nursery, with special support regarding breastfeeding, oxygen administration at home, and home care for tracheostomy or colostomy. Contact: Cindy Cleveland, R.N., family care coordinator, 303-861-6883, or Emily Selig, 303-377-9548.

Parent-to-Parent Group
320 East Highland Drive
Grand Junction, Colorado 81503

Meets monthly at St. Mary's Hospital, sometimes with professionals, and offers counseling to new parents through phone, letter, or personal visit. Volunteers also make special holiday gifts for babies in the intensive care nursery and visit the babies of parents who are too far away to visit frequently. Contact: Bonnie Bruhn, 303-243-4303.

DISTRICT OF COLUMBIA
Parents of Premies
Georgetown University Intensive Care Nursery
3700 Reservoir Road
Washington, D.C. 20007
> Provides one-to-one counseling for parents of premies in the intensive care nursery, rides to the hospital and babysitting for older children when parents are visiting the premie, and after-discharge support such as babysitting exchanges and information about other community resources and sources of diapers and clothes. Contact: Diane Saulter, 301-493-8780.

ILLINOIS
Parent-to-Parent Group
Rush-Presbyterian-St. Luke's Medical Center
1753 West Congress Parkway
Chicago, Illinois 60812
> Weekly Sunday evening meetings for parents of babies currently or formerly in the hospital's intensive care nursery. Also supplies the hospital's Parent's Room with articles and stories about premature infants and their parents. Contact: Judy B. Friedrichs, coordinator, special care nursery, 312-942-5000.

Will County High-Risk Infant Parent Association
422 Connor Avenue
Lockport, Illinois 60441
> Meets bimonthly to discuss topics on adjusting to premature parenthood, including dealing with stress, spouse, siblings, and relatives. Graduate parents contact parents with babies currently in the special care nursery. The group also publishes a monthly newsletter, "Transport News." Contact: Jimmy Jackson, chairman.

High-Risk Parent Support Group
Christ Hospital
Nursing Services Department
4440 West 95th Street
Oak Lawn, Illinois
> Weekly evening meetings for parents of babies in the hospital. Contact: 312-425-8000, extension 5734.

Premature and High Risk Infants
P.O. Box 3714
Peoria, Illinois 61614
> Contact: 309-673-5911

INDIANA

Neo-Fight
130 Red Oak Court
Carmel, Indiana 46032
> Graduate parents serve as hospital hostesses for new parents of infants in the intensive care nursery and provide counseling and support through telephone contacts. Active in hospitals throughout the Indianapolis region. Contact: Debbie Snyder, 317-844-2212.

KANSAS

Parents and Friends of Special Care Infants
1452 Melrose
Wichita, Kansas 67212
> Offers practical and emotional support to families and friends of infants requiring neonatal intensive care. Monthly newsletter. Contact: Jude Langhurst, 316-722-4372.

LOUISIANA

NICU Parents
1346 Havenwood Drive
Baton Rouge, Louisiana 70815
> Sponsors monthly meetings, including a rap session and a guest speaker, and a telephone network for parent support. Also operates a clothing exchange. Con-

tacts: Katherine Tobey, 504-275-2590, and Margie Roth, 504-769-2331.

MARYLAND

Parents of Special-Care Infants (PSCI)
Sinai Hospital
Department of Social Work
Baltimore, Maryland 21215
Sponsors two annual eight-week training workshops to teach graduate parents of intensive care nurseries how to provide one-on-one support for parents of premies now in the hospital. Also publishes newsletter and sponsors monthly lectures. Contact: Ann Oster, 301-323-1238.

MASSACHUSETTS

Coping with the Overall Pregnancy/Parenting Experience (COPE)
37 Clarendon Street
Boston, Massachusetts 02116
Offers counseling and support for expectant and new parents regardless of pregnancy outcome. Sponsors twelve-week seminars in perinatal psychology for professionals and paraprofessionals. COPE groups and programs are found in Boston and twenty metropolitan communities, including North and South Shores and Western suburbs. Contact: Isobel Freeman, 617-357-5588 or 357-5591.

Wee Touch
17 Merriam Road
Grafton, Massachusetts 01519
Provides emotional support to parents of premature or critically ill infants and sponsors monthly meetings, home visits, and an equipment exchange. Contacts: Nancy Poland, 617-839-4292, or Maria Hilton, 617-754-3787.

MISSOURI
Freeman Hospital
Social Services Department
1102 West 32nd
Joplin, Missouri 64801
Social work follow-up for graduates of the intensive care nursery, as well as a formal support group, Mothers in Crisis, for mothers whose infants died. Contact: Terry Weston, 417-623-2801.
Children's Mercy Hospital
24th and Gillham Road
Kansas City, Missouri 64108
Support group for parents of infants in the intensive care nursery, led by a nurse practitioner. Contact: Mary Kay Leick, 816-234-3000.

NEBRASKA
Infants in Crisis
c/o Self-Help Information Service
1601 Euclid
Lincoln, Nebraska 68502
Contacts: Judy, 402-489-7760, or Lorna, 402-488-2928.
Helping Other Parents Endure (HOPE)
Creighton Health Center/St. Joseph Hospital
601 North 30th
Omaha, Nebraska 68131
Meets weekly at a local church to offer support for parents of special care infants throughout the community. Contact: Norma Mae Nelson, 402-449-4000.

NEW JERSEY
POINT (Parents of Intensive Care Nursery/Tots)
Department of Neonatology
Beth Israel Medical Center
201 Ryans Avenue
Newark, New Jersey 07112
Offers support for parents of infants in the intensiv care nursery, both during hospitalization and after d

charge, as well as providing forums for education and phone outreach. Contacts: Millie Bier, 201-238-5918, Mildred Sarono or Jane Saylivitz, 201-926-7278.

NEW MEXICO

Action for Newborns of New Mexico
5605 Bentwood Trail, N.E.
Albuquerque, New Mexico 87109
Consists of local volunteers in twenty-five cities across the state, who serve as community support for parents of newborns transferred to the intensive care nursery at the University of New Mexico. Activities include lobbying, providing public information, and sponsoring a semiannual reunion of intensive care graduates. Contact: Sharon Curry, 505-821-3349.

PENNSYLVANIA

Famlee (Fathers and Mothers Learning through Education and Experience)
Box 15
Telford, Pennsylvania 18969
Parent support for parents of premature, high-risk, or handicapped children, providing twenty-four-hour parent-to-parent telephone counseling, a library and community resource center, referrals to other organizations, and volunteer counselor training. One volunteer also makes premie clothing. Contacts: Lenette S. Moses, 215-723-8274, Mary Catherine Reilly, 215-855-4074, and Mary Schnaubalt, 215-368-5443.

TEXAS

Parent Love
10729 Benbrook
Dallas, Texas 75228
Provides crisis counseling, in person and through twenty-four-hour phone assistance, for parents of special care newborns, monthly group sessions, occasional lectures, and attractive "love packets" to hang near the isolette, including a hand-embroidered tee shirt, boo-

ties, an audiovisual stimulation toy in bright colors, and some pamphlet information. Contact: Janell Myers, 214 270-5095.

Parents of *Prematures*
Houston Organization for Parent Education, Inc.
3311 Richmond, Suite 330
Houston, Texas 77098

Researched, wrote, and now distributes a book for parents, *Premature Babies*, and offers supportive services such as patterns for premie clothes, referrals, and information. Contact: Sherri Nance, 713-524-3089.

UTAH

Parent-to-Parent
Intermountain Newborn Intensive Care Center
University of Utah Medical Center
Salt Lake City, Utah 84132

Offers individual and group support to parents of critically ill newborns from the five-state area served by the hospital. Working now on a project to provide housing for out-of-state parents of hospitalized newborns. Contact: Sandy Garrand, 801-581-7705.

WASHINGTON

Parents of Prematures
13613 N.E. 26th Place
Bellevue, Washington 98005

Offers emotional and educational support to parents of high-risk babies, especially prematures. Provides a newsletter, information on local resources, and monthly lectures. Contacts: Lauri Lowen, 206-883-6040; Kathy Ormbrek, 206-522-6941.

Inland Empire Perinatal Parent Support Group
W. 1662 Fairway Drive
Spokane, Washington 99218

Offers one-to-one support for parents experiencin high-risk pregnancies or delivery of a high-risk ne born. Also sponsors a grief group for parents periencing miscarriage, stillbirth, and neonatal death. Contact: Elsa Distelhorst, 509-456-8885.

CANADA

Toronto Perinatal Association
80 Ranleigh
Toronto, Ontario M4N 1W9
Holds regular meetings for parents of premies at the Hospital for Sick Children. Contact: Carol Fraser, 416-489-8227.

Other Resources

PREMIE DIAPERS

Premie Pampers (for babies under six pounds)
Proctor & Gamble, 11015 Kenwood Road, Cincinnati, Ohio 45242
Toll-free number: 800-543-4932

PREMIE CLOTHING

Lil Bits
Carol Meredith, 550 Herschel, Wichita, Kansas 67209, 316-722-7824
Littletot
Judy C. Mickelsen, 1880 Coronando, Ann Arbor, Michigan 48103
Parents of Prematures Clothing Committee
Margo Olson, 18030 Eighth Street, N.E., Seattle, Washington 98155, 206-367-5301
Patterns for premie clothes
Patricia Silvers, P.O. Box 217, Department P, Lopez, Washington 98261
Premie Petites
Francis & Associates, 3318 Western #117, Amarillo, Texas 19109, 806-353-4206
Tiny Mites
Janet Thayer, P.O. Box 6346, Glendale, California 91205.

PREMIE BABY CARRIERS
Snugli Premie Packs
> Snugli, Inc., 1212 Kerr Gulch, Evergreen, Colorado
> 80439, 303-526-0131
> The popular Snugli soft front carrier is available with
> extra tucks and snaps to fit premies and can be adjusted
> for use through the child's third year. Snugli, Inc., also
> has other front carriers for children with special needs,
> including the Snugli Twin Pack.

Associations for Children with Special Needs

The Alexander Graham Bell Association for the Deaf
The Volta Bureau
> 3417 Volta Place, N.W.
> Washington, D.C. 20007

American Foundation for the Blind
> 15 West 16th Street
> New York, New York 10011

American Speech, Language, and Hearing Association
> 10801 Rockville Pike
> Rockville, Maryland 20852

Association for Children with Learning Disabilities
> Suismon and Middle Streets
> Pittsburgh, Pennsylvania 15212

Association for Neurologically Impaired Brain Injured
Children
> 217 Lark Street
> Albany, New York 12210

Council for Exceptional Children
> 1920 Association Drive
> Reston, Virginia 22091

Directory of Services for the Deaf
American Annals of the Deaf

Gallaudet College
7th Street and Florida Avenue, N.E.
Washington, D.C. 20002

Foundation for Child Development
345 East 46th Street
New York, New York 10016

National Association for Retarded Citizens
2709 Avenue E East
Arlington, Texas 76011

National Association of Hearing and Speech Agencies
919 Eighteenth Street, N.W.
Washington, D.C. 20006

National Easter Seal Society for Crippled Children and
Adults, Inc.
2023 West Ogden Avenue
Chicago, Illinois 60612

National Organization of Mothers of Twins Clubs
5402 Amberwood Lane
Rockville, Maryland 20853

National Perinatal Association
52nd and F Streets
Sacramento, California 95819

United Cerebral Palsy Associations, Inc.
66 East 34th Street
New York, New York 10016

Appendix D
A Growth Chart
For the Next Twelve
Months

By one month corrected age:

Vision:
- The baby is sensitive to bright light or sunlight; they cause her to flinch and close her eyes tightly.
- She can see objects six to twelve inches from her nose.
- She shows signs of the "doll's eye effect"—her eyes open when she's lifted and held upright.
- She prefers to look at patterns, especially those that evoke the human face, and at bright colors and sharp contrast.
- She'll gaze for long periods at a face or a picture of a face—especially the region between the eyes and hairline.

Touch:
- She grasps objects placed in her open hand—a reflex over which she has no control.

- For most of the time, especially when she's awake, the baby's hands are curled into fists.

Movement:

- On her back, the baby most often lies in the "tonic neck position," with her head turned to one side (usually the right), the arm extended on that side, and the opposite arm flexed so that it comes close to the shoulder.
- On her belly, she lies with her face down, but she's able to lift her head for very brief periods.

Sounds:

- The baby begins to make small "throaty" sounds.

Socializing:

- The baby spends most of her time sleeping. She's in her "quiet alert state"—when she's awake, comfortable, not hungry, and ready for some social play—for only about five minutes out of every hour during the day.
- She stares at adults' faces, especially their eyes, for long periods.

By two months corrected age:

Vision:

- She will look at objects and follow a moving object or face within her eight- to twelve-inch visual range.
- She can differentiate between a real face and a picture of a face, and, although each will get a smile, the real face will get a bigger smile.

Touch:

- The baby can hold a rattle that is placed in her hand and can wave it around. The sound it makes will attract her attention; as she looks for the rattle, she takes a step toward the "discovery" of her own hands.

Movement:

- She is gaining control of her head. When she is held upright, her head will jerk and bob, but it will not sag forward as it used to.

Sounds:

• The baby babbles to herself, playing with the sounds she can make and endlessly repeating the same odd-sounding trills and coos. At this age, the babbles are universal; Chinese babies, French babies, and American babies all utter identical sounds. Soon, though, the babbling will begin to shift toward the sounds made only in the baby's native language.

Socializing:

• The baby begins making spontaneous smiles, and, as they are encouraged by returned smiles from her loved ones, she learns to smile some more.

By three months corrected age:

Vision:

• The baby is better able to keep a slowly moving object within sight, a process known as "tracking." When a large, bright object is held about a foot away and moved slowly from one side to the other, the baby can follow it smoothly and reliably.

• The baby will have found her hand and spends long periods looking at it, waving it in front of her face and exploring it with her other hand.

• She shows signs of recognizing familiar things.

Touch:

• Reflex grasping has been replaced by voluntary grasping.

• The baby experiences "touch hunger"—she so loves holding and touching objects that she will fuss and reach for things until she can hold still more.

• She swipes at objects within reach.

Movement:

• The baby's control of her head is just about complete

• She has uncurled totally from her earlier postures a

can now lie flat either on her back or her belly. This allows her to move her limbs more freely, and she begins pumping her legs happily in a "bicycling" motion when she gets excited.

• When lying on her belly, she places some weight on her forearms, so that not only her head but soon her shoulders and even chest rise above the mattress.

• She can bring her fist to her mouth intentionally and keep it there.

Sounds:

• The baby has a large repertoire of sounds: squeals, chuckles, coos, clicks, bubbles, gurgles. When an adult imitates the sound, the baby becomes excited and tries to repeat the sound in turn, creating a sort of dialogue.

• She will make long "speeches" when looking at something interesting.

Socializing:

• She begins to flash her first "social smile"—a smile meant simply to tell her parents or other loved ones that she's happy. In the months to come, that smile will appear more and more often.

• She's awake and alert for longer periods of time—about fifteen or twenty minutes out of each daytime hour.

By four months corrected age:

Vision:

• She can focus easily on brightly colored objects.

• She looks at toys as she holds them in her hand—a first step in the development of hand-eye coordination.

• The sight of food is a cue to her that she soon will be fed.

• She brings her hands to the middle of her body and plays at intertwining them.

Touch:
- The baby might begin to use her fingers separately.
- She generally uses both hands together to reach for an object.
- A great deal of her attention is devoted to watching and playing with her hands.

Movement:
- When the baby is held upright, her legs will support some of her weight.
- When she is propped into a sitting position, she can remain upright for ten to fifteen minutes.
- She is working hard at learning to roll over.

Sounds and Socializing:
- The baby has developed a belly laugh.
- She turns her head at the sound of voices.
- She knows a loved one's voice from the voice of a stranger and prefers it.

By five months corrected age:

Vision:
- She uses her vision in a new way—coordinating it with all her other senses. If she sees a nearby object, a predictable, smooth sequence of events follows: she reaches, grasps, and pulls the object to her mouth, completing her exploration by gumming and chewing it.
- Her ability to see is equal to that of an adult. She can see objects across a room.
- The baby is interested only in the things she can see. She loses interest in a toy if it is covered up or hidden.

Touch:
- Much of her time is spent playing with her hands, squeezing one with the other as she learns to distinguish her own body from all other objects she can see and touch.

- She begins voluntary reaching.
- She reaches in different ways for different objects, anticipating their size, shape, and distance.
- She can hold onto only one object at a time.

Movement:
- The baby learns to roll deliberately from her belly to her back.
- She can reach for things within range of her hands. Sometimes she manages to grab them; more often, though, she "swipes" at them in an unsuccessful effort to catch hold.
- The baby has outgrown her "tonic neck reflex." When she lies on her back now, her head usually is centered, and she is able to move it freely from side to side.
- She uses her hand to grasp objects much as though she were wearing a mitten, with her thumb used in opposition to her other four fingers.
- Her back is much stronger, and she can sit erect with support for up to one-half hour.
- She can often grasp a toy she wants, but she cannot yet transfer it from one hand to the other.
- Hand-eye coordination is vastly improved and allows the baby to move her hand wherever she wants it to go. She most frequently brings it to her mouth, preferably with an object or toy, so she can "mouth" her fist or rattle in a feast of sensory exploration.

Sounds:
- The baby talks to herself when she's left alone.
- She experiments with certain favorite sounds, such as growling, blowing bubbles, or gurgling.
- She likes to make sounds when something is in her mouth.

Socializing:
- She recognizes people and smiles at the approach of Mother, Father, or others who are familiar. The smile may disappear at the approach of a stranger.

By six months corrected age:

Vision:
- She spends less time looking at objects that are far away, concentrating instead on things within her reach.
- She shifts her attention from large objects to small.
- She begins to prefer pictures with more realistic detail, rather than the cartoons and patterns she liked a few months earlier.

Touch:
- She works to reach a toy that is out of easy reach.
- She can hold an object between her extended fingers.
- She uses her hands to explore all parts of her body, including her toes, feet, face, and genitals.

Movement:
- The baby will move toward objects.
- She can roll deliberately from her back to her belly.
- She likes to wave her arms, with or without an object in her hand, up and down and from side to side.
- She will try to transfer objects from one hand to the other.
- She will lift her chest completely and might be able to support herself on hands and knees.

Sounds:
- The baby's sounds are beginning more closely to resemble speech.
- Her vocalizations are different depending on whether they're directed at toys or people.
- She babbles the most when playing with a familiar toy; if the toy is new, she is too immersed in it to be able to babble at the same time.

Socializing:
- She has an increased interest in the outside world.
- She does not like to be left alone.

• She looks up from what she's doing when people enter the room.

By seven months corrected age:

Vision and Touch:
• She reaches purposefully for a toy when she sees it and can grasp it not only from a flat surface or from your hand but also as it dangles above her.
• She is much more dexterous. She can grasp small objects or pieces of food in a pincerlike grasp, using her thumb in opposition to two fingers.
• She may be able to retrieve small objects using a raking movement of her hand and arm.
• Small objects, such as keys and beads, especially fascinate her.

Movement:
• The baby can sit without support, although she cannot yet get herself to a sitting position alone.
• She can bear weight on her legs when placed standing in a walker or against a piece of furniture.
• She may rotate her wrist to see the bottom of a toy she is holding.
• She can hold an object in one hand instead of two and can bang it against another object.
• She can transfer objects from one hand to the other.
• She can feed herself crackers.

Sounds:
• The baby imitates her own sounds when you say them back to her, engaging you in a kind of dialogue.
• The sounds the baby makes begin to sound more and more like speech, including occasional use of such words as "mama" and "dada," although not meant specifically to mean Mother and Father.

Socializing:
- She enjoys playing peek-a-boo.
- She likes to be included in social interactions.
- She begins developing a sense of humor, and she likes to tease and be teased.
- She resists doing things she doesn't want to do.

By eight months corrected age:

Vision and Touch:
- The baby's ability to discern detail has improved dramatically, leading to a fascination with tiny objects, including crumbs, blades of grass, and insects.
- She begins to develop a perception of depth.

Movement:
- She puts her toes in her mouth.
- She can bang a bell.
- She reaches with one hand.
- She may begin crawling, both forward and backward.
- When held upright, she frequently makes bouncing movements.

Sounds:
- She talks to her toys, using a different tone than the one she uses to talk to herself or to people.
- She enjoys noisemaking toys, such as bells and chimes.
- When she recognizes a familiar person, her vocalizations change.
- She imitates adult speech patterns, varying her intonation and pitch in the same way her parents do.

Socializing:
- She stretches her arms to be picked up.
- She loves looking into mirrors. She will smile at her reflection and try to pat it.
- She vocalizes to state her demands, get attention, express pleasure or displeasure, or simply to socialize.

By nine months corrected age:

Vision:

• She retains interest in an object even after it is covered up, and she tries to find it to get it back.

• She allows herself to be interrupted during crawling when a new object appears; she'll stop for a while and stare at it.

Touch:

• The baby uses her hands to explore her environment. She has great control of her hands and can grasp and manipulate two or three objects at a time.

• Her forefinger is the device through which she explores objects. She uses it to poke, prod, and manipulate anything new, especially if it has holes in it.

• She can pick up small objects using two fingers (thumb and forefinger).

• She will try to build a tower of blocks, probably without success, though she might manage a "tower" of two.

Movement:

• The baby is able to crawl, usually distributing her weight evenly among her two hands and two knees.

• She can get herself from a sitting position to a crawling position and might even be able to get herself from a crawl to a sit.

• She can stand while holding onto a stable object.

Sounds:

• She enjoys hearing and moving to music.

• She recognizes the differences among speech sounds; she can recognize the voice melodies of her parents, for instance, and knows which tones of voice are happy and which are mad.

Socializing:

• The baby can use her voice to get what she wants. She is learning that a particular call can elicit a helpful parent more effectively than can a cry.

• She is initially shy with strangers.

• She might insist on feeding herself, grabbing the spoon and trying messily to get it to her mouth.

• She can feed herself many finger foods.

• When certain behaviors are positively reinforced, she "performs" to have adults laugh with her and applaud her.

• She might begin asserting herself and protecting her possessions, such as by fighting to keep her toys from another child.

By ten months corrected age:

Vision:

• The baby likes watching scenes as much as she likes watching people or objects.

Touch:

• She will be able to place small objects inside a large container.

• She may be able to build a tower of two blocks.

Movement:

• The baby will grasp a bell by its handle, pull on a string, and roll or throw a ball.

• She can maintain her balance easily from a sitting position, turning from side to side and even leaning far over to retrieve a toy before returning to an upright posture.

• Her crawling improves, and she may be able to climb up and down stairs.

• She practices using both sides of her body to do the same thing, and practices using each hand for a separate activity.

• She begins to release objects voluntarily.

Sounds:

• The baby will imitate sounds such as coughing and laughing.

• She may try to hum or sing when she hears music.

Socializing:
- The baby likes to play pat-a-cake.
- She can wave "bye-bye."
- She will relinquish a toy on request.
- She responds to her name.
- She seems to understand the concept of "no."

By eleven months corrected age

Vision:
- She can sit and stare for long periods, especially if she's watching a lot of action, such as other children playing.
- She likes to look at picture books.
- She remembers objects that have fallen out of sight (this is an intellectual concept called "object permanence") and tries to retrieve them.

Touch:
- The baby enjoys games of throwing objects and having them returned to her to be thrown again.
- She likes to try turning the pages of books.

Movement:
- The baby can pull herself to a standing position, using a crib rail, coffee table, or other stable object for support.
- She likes to climb up stairs.
- She is able to "cruise," moving around the room sideways while edging from one piece of furniture to the next.
- She might take a few steps while holding onto an adult's hand or pushing a stroller or sturdy "toddling" toy.

Sounds:
- She can imitate new sounds.
- She makes sounds that for the first time sound like words.

Socializing:
- She can amuse herself for as long as one hour but is

happier playing alone when other people are in the room with her.

• She seeks the approval of her loved ones and may follow simple commands.

By twelve months corrected age:

Vision:

• The baby still smiles at herself in the mirror and also may reach for objects reflected there.

• She likes observing details.

• She will imitate the facial expressions and gestures of others, especially adults.

Touch:

• She can pick up and hold small objects in a "prehensile" grip, between the tip of the thumb and the tip of the index finger.

Movement:

• The baby can walk unassisted. (Note: the average age for this much-awaited accomplishment is about 12.5 months corrected age. But some perfectly normal babies do not walk alone until as late as sixteen to eighteen months. Your baby's slow walking should not be a matter of concern until it's delayed beyond eighteen to twenty months *corrected age* and then only if the baby is not showing signs of moving in the direction of walking, such as pulling to a stand and cruising.)

• She can stoop when standing and then stand up again.

Sounds:

• She babbles with more complicated sounds, and the melody of her "speeches" sounds more like conversation.

• She might have a few simple words that she uses appropriately, including "mama," "dada," "dog," "cat," and "book."

Socializing:

• She recognizes her own name and the names of familiar people.

• She tries to follow instructions.

• The baby can drink well from a cup, and she tries to feed herself with a spoon.

Notes

Chapters 1 and 2

Most of the information in these chapters comes from actual experience in the intensive care nursery. Additional references include, especially, Marshall H. Klaus and Avroy A. Fanaroff, eds., *Care of the High-Risk Neonate* (Philadelphia: W.B. Saunders Company, 1979); and Catherine Caldwell Brown, ed., *Infants at Risk: Assessment and Intervention. An Update for Health Care Professionals and Parents* (Piscataway, N.J.: Johnson & Johnson Baby Products Company, 1981).

Chapter 3

The information on bonding beginning, "The leaders in the study of parent-infant attachment are Drs. Marshall Klaus and John Kennell," comes in part from Marshall H. Klaus and John H. Kennell, *Maternal-Infant Bonding* (St. Louis: C.V. Mosby Company, 1976). The study by A. C. Turnbull was reported on in *Lancet* 1 (1974):101–3, and cited in Klaus and Kennell, *Maternal-Infant Bonding*, p. 35.

Ann Dixon's quote beginning, "It was terrible in the hospital," appears in Klaus and Kennell, *Maternal-Infant Bonding*, p. 142.

The newspaper article with the quote, "Somewhere in her brain," is "Forming a Bond with the Newborn," Nadine Brozan, *New York Times*, January 19, 1981, p. B10.

The quote about mothers' behavior during living-in arrangements beginning, "It was interesting to observe," is from Klaus and Kennell, *Maternal-Infant Bonding*, p. 135.

The quote from Dr. Marjorie Seashore beginning, "For mothers of premature infants," is from "The Effects of Denial of Early Mother-Infant Interaction on Maternal Self-Confidence" (with Aimee Dorr Leifer, Clifford R. Barnett, and P. Herbert Leiderman), *Journal of Personality and Social Psychology* 26, no. 3 (1973):369–78 reprinted in Jane Linker Schwartz and Lawrence H. Schwartz, eds., *Vulnerable Infants: A Psychosocial Dilemma* (New York: McGraw Hill, 1977), p. 137.

The "four stages of premie parenthood" were first described by Gerald Caplan, Edward A. Mason, and David M. Kaplan in "Four Studies of Crisis in Parents of Prematures," *Community Mental Health Journal* 1, no. 2 (summer 1965): 149–61, reprinted in Schwartz and Schwartz, eds., *Vulnerable Infants*, p. 98.

The study of "a tape recording of their mothers' voices to a group of premies" was reported by V. Katz, "Auditory Stimulation and Developmental Behavior in the Premature Infant," *Nursing Research* 20, (1971):196–201, and cited in Tiffany Martini Field, ed., *Infants Born at Risk: Behavior and Development* (New York: Spectrum Publications, 1979), p. 371.

The study comparing handled premies to nonhandled premies, beginning, "One recent study found that just by stroking and flexing premies' legs," was reported by N. Solkoff and D. Matuszak, "Tactile Stimulation and Behavioral

Development among Low Birthweight Infants," *Child Psychiatry and Human Development* 6 (1975):33–37, and cited in Field, ed., *Infants Born at Risk*, p. 370.

Dr. Allan Gottfried's quote beginning, "Although infants in special care units do not suffer," is from "Physical and Social Environment of Newborn Infants in Special Care Units" (with Patricia Wallace-Lande, Susan Sherman-Brown, Jeanne King, Carolyn Coen, and Joan E. Hodgman), *Science* 214 (November 6, 1981):674.

Chapter 5

The description of iatrogenic anemia comes in part from Jerri M. Oehler, *Family-Centered Neonatal Nursing Care* (Philadelphia: J. B. Lippincott Company, 1981), p. 296.

The description of bronchopulmonary dysplasia in the section "Chronic Lung Disease" is from William H. Northway, Jr., "Observations on Bronchopulmonary Dysplasia," *Journal of Pediatrics* 95, no. 5, pt. 2 (1979):815.

Jerri Oehler's quote that BPD babies are "small tyrants" is from her book, *Family-Centered Neonatal Nursing Care*, p. 218.

Statistics about mortality from hyaline membrane disease beginning, "Even as recently as ten years ago," come in part from Victor C. Vaughan III, R. James McKay, Jr., and Richard E. Behrman, eds., *The Nelson Textbook of Pediatrics* (Philadelphia: W. B. Saunders Company, 1979), p. 430.

Additional information for the section beginning, "The blood gas measurements": The blood level of oxygen is called pO_2 and usually should be maintained in the range of 50 to 70 Torr. (The designation "Torr" reflects the partial pressure of the substance being measured.) The blood level of carbon dioxide is called pCO_2, and the normal range is about 40 to 45 Torr. A balanced pH for a premie is in the range of 7.35 to 7.45, slightly higher than the range consid ered normal for full-term newborns. These readings are averages only and are presented here to help you interpret the readings your doctors and nurses might be reporting to you. There are many reasons why, for treatment purposes, your doctor might deliberately keep your baby's blood gases outside the normal range. If this is the case, ask your doctor to explain his reasoning to you.

Additional information for the section "Oxygen Hoods": A baby under an oxygen hood usually should maintain a pO_2 of 55 to 60 Torr. If the oxygen level cannot stay in this range, the doctor might increase the percentage of oxygen going into the hood. The doctor will probably switch to CPAP when the concentration gets above 70 percent oxygen. He will probably consider mechanical ventilation for babies on CPAP at about 80 percent oxygen whose pO_2 is less than 50 Torr, whose CO_2 is more than 60 to 70 Torr, and whose pH is less than 7.2 (Klaus and Fanaroff, eds., *Care of the High-Risk Neonate*, p. 206).

Dr. Tetsuro Fujiwara described his research in "Artificial Surfactant Therapy in Hyaline-Membrane Disease" (with H. Maeta, S. Chida, et al.), *Lancet* 1 (1980):55,

The description in the section "Jaundice" comes in part from Oehler, *Family-Centered Neonatal Nursing Care*, p. 313.

Additional information for the section beginning, "At birth, newborns produce bilirubin at a rate more than twice that of an adult": In general, the normal values for bilirubin and conjugated bilirubin in the newborn are 10 mg/100 ml of blood and 1.5 mg/100 ml of blood, respectively. Doctors usually do not like to see the rates of either value increasing by more than 5 mg/100 ml per day.

The description of NEC comes in part from Klaus and Fanaroff, eds., *Care of the High-Risk Neonate*, p. 136.

Statistics about RLF beginning, "A recent study of premies," come in part from Dale L. Phelps, "Retinopathy of Prematurity: An Estimate of Vision Loss in the United States—1979," *Pediatrics* 67, no. 6 (1981):924.

Chapter 6

"A generation ago, most premies were not fed for the first several days," is from Sydney S. Gellis, "The Problem in Historical Perspective," from Tom D. Moore, ed., *Iatrogenic Problems in Neonatal Intensive Care* (Columbus, Ohio: Ross Laboratories, 1976), p. 16.

Studies comparing the breast milk of premie mothers with that of nonpremie mothers were reported by Stephanie A. Atkinson, M. Heather Bryan, and G. Harvey Anderson, "Human Milk Feeding in Premature Infants: Protein, Fat, and Carbohydrate Balances in the First Two Weeks of Life," *Journal of Pediatrics* 99, no. 4 (1981):617–24.

The "recent study at the Rainbow Babies' and Children's Hospital" of the effects of colostrum on premies was cited in Ruth A. Lawrence, *Breast-feeding: A Guide for the Medical Profession* (St. Louis: C. V. Mosby Company, 1980), p. 188.

The quote beginning "The first few nursing sessions are for getting acquainted," is from Paula Meier, "A Program to Support Breast-Feeding in the High-Risk Nursery," *Perinatology-Neonatology* 4 (March/April 1980):45.

The AMA's policy statement beginning, "The decision whether to treat . . . should be the choice of the parents," appears in *Current Opinions of the Judicial Council of the AMA*, a copy of which can be obtained from the American Medical Association, 535 North Dearborn Avenue, Chicago, Illinois 60610.

Chapter 8

The quote beginning, "Evidence is accumulating," from Dr. Anneliese Korner is from her chapter, "Sensory Responsiveness and Social Behavior in the Neonatal Period," in Sarah L. Friedman and Marian Sigman, eds., *Preter*

Birth and Psychological Development (New York: Academic Press, 1981), p. 211.

Chapter 9

The quote from Dr. Penelope Leach on "constructive resignation" is from *Your Baby and Child* (New York: Alfred A. Knopf, 1980), p. 102.

The rehospitalization rate for premies was reported by Marie C. McCormick, Sam Shapiro, and Barbara H. Starfield, "Rehospitalization in the First Year of Life for High-Risk Survivors," *Pediatrics* 66, no. 6 (1980):991–99.

The section beginning "Obstetricians often advise partial or complete" bedrest for mothers carrying twins is from Klaus and Fanaroff, eds., *Care of the High-Risk Neonate*, p. 71.

Chapter 10

Dr. T. Berry Brazelton's quotation beginning, "Practicing physicians tend to postpone the referral of damaged infants," is from his introduction to Brown, ed., *Infants at Risk*, p. xv.

Statistics about the incidence of cerebral palsy among premies beginning, "Approximately three hundred thousand children," are from Vaughan, McKay, and Behrman, eds., *Nelson Textbook*, p. 1759.

The quote from Dr. Lawrence Taft beginning, "The symptoms of cerebral palsy," is from his chapter, "Intervention Programs for Infants with Cerebral Palsy: A Clinician's View," in Brown, ed., *Infants at Risk*, p. 79.

The quote from Dr. Eric Denhoff beginning, "Most high-risk, low birth-weight infants," is from his chapter, "A Sensory-Motor Enrichment Program," ibid., p. 117.

The quote from Dr. Kathryn Barnard beginning "It is

difficult in a dynamic interaction," is from her chapter, "An Ecological Approach to Parent-Child Relations," ibid., p. 93.

The quote from Dr. Tiffany Martini Field beginning, "Slowing down, exaggerating and repeating," is from her chapter, "Interaction Patterns of Pre-Term and Term Infants," in Field, ed., *Infants Born at Risk*, p. 337.

Statistics on hearing loss in premies, estimated by Dr. Robert Galambos, are from Brown, ed., *Infants at Risk*, pp. 102, 117, and 91.

Chapter 11

The "vulnerable child syndrome" was first described by Morris Green and Albert J. Solnit in "Reactions to the Threatened Loss of a Child," *Pediatrics* 34 (1964):58–66, reprinted in Schwartz and Schwartz, eds., *Vulnerable Infants*, pp. 183–95. The story of "Jerry A." appears in ibid., pp. 184–87.

Dr. Benjamin Spock's quotation beginning, "Overprotective feelings," is from *Baby and Child Care* (New York: Pocket Books, 1977), p. 390.

Chapter 12

The information in the section, "Early Labor: The Warning Signs" comes in part from Dianne Hales and Robert K. Creasy, *New Hope for Problem Pregnancies: Helping Babies BEFORE They're Born* (New York: Harper & Row, 1982).

Chapter 13

Information in the section "A Brief History of Premie Care" comes from Klaus and Kennell, *Maternal-Infant Bonding*, pp. 4–7.

The early follow-up study for premies born in the 1960s is C. M. Drillien, "The Long Term Prospects of Handicap in Babies of Low Birth Weight," *Hospital Medicine* 1 (1967):937.

The 1980 report to Congress is by Peter Budetti, Peggy McManus, Nancy Barrand, and Lu Ann Heinen, *The Costs and Effectiveness of Neonatal Intensive Care"* (Washington, D. C.: U. S. Government Printing Office, 1980).

Dr. Albert Jonsen describes the ethical aspects of neonatology in "Critical Issues in Newborn Intensive Care: A Conference Report and Policy Proposal" (with R. H. Phibbs, W. H. Tooley, and M. J. Garland), *Pediatrics* 55, no. 6 (1975):756–69, which is reprinted in Schwartz and Schwartz, eds., *Vulnerable Infants*, pp. 312–34.

The per-baby cost of neonatal intensive care was calculated in C. S. Phibbs, R. L. Williams, and R. H. Phibbs, "Analysis of Factors Associated with Costs of Neonatal Intensive Care," *Western Society for Pediatric Research*, and in S. A. Schroeder, J. A. Shostack, and H. E. Roberts, "Frequency and Clinical Description of High-Cost Patients in 17 Acute-Care Hospitals," *New England Journal of Medicine* 300 (1979):1300–1309. Both articles were cited in Budetti et al., *Costs and Effectiveness*.

Appendix D

The information assembled in these growth charts comes in part from Frank Caplan, ed., *The First Twelve Months of Life* (New York: Grosset and Dunlap, 1973), and from Richard A. Chase and Richard R. Rubin, eds., *The First Wondrous Year* (New York: Collier Books, 1979).

Index

About the Authors

Robin Marantz Henig is a medical journalist whose work appears in many national magazines, including *The New York Times Magazine, Woman's Day, Redbook,* and *Mademoiselle.* Her first book, *The Myth of Senility: Misconceptions About the Brain and Aging,* won the 1982 Media Award of the American Psychological Association. She is currently at work writing *How a Woman Ages* with Esquire Press. Ms. Henig lives outside Washington, D.C., with her husband and family.

Anne B. Fletcher, M.D., is a neonatology specialist and chief of the Neonatology Unit at Children's National Medical Center in Washington, D.C.